G000139019

IN THE COMPANY OF COWARDS

Michael Dante Mori recently retired as a Lieutenant Colonel in the United States Marine Corps after completing his final tour of duty as the Navy-Marine Corps Military Judge in Hawaii. His military career began in 1983 when he enlisted in the Marine Corps at eighteen years of age, completing boot camp at Marine Corps Recruit Depot, Parris Island, South Carolina. In pursuit of his commission as a Marine Corps Officer, he completed Officers Candidate School and obtained a Bachelor of Science degree in Communications from Norwich University, located in Northfield, Vermont. Upon receiving his Commission in May 1991 as a Marine Corps Second Lieutenant, Mori remained in a reserve status to attend Western New England College School of Law in Springfield, Massachusetts, graduating in 1994. After completing the bar examination and admittance to the Bar for the Commonwealth of Massachusetts, Mori commenced his career as a Marine Corps Officer serving predominantly as prosecutor and defence counsel. In 2003, the United States Department of Defense assigned Mori to the Office of the Chief Counsel for Military Commissions, which was to provide representation to detainees held at the Naval Base in Guantanamo Bay, Cuba. Mori became the first Military Lawyer assigned to represent a detainee. Mori has since moved to Melbourne and is working in Shine Lawyers's Social Justice Department, having completed the requirements to obtain his Australian law license.

MICHAEL MORI

IN THE COMPANY OF COWARDS

Bush, Howard and injustice at Guantanamo

VIKING
an imprint of
PENGUIN BOOKS

VIKING

Published by the Penguin Group
Penguin Group (Australia)
707 Collins Street, Melbourne, Victoria 3008, Australia
(a division of Penguin Australia Pty Ltd)
Penguin Group (USA) Inc.
375 Hudson Street, New York, New York 10014, USA
Penguin Group (Canada)
90 Eglinton Avenue East, Suite 700, Toronto, Canada ON M4P 2Y3
(a division of Penguin Canada Books Inc.)
Penguin Books Ltd
80 Strand, London WC2R 0RL England
Penguin Ireland
25 St Stephen's Green, Dublin 2, Ireland
(a division of Penguin Books Ltd)
Penguin Books India Pvt Ltd
11 Community Centre, Panchsheel Park, New Delhi 110 017, India
Penguin Group (NZ)
67 Apollo Drive, Rosedale, Auckland 0632, New Zealand
(a division of Penguin New Zealand Pty Ltd)
Penguin Books (South Africa) (Pty) Ltd
Rosebank Office Park, Block D, 181 Jan Smuts Avenue, Parktown North,
Johannesburg 2196, South Africa
Penguin (Beijing) Ltd
7F, Tower B, Jiaming Center, 27 East Third Ring Road North, Chaoyang District,
Beijing 100020, China

Penguin Books Ltd, Registered Offices: 80 Strand, London WC2R 0RL, England

First published by Penguin Books Australia Ltd, 2014

10 9 8 7 6 5 4 3 2 1

Copyright © Michael Mori 2014
The moral right of the author has been asserted

All rights reserved. Without limiting the rights under copyright reserved above, no part of this
publication may be reproduced, stored in or introduced into a retrieval system, or transmitted, in
any form or by any means (electronic, mechanical, photocopying, recording or otherwise), without
the prior written permission of both the copyright owner and the above publisher of this book.

Cover design by John Canty © Penguin Group (Australia)
Text design by Samantha Jayaweera © Penguin Group (Australia)
Cover photograph of Michael Mori by Andrew Sheargold/Fairfax; of barbed wire
Chip Somodevilla/Getty Images.
Typeset in Adobe Garamond 12.5pt/18pt by Samantha Jayaweera, Penguin Group (Australia)
Printed and bound in Australia by Griffin Press, an accredited ISO AS/NZS 14001 Environmental
Management Systems printer.

National Library of Australia Cataloguing-in-Publication data is available.

ISBN: 9780670077854

penguin.com.au

For Dante, Enrico and Antonio

He that would make his own liberty secure, must guard even his enemy from oppression; for if he violates this duty, he establishes a precedent that will reach unto himself.

Thomas Paine

Great as the provocation has been in dealing with foes who habitually resort to treachery, murder and torture against our men, nothing can justify or will be held to justify the use of torture or inhuman conduct of any kind on the part of the American Army.

Elihu Root
US Secretary of War (1899-1904)
US Secretary of State (1905-1909)
US Senator (1909-1915)
Nobel Peace Prize Winner (1912)

Courage, acted out in our lives, watches out for the oppressed, speaks up for the weak, takes a stand against injustice and immorality and does so at our own expense. But the courage to take a stand against what is popular and easy, when required, is the key to experiencing a clear and uncluttered conscience.

General C.C. Krulak, 31st
Commandant of the Marine Corps

Author's Note

I see this book as a small part of the historical record by someone who was on the ground for one part of George W. Bush's War on Terror.

Following the attacks of 9/11, Bush's decision to establish flawed Military Commissions affected my life profoundly.

While many may like to see political conspiracy around every corner, I suggest that before giving credence to governmental conspiracy theories, you need to rule out government incompetence. The depth of the incompetence surrounding the tragic events of 9/11 includes the failure to lock the cockpit doors of commercial airliners even though the Israelis had warned the United States government to do so before 9/11, and the failure to institute many other policies and practices that may have prevented the 9/11 tragedy.

This book focuses on the continued governmental incompetence post-9/11, when the Bush administration detained hundreds of prisoners at Guantanamo Bay, an outpost erroneously believed to be free from US Constitutional and international law protections, and created an illegal Military Commission to try those alleged to be responsible for 9/11. Of the approximately 770 individuals ever detained there, fewer than 3 per cent have faced trial, even over a decade later. In using Military Commissions for the first time since World War II, Bush turned his back on the US Federal Court system, its federal judges experienced in terrorism cases, and federal prosecutors experienced in successful terrorism prosecutions. Bush's opting for the sluggish Military Commissions was at best incompetence, and at worst, a deliberate political decision to pervert justice.

The Military Commissions have not brought justice to the victims of 9/11 or to their families. The Military Commissions have not made the world safer, contributed to US military power, or increased the reputation of the United States abroad. If anything, the Military Commissions have done the exact opposite, which bothers me, especially when easy alternatives to the Military Commissions were, and are, available.

I struggled with how much detail should go into this book since I wanted it to be of interest to readers with no legal or military experience, and equally of interest to those with such experience. This book is not an all-encompassing history of Military Commissions or of the Guantanamo Bay detention policy. I was not able to chronicle each minute detail of the legal aspects of David Hicks's case. This book shares my view of what happened and why.

The David Hicks case was not one of 'who done it' but more 'what was the crime'. While this book covers a court case that involved legal proceedings in courtrooms in multiple countries, there's not much courtroom drama because much of what occurred happened outside of a court, in places such as the Pentagon, the White House, the US Congress, the Australian Parliament and even 10 Downing Street.

I worked on only one case for almost four years, whereas defense counsel in the US civilian world and military are generally responsible for many cases at any given time. After I had left the Military Commissions, I was teaching a class of military lawyers and a student asked me, 'What did you do for four years on one case?' In this book I try to answer that question.

Almost seven years have passed since my involvement in the US case against David Hicks. Publicists, agents and publishers approached me about writing a book while I was still working at the Military Commissions but I had no desire to do so at the time, and even if I wanted to write a book I had too much work to do. Years passed and I was approached again, but I felt it would be wrong for me to write a book until David Hicks had an opportunity to tell his story, and he did so in 2010, with *Guantanamo: My Journey*. While my story is different to his, it covers the same time period and events, though for that time, Hicks sat in a cell at Guantanamo Bay.

I, like so many others, wondered how a young man from Salisbury, South Australia ended up in Afghanistan. But I do not answer this question here. I have not told Hicks's story. Anyone who wants to know David's story can read his book. I try to address how an Australian was left by the Australian government at Guantanamo Bay (GTMO) to face made-up charges before an illegal United States Military Commission.

This book reveals no secrets, and does not breach the privileged attorney-client relationship Hicks and I had. Additionally, I had to submit this book for review by the US Department of Defense that sought to ensure I did not disclose any government secrets. I have not named anyone unless individuals chose to insert themselves into the public eye, were already named in the media or served in a public office. I have kept private conversations private, and not identified certain people even when no legal requirement exists.

This book offers my opinion and only mine. Any mistakes in it are mine. The views reflected in the book are not those of the US Department of Defense or the United States Marine Corps.

I

Freedom

Cuban nights are often beautiful, with a soft warmth left over from the day and the salt from the ocean still in the air. I had known more than my share of evenings at Guantanamo Bay, but none was more satisfying than the night in May 2007 when I sat in the dark at the airstrip on the leeward side of the bay, waiting for an Australian aircraft to land.

The security arrangements were as tight as if a head of state were preparing to depart. Although I had been a regular visitor to the American outpost in southern Cuba for several years, I was now on the outside of the cordon and was only able to be at the airstrip thanks to the kindness of the local military staff. When the Australian plane touched down and the crew and police officers came out, I wanted to give them some US Marine Corps Security Force T-shirts as souvenirs. I only had a moment to thrust the shirts towards them before American security shooed me away. I was a defence counsel and not supposed to be there.

I watched the big event as an outsider. Strong outdoor lights were set up around the base of the stairs leading up to the plane. Lines of armed military staff formed as if Hannibal Lecter were being moved.

When the convoy arrived, the guards stiffened. A small dark-haired man was led out of the armoured vehicle that pulled up on the tarmac. He shuffled, his legs still clasped by the iron shackles that had held him for most of the previous five and a half years. At the bottom of the stairs he stopped. The Australian police asked the US security to remove the chains.

Somewhere on his way up those steps, David Hicks ceased being a detainee of the United States and regained his rights as a citizen of Australia. At the top of the stairs, which he mounted slowly, he turned to take a last look at the place that had been his personal hell. He looked to one side of the security cordon. I was not sure if he saw me at the back of the large crowd; then, in an instant, he disappeared into the plane.

Minutes later, it took off, and the Cuban night was quiet again. The convoy drove away and the security guards disassembled the lights and wheeled away their generator. The purpose of my last four years had just gone. I had no idea what my future held, and the past had been jerked away like a rug being pulled out from under me. David Hicks was no longer my client. I didn't know what to feel. There was no elation. I couldn't have said if I'd succeeded or failed. David Hicks was going home, which was what I had strived for, day and night, since 2003. But I found it hard to even contemplate how much I had really achieved for him, let alone make an assessment. The strangest journey had brought me to this pass. I had seen the inner workings of my country's political system, and it wasn't always pretty.

I caught a lift back into the main base, and returned to my room to spend my last night in Guantanamo Bay. I couldn't wait to get off the island, and yet, in another way, I did not want to leave. This final trip would be relatively simple and straightforward. What was more complex was understanding how I had got there in the first place.

2

The Honour Code

A lot of young men who reach a point of crisis yearn for some drastic change. David Hicks, as the world would find out, had chosen his course. I wasn't all that different, except the military group I had joined was the US Marine Corps.

There were no hints of a military future for me in my schooling or upbringing. My stepfather had been a Marine for three years, a long time before I knew him, and he didn't parade the fact or even talk about it much. There were no notable military figures in our family.

That said, I grew up a proud American. When you come from Massachusetts, the birthplace of America's independence, your pride in America gets under your skin and becomes so much a part of you that you don't fully recognise it. But in American patriotism there has always been a tension between a love of the ideals that

America has stood for and practised under the banner of democracy and liberty, which have made it a beacon for freedom in the world, and the more unconditional and unthinking 'my country right or wrong' form of patriotic belief. Belief in a fair trial for an accused, regardless of who that person is or where they have come from, and justice for victims should not be at odds, but there have been times in history when they have pulled in opposition to each other. That tension has played out through my adult life as a lawyer, and to some extent has come to define who I am. I believe I have served and defended my country's highest principles, even if that has left me open to the accusation of helping those who would attack our nation.

My family's story is is common in American history. In 1912, my father's grandfather, Enrico Mori, was one of thousands of poor Italians who made the journey across the Atlantic to Ellis Island. He settled in Barre, Vermont, a town so Italian that if you go to the cemetery and look at the names, you would think you were in a city in Italy. Enrico was a stonecutter by trade who gravitated to Barre to quarry the town's grey granite. Ultimately, he became a sculptor involved in creating the Soldiers' and Sailors' World War I Memorial and the entrance to the Hope Cemetery, both in Barre.

My great-grandfather helped his wife, Maria, and their son, Dante, to migrate to Vermont, and as a child I loved visiting my great-grandmother. I was named after Dante, my grandfather, and when I was little I could speak a little Italian because that's what my great-grandmother spoke as we sat and talked and made fresh pasta.

Dante's son, my father Donald Mori, was the first person in his family to go to college, and was a practising dentist by the time I was born in 1965.

My mother Patricia's paternal family came to Beaver Falls, Pennsylvania, from Canada in a horse drawn carriage. Her grandfather had come from England and her grandmother's family, originally from Holland, had been in Canada for many generations. Her maternal family was Irish and migrated to the US before the war for independence. Her father, Walter, and his three brothers all worked in the Western Pennsylvania steel industry.

I saw a lot of Dad's family as I was growing up; my Aunt Donna and her daughters lived in Barre, only a three-hour drive from where we lived on the north shore of Massachusetts. My mother's parents moved to Florida, so while I enjoyed spending time with them, visits were a lot less frequent than visits with my father's family.

The separation between the families widened when I was nine years old and my parents divorced. My sister Pam, who is three years older than I am, and I stayed with our mother. Dad still lived locally, so I was shuttled back and forth between my parents' homes. I was luckier than other kids whose divorced parents lived on opposite sides of the country. When I was in my early teens, my mother married Dana Goodwin, a man who, with his former wife, had been a family friend of ours. We all moved to Kennebunk, a coastal town in Maine, where we'd gone on holidays when I was a young boy. This was still only a little over an hour away from my dad's house. He was also remarried, to my stepmother Villa, so I got to have a pretty normal, happy childhood. When I was fifteen, I got my motorcycle licence in Maine and was able to travel between the houses on my own, with maybe a little more independence than some; I cannot claim that I *never* told my mum I was with Dad, while telling Dad I was with Mum, and going off to stay with my friends. Children in divorced families have some small perks.

Politics didn't feature in our family conversations, whether I was in my dad's house or my mum's. If I leaned either way politically, it would have been Republican. Part of this was due to a sentimental affinity for the Bush family.

Kennebunkport was where the Bushes had their summer home. When they arrived, the buzz would go around: 'The Bushes are in town.' My stepbrothers worked for Chick's Marina, where some of the Bush boys had put in some hours. As a child I would take my little whaler boat out to grab a close look at the Bush compound, and get chased away by security – this was when George Bush, Senior, was director of the Central Intelligence Agency. I often saw members of the Bush family during summer, and, like many residents of small towns with famous residents, developed a kind of pride in the fact that we almost knew them.

I always thought George Bush, Senior, was wonderful. He'd served in the military, and had been vice-president to Ronald Reagan, who I thought had the perfect presidential persona. In 1988, when George Bush, Senior, was running for president against the Democrats' Michael Dukakis, I was solidly cheering for Bush, even though Dukakis had been governor of our own state, Massachusetts. I later worked as a summer cop in Kennebunk, and was part of the detail looking after President Bush when he came up there. In 1992, I wanted Bush to beat Bill Clinton. Although I didn't regard myself as politically engaged, I clearly leaned towards Republican candidates.

Growing up, I worked on a paper route, pumped gas and did lots of small jobs to earn money. When you grow up in New England, you can't help imbibing the place's deep roots in the American Revolution. You learn about the abuse of power, and how it was resolved by revolting against the British. I'm sure it played a role in shaping me. I was a cub scout and boy scout, and my football coaches at high school all held mainstream American views on the importance of fair play.

Even after my parents' divorce, I enjoyed a relatively stable upbringing, going to the same school in Massachusetts through the eighth grade before being sent to a boarding school, Proctor Academy, in New Hampshire. Kids came from all over the country to attend Proctor. It wasn't a super-elite or preppie school, more what you might call an 'earthy crunchy' private school, where we spent our extracurricular time building sweat huts, canoeing, playing sports and engaging in other outdoor activities. At school, I didn't get into any more trouble than I deserved, and generally did the right thing. At Proctor, we had an honour code, a sort of creed that focused on honesty in your school work, reminding you of some basic moral principles, such as playing games with good sportsmanship, never lying, stealing or cheating, and so on. It was all part of the school's philosophy.

I wasn't an exceptional athlete, even though I loved playing sports. I really didn't fill out physically until after my senior year, and then I was one of those kids who tend to go a bit wild when they start college. In September of 1983, I attended Wittenberg University in Springfield, Ohio, and soon wasn't going to a lot of classes. I was on the football team and practising lacrosse and partying. I was enjoying myself – too much – and after a while I realised that if I didn't change direction, I was in danger of wasting these years.

For the winter break in 1983, I went home to Massachusetts in a state of private upheaval. I knew I needed to grow up, but couldn't see it happening while I remained in the college environment. The only effort I was putting in was to sports and recreation. I'd been at boarding school for a long time, and probably was tired of the academic demands. It wasn't a moment of epiphany that hit me with a blinding light one day; I just knew I needed a drastic change in my life, and joining the military would be such a change. I went to all the different recruiting offices for the armed services, asking, 'Who can send me off to boot camp before Christmas?' Most of the services had filled their quotas, and the only one interested in getting me shipped off that quickly was the Marine Corps's Sergeant Brown, in the recruiting office in Salem, Massachusetts. By early December 1983, I had taken the entrance test and was signed up. I was shipped off and arrived at Parris Island on 21 December. I had no idea I had just set the path for the next twenty-nine years of my life.

3

Stumbling into My Future

I've never had a grand plan for what I wanted to do with my life. At any particular moment, it's just, 'What's the next step?' If the Marine Corps hadn't taken me, I might have gone back to college in Ohio and got the partying out of my system. Who knows? But I joined the Marines on an impulse, and it changed the direction of my life.

When I told my mother I was joining the Marines, she was horrified. The bombing of the Marine Barracks in Beirut, Lebanon, had happened just a month earlier, and she was thinking, 'Oh God, 200-plus Marines have just been killed.' Dad joked about not having to pay my college fees, but actually he thought the military was a good idea: after twenty years, I would have a pension for the rest of my life. I was not thinking that far ahead.

Parris Island, on the south-east coast of South Carolina, has been the traditional location for Marine Corps Recruit training since 1915. When I showed up in December 1983, there were yellow footprints on the pavement outside the Receiving Barracks, to remind us of the generations of Marines we were following. Boot camp itself was everything we had been warned it would be, and everything we might have hoped and dreaded: like the first part of the movie *Full Metal Jacket*, just without as much violence. But I got through, and found that I liked the athleticism of training: the running, the obstacle courses, even the drill. After boot camp I was off to electronics school and then to my duty station at the Marine Corps Air Station at Cherry Point, North Carolina, where I worked on testing and repairing electronics for aircrafts.

As for actual combat, that seemed a distant prospect. As any infantry Marine would tell you, those in the 'Air Wing' had little chance of hearing any shots fired in anger. Nothing was happening in terms of overseas military action but, of course, most Marines couldn't help wanting to deploy. If I remained in the Marines, I thought I might get to be an embassy guard and travel the world. That was about as far as those ideas went.

Without a war to fight, I discovered rugby. The sport grabbed hold of me for the next eighteen years. I played number eight and flanker, having grown a bit since my school days, and loved the game's demands on the brain as well as the body, the way you have to think clearly when you're exhausted.

There were sacrifices, occasionally. At one point I was in Colorado and my friends were going to a concert at Red Rocks, and due to my Marine commitments I missed going to U2's celebrated Red Rocks show. Little did I know, thirty years later Bono would play another significant part in my life when he called for David Hicks to be released.

During almost four years in the Marine Corps, I matured – a little bit. After finishing my active duty enlistment, I transferred to the Marine Reserves. I went back to obtain a college degree, at Norwich University in Vermont, majoring in communications. At Norwich I got more involved in rugby and the camaraderie of the rugby club made the years fly by. A real highlight was going on a rugby tour to New Zealand and Australia. I didn't know much about Australia besides *Crocodile Dundee* and Olivia Newton-John, but as a rugby player I'd have given my right arm to live in New Zealand, Australia or South Africa. We had a ball playing in Rotorua and Auckland, and then travelling up the Australian eastern seaboard for matches against university teams in Sydney, Brisbane and Cairns. My memories are all a bit of a blur when it comes to the activities that occupied us between games, although I do recall falling down some stairs in Kings Cross. Anyway, what happens on tour stays on tour, and I wouldn't tell tales even if I could remember them. I'll never forget what a great time I had with the locals and how I developed a real affinity for Australia and its people. For years after that trip, I was hoping and dreaming to get back Down Under.

During college, I completed Marine Corps Officers Candidate School (OCS) at Quantico, Virginia, in two of my summer breaks and worked as a reserve police officer during the summers. As I began my senior year of college, I pondered what to do next. With OCS completed, I was qualified to accept a commission and return to the Marines as an officer. Several of my friends were doing this; the only reason I hesitated was that unless you had a flight contract (to be a pilot), you wouldn't know what specific job you'd have in the Marines until you were already committed. Not to knock any of these roles in the Marines, but I was not that excited about becoming an administrative or motor transport officer.

One way of seizing control of your destiny was to get the flight contract. In the Marines you had to have 20:20 vision to be a pilot or backseater, the guy in a jet who sits behind the pilot and operates the electronics. (For any *Top Gun* fans, that's Goose.) That ruled me out, as I am short-sighted, but the Navy was also advertising for their flight test and didn't require 20:20 vision for potential backseaters.

I met my Marine Corps recruiter and told him what I was thinking. He said, 'Why would you want to join the Navy?' and I told him it was because I didn't want to be a motor transport officer.

'I can't let you fly,' he said, 'but I do have a law slot. Do you want to be a Judge Advocate?' That's what the military calls a lawyer.

Huh? It had never crossed my mind. I'd never thought of being a lawyer.

'What do I have to do?' I asked.

'If you can get into a law school,' he said, 'the slot's yours.'

So, stumbling along from one thing to the next, I found myself taking the Law School Admission Test (LSAT), a quiz of raw intelligence and thinking ability (which had no real reflection on how someone would perform as a practising lawyer), and applying to a couple of law schools. Luckily, I was accepted. That's how I became a lawyer – almost by accident.

I graduated from Norwich University and received my commission as a Second Lieutenant. While my friends went off on active duty, I went on reserve status to attend Western New England School of Law in Springfield, Massachusetts, for the next three years. My abiding love in law school quickly became criminal law. In the basic first-year courses, my favourites were criminal procedure and evidence. I had a really good professor for several criminal law subjects, and I'd always read books involving true crime. Plus, I knew that once I was in the Marine Corps, criminal law would mean litigation and being in court, which really enticed me.

A rugby tournament clashed with my graduation date, so, to my mother's disappointment, I didn't attend the ceremony in May 1994. I studied for two months for my Massachusetts bar exam, the professional qualification required to obtain a law licence in Massachusetts, which was a requirement for me to go on active duty in the Marines. I took the exam in July but had to wait until December before receiving my results: I passed.

With my law licence in hand, I got in line for a spot on active duty to attend the Basic School in Quantico, Virginia, which was a six-month school that all Marine officers had to complete. I had to wait until June of 1995 for a spot to open up. After the Basic School, I was off to Naval Justice School, where all Navy, Marine Corps and Coast Guard lawyers complete a course to learn about the various areas of military legal practice they might encounter. Finally, after eight months of training, in March of 1996, I was heading off to my first duty station as a lawyer: back to Parris Island.

Having been at Parris Island for boot camp, I was feeling nostalgic to be heading back. It was good not to be heading there as a recruit, though. Parris Island for a lawyer was ideal: not too busy, but busy enough to gain valuable court experience. I started in the legal assistance office, which was a walk-in legal clinic for all the Marines and their spouses on the base. You never knew what was going to come through the door. One Marine might come in complaining that he was getting ripped off by his landlord; someone else was going through a divorce; another had a legal letter from his home town that he didn't understand. It was good, useful work, and provided me with a solid grounding in legal practice.

I hungered to do trial work, though, in the military courts. I started by doing some guilty pleas for the prosecution office and administrative discharge boards representing Marines and Sailors who were facing a hearing on whether they should be discharged from the service. After about a year, I was assigned to the defence office under Captain Gary Baumann to provide representation in courts-martial. I am always shocked when I hear civilians express a concern that a court-martial is an unfair system. Military courts-martial operated very much like a US civilian criminal trial in a state or federal court. Courts-martial have a jury and judge structure and a very expansive requirement of the prosecution to turn over evidence to the defence. F. Lee Bailey, of the O.J. Simpson trial fame, said if he were guilty he'd rather be tried in a civilian court, and if he were innocent in a court-martial.

Parris Island provided great opportunities for trial work as a defence counsel. Most of the clients were mid-career Marines who had a lot at stake. If drill instructors with ten or fifteen years behind them had been accused of, let's say, adjusting a recruit's body position a bit too hard – and charged with assault – they might not be facing a punishment as serious as years in prison, but could lose everything they had worked for: reputation, career and retirement benefits. As a defence counsel, I would be wearing the white hat, coming in on the side of the hard-working Marine against the prosecutorial powers of the institution. There were all sorts of other matters as well, similar to civilian life, such as drugs charges, sexual assault and other offences covering the full range from petty to serious.

And the defence counsel were not very popular. It is hard for a commander to send someone to court unless they strongly believe the Marine or Sailor has committed the offence he's been charged with. Once they've made the decision, the commander is vested in getting a conviction. It takes a good commander to stand back and say, 'Look, there's some evidence, but it's got to be a fair process, so we want the defence to be well resourced because they're defending our Marine.' In many instances, commanders went the other way and were too personally involved in the success of the prosecution.

This first tour taught me there is no love lost for defence counsel in the military. When I finished my three years at Parris Island, I didn't receive the traditional end-of-tour award. The prosecutor who left before me and the prosecutor who left after me received theirs, while neither I nor my friend, who was also a defence lawyer and finished after me, got ours. It was a subtle sign of what happens if you fight the system too hard. So being the white-hat lawyer might have been stimulating and ethical work, but it wasn't great for your military career prospects.

At Parris Island, I learnt as much from the bad lawyers as from the good ones. I saw prosecutors who were not necessarily deceitful, but who did everything they could to win, stretching the rules to their limits. On the positive side, I was exposed to some outstanding lawyers, such as Major John Ewers, who in 2014 attained the rank of Major-General as the Staff Judge Advocate to the Commandant of the Marine Corps. His advice on fighting hard but fair in court and always doing the right thing reinforced the values I had learnt growing up. There was a message sent from the Commandant of the Marine Corps, General C.C. Krulak, in January 1997, which would never leave me:

> Courage, acted out in our lives, watches out for the oppressed, speaks up for the weak, takes a stand against injustice and immorality and does so at our own expense. But the courage to take a stand against what is popular and easy, when required, is the key to experiencing a clear and uncluttered conscience.

Those are words I've tried to live up to. They would echo throughout my military career, even though I may not always have achieved that high standard.

By 1998, when I was coming to the end of my time at Parris Island, I was planning to get out of the Marine Corps. I wanted to try starting a civilian legal practice in Massachusetts. While on leave, I put in a bid to buy a house with an old dental office, which I wanted to convert into my own law office, when a small wrinkle arose: a possibly leaking oil tank that might require a large environmental clean-up stalled the purchase contract. Then fate came calling in the form of a phone call from a Marine lawyer who had attended my law school and was now working at the legal headquarters for the Marines, putting lawyers in different jobs around the world. He had a 'hot-fill' – they needed someone urgently – to go to work at the Navy legal office in Japan.

'OK,' I said. I didn't really want the hassles with the house; I hadn't made any other commitments; Japan sounded interesting. Everything else could wait. Adventure beckoned.

4

The Turning Point

Japan was everything I'd hoped for. I was living in a local Japanese community a few miles from the base and this gave me an opportunity to experience the real culture, the local events and festivals, which can sometimes be missed when people visit countries on a two-week holiday. Japan was also a wonderful location to get out and visit other countries in Asia. In my first year I headed the Civil Law Department, overseeing legal assistance for military members and their families, as well as Japanese compensation claims. For the next two years, I served as senior defence counsel, a job that was everything I'd hoped being a military lawyer would be. It was not quite as exciting as the television show *JAG*, but my lawyers and I were flying around the South Pacific and other parts of the world, working on cases. The catchment area for the office covered everywhere from Hawaii to Australia. (Having loved the place so much on my earlier rugby trip, I was dying for a client in Australia, but it never happened!) I would fly onto an aircraft carrier for a hearing, or to the middle of the Indian Ocean to the base at Diego Garcia to defend a client, and then go back to Japan. I also had the opportunity to teach new lawyers the skills I had learnt. This was why I enjoyed the military. I also found another great rugby team at the Yokohama Country and Athletic Club, and another instant group of friends from around the world.

My tour in Japan lasted three years. At the end I was again thinking about switching to the Marine Reserves and pursuing the challenge of a civilian law career. Again fate intervened. I had let it be known that I was thinking of getting out, but then got a call from a former colleague at Parris Island who had taken over the role of assigning lawyers to bases.

'Why are you getting out?' he asked. 'We're going to send you to Hawaii. People save money all their lives to spend two weeks in Hawaii, and the Marine Corps is going to pay you to live there for three years!'

His logic convinced me. In Hawaii, I would be switching to the prosecuting side of military law, as a Military Justice Officer. It was important to keep gaining experience and expanding my skills.

Marine Corps Base Hawaii (MCBH), where I was posted in August 2001, is at Kaneohe Bay, on the windward side of Hawaii's most populous island, Oahu. Waikiki Beach and Honolulu are to the south-west, and the famous surf spots of Pipeline, Sunset and Waimea Bay are on the north shore, while Kaneohe Bay sits at the east end of the H-3 Highway. On 7 December 1941, the Naval Air station on the MCBH site at Kaneohe Bay was attacked minutes before Pearl Harbor. The first Japanese aircraft was shot down by Marines and Sailors at Kaneohe, and one of the first Medals of Honor earned during World War II was for the heroic actions of Lieutenant John Finn. His Medal of Honor citation reads, in part, that he 'manned a 50-caliber machine gun mounted on an instruction stand in a completely exposed section of the parking ramp, which was under heavy enemy machine-gun strafing fire. Although painfully wounded many times, he continued to man this gun and to return the enemy's fire vigorously.'

In August, when I was driven from the Honolulu side of Oahu through the Pali Mountains, exiting the tunnel and catching my first glimpse of the base, it looked like paradise. And in Marine Corps terms, it was! The MCBH seemed like an ideal duty station for a Marine lawyer. My predecessor said it was busy enough with work to get good trial experience, but not so busy that you couldn't enjoy the island. I couldn't believe my luck. Little did I know how my life was about to change.

Not being one for watching the morning news, I had no idea what was happening, as the traffic was backed up for nearly a mile outside the base, just one month into my new job. Hawaii is six hours behind East Coast time, and I might have been the last person in America not to know what was going on. It was 11 September 2001.

I was sitting in this traffic jam when a Navy guy walked past.

'What's going on?' I said.

'There have been some attacks, so parts of the base are being secured,' he said. 'Only essential personnel are needed.'

I pulled a U-turn and headed back home, where I turned on the news and phoned the office. It was already early afternoon in New York and Washington DC, and although the terrorist attacks were over and the World Trade Center towers had fallen, nobody knew exactly what had happened yet, and there was a lot of speculation about what might happen next and who was behind it. There were suggestions in those first hours that as many as 40000 people had been killed. Nobody knew any more than they were getting from the constant repetition of the same footage and the wild suppositions of the news media. Like everyone else, I was most worried about whether any of my friends or family had been killed. But I was also wondering what role we (the military) might play in pursuing those responsible for the attacks.

Over the next few weeks, events moved quickly. President George W. Bush gave the Taliban his ultimatum to hand over Osama bin Laden, the leader of al-Qaeda, the organisation being reported as behind the attack. When the US Congress passed its resolution to authorise the use of the armed forces to retaliate, I was concerned for my friends and fellow service personnel serving overseas, who might end up in Afghanistan. I also wondered if I would get the opportunity to become involved. An idyllic three years on the islands suddenly seemed a bit inconsequential.

The ground war in Afghanistan began in October 2001 and ended just as quickly. The hunt for bin Laden was on and, while a few of my friends headed off to Afghanistan, all I could do was focus on my duties in Hawaii and wait for an opportunity to arise. The media liked to report on who was responsible for 9/11 and what could have been done to prevent it, but as the months rolled on Iraq began to be reported on more frequently and the focus shifted to Saddam Hussein as bin Laden proved elusive.

We had an important visitor to the base in late 2002. The most senior uniformed lawyer in the Marine Corps was Brigadier

General Kevin M. Sandkuhler, the Staff Judge Advocate to the Commandant of the Marine Corps. Sandkuhler came to the MCBH at Kaneohe Bay on his annual inspection of all legal offices within Marine bases, and briefed the Marine lawyers about the Military Commissions that were being set up to try enemy fighters who had been captured in the Afghanistan conflict. Lawyers from the Army were taking the lead in the commissions, and at the time the Marines were being told not to provide any more legal staff.

I had no real interest in and little knowledge of Bush's Military Commissions, beyond what I'd occasionally seen in the media. The one thing that I did wonder about was that the United States was not calling the enemy fighters captured in Afghanistan 'prisoners of war', but instead had given them new labels: 'unlawful enemy combatants' or 'illegal combatants'. In the basic law-of-war training I had received in Hawaii, there was never any mention of such a thing. Captured fighters in a war were enemy prisoners of war, retained persons, such as enemy doctors or chaplains, or civilian internees. In retrospect, it would become obvious that this was the administration's foundation for ignoring the Geneva Conventions. At the time, though, as Sandkuhler told us, our chances of being involved were slim to non-existent, so I didn't pay as much attention to it as perhaps I should have.

Instead, I was focused on the growing call for war in Iraq, which was going to start in early 2003. Lieutenant Colonel Ewers, who I knew from my Parris Island days, was wounded during the first weeks of fighting in Iraq. I had other friends engaged in both Afghanistan and Iraq, and many more who were preparing to go. For me personally, it was a matter of waiting. The senior legal staff were deciding who was going on an upcoming deployment for

Iraq. If I missed out on that, I would either be left in Hawaii to run the law centre or would be deployed to an annual military exercise in Thailand called Cobra Gold.

It came out of left field when my Staff Judge Advocate in Hawaii, Lieutenant Colonel Laulie Powell, told me that she, along with all the Staff Judge Advocates in the Marine Corps, had received an email seeking nominations for potential defence counsel for the Military Commissions. This came as a surprise after Brigadier General Sandkuhler's earlier advice that Marine lawyers were not going to be required. But as it turned out the Department of Defence (DOD) wasn't happy with the Army lawyers' model for the commissions, which was based on courts-martial. The DOD, it later emerged, wanted a more fluid set of rules that it could influence.

Lieutenant Colonel Powell asked me if I wanted her to put my name forward, and I initially asked her for some time to consider it. I really didn't want to leave Hawaii unless it was for a deployment to a combat zone, which is where I think every Marine lawyer wants to go; that is why we joined the Marines. I enjoyed my duties in Hawaii, which included serving as a Special Assistant US Attorney working out of the US Attorney's office in Honolulu, reviewing and prosecuting alleged violations of federal law by civilians that had occurred on the Marine bases. Lieutenant Colonel Powell thought I would be able to work Military Commission cases out of Hawaii. If I had known that this was actually not going to be possible, I might not have put my name forward.

I sought some guidance from my military judge at the time, Lieutenant Colonel Bob Fricke, who pointed out that I had been involved with military courts-martial for almost eight years and might be stimulated by a new challenge. You never know what lies ahead, but new is not always bad, he suggested.

Finally, thinking no more deeply or long term than to ask myself, 'Why not?' I told Lieutenant Colonel Powell to put my name in. It was a stab in the dark. I was being asked to volunteer to represent a type of client I did not know, on charges of a yet-to-be-determined nature, before a tribunal whose status and procedures were unclear. I had been told that the Military Commissions would be a lot like courts-martial, though, and I had the expertise for that.

My lack of engagement with politics meant I was relatively unaffected by the government's rhetoric on the captured fighters. President Bush might have labelled them as terrorists and 'the worst of the worst', but that had no impact on me. I loved the law, and wholly believed that whoever the defendants were and whatever they had been accused of, they were entitled to proper representation and due process. I believed, as an article of faith, in the words of Dr R. John Pritchard, who wrote in the *Military Law Review* in 1995, 'For any lawyer, the issue of due process ought to be the main concern: it defines the strength or weakness of these proceedings. Due process stands apart from the substantive issues of the trial.' Due process, the inherent fairness of the system, is what stands between us and authoritarian or corrupt regimes. That was my overriding principle.

In any case, I'd put my name forward knowing that the chances were that I would not be selected. So having said yes to Lieutenant Colonel Powell, I promptly put it to the back of my mind.

It turned out that Lieutenant Colonel Powell was to deploy to Operation Iraqi Freedom, my friend was given the law centre to run in her place, and I was sent to Thailand for the military exercise

Cobra Gold as an Executive Officer for Brigade Service Support Group-3. While it was not Iraq or Afghanistan, it was a rare leadership opportunity for a lawyer. Just before I left for Thailand, I was told that I was one of four Marine lawyers whose names would be submitted to the DOD General Counsel's office (DOD GC) for consideration as a defence lawyer at the Military Commissions. I went to Thailand, where I soon received an email telling me to call Colonel Will Gunn, an Air Force lawyer who had been selected as the Chief Defense Counsel for Military Commissions (CDC), to be interviewed for the job. In the telephone interview, I outlined to Colonel Gunn my background in the Marines and my litigation experience, and he advised me that someone would be in touch. I wasn't sure if I would hear back from him, and I kind of dreaded working for the Air Force, the so-called 'Chair Force', which has a reputation for being slightly more military than the US Postal Service. (Sorry, cheap shot at the Air Force.)

When I flew back to Hawaii in June 2003, I was informed that I was the Marine Corps' representative selected to assist in the defence of the detainees at the Naval Station Guantanamo Bay (GTMO). I wanted to know when the job would start and, most importantly, whether it was still OK for me to do it from Hawaii. Nobody knew. I started trying to gather as much information as I could find on the commissions, and get a sense of what I was in for.

5

The Military Commissions

My understanding of the Military Commissions' history, rationale and main purpose would take several years to come together. Looking back, it was an education of slowly unfolding puzzlement. I began as a military lawyer looking for a new opportunity. I went through periods of questioning and disbelief, as if what I was learning were things that could not possibly be true, or as if I had awoken at some time in the past. Finally, I arrived at a somewhat jaded disillusionment. But that would take some time. I didn't start out as a cynic: I was proud of the military courts-martial system and expected to be involved in a process that upheld the same tradition. I have always remained committed to the same principles of law and justice as when I started out. What changed was my exposure to how far those in power would go to further their own aims, and how easy it was for others to go along with them to further their own careers.

The first retaliatory step President Bush took after the 9/11 attacks was to invade Afghanistan in October 2001. A month later, he issued a President's Military Order (PMO), resurrecting a type of tribunal that had not been used since World War II.

American military tribunals of one kind or another went back to the birth of the United States, but on 2 July 1942 President Franklin Roosevelt created the 'modern' version, issuing an 'Order Establishing a Military Commission to Try Eight Captured German Saboteurs'. The commission had a strictly limited jurisdiction, hearing only 'violations of the laws of war and other applicable laws by military tribunals'. But although its scope was limited, its powers were not. Unlike a civilian criminal court – where a jury decides questions of fact and a judge oversees questions of law – the Military Commission would combine both functions. That was an extraordinary departure from American criminal law. The German saboteurs were tried and six were executed. This case would be the cornerstone of the Bush administration's justification for its new commissions.

While Military Commissions were used on occasion throughout World War II, during the Korean conflict in 1950, new rules were written by the United Nations for the commissions. In an advancement from the WWII commissions, and showing that the United States led the way in principles of justice, the US rules of evidence used in courts-martial would be the standard applied by the United Nations.

Now, President Bush was reintroducing a system unused for more than half a century, saying courts-martial, which had a long and strong history of use in combat situations, were not sufficient to counter 'the danger to the safety of the United States and the nature of international terrorism'. According to his PMO and the instructions that followed it, the Military Commissions would not apply the basic rules of evidence common to courts-martial and civilian criminal courts. Hearsay (testifying to what someone else said), for instance, and statements obtained through coercion, which are not admissible as evidence in criminal courts, would be allowed. The Military Commissions would have just one such rule: evidence would be admissible if it would, in the opinion of the presiding officer or the majority of the commission, have probative value to a reasonable person. That is, if a reasonable person thought the evidence was relevant, it could be admitted, no matter how it had been obtained or how reliable it was.

This elimination of the rules of evidence really bothered me. Were the architects of the commissions worried that if they didn't relax the rules of evidence, they couldn't prove that crimes had actually taken place? I could see that the playing field was tilted strongly in favour of the prosecuting authority, and the United States was abandoning the long-held principle that our courts treat everyone equally. (Although I was probably a little idealistic if you consider how minorities have been treated.) The Bush administration was reaching back to a system that could be used only against non-US individuals whom the President personally selected in writing. If Bush had permitted US citizens to be tried by the commissions, they might claim constitutional rights, which would highlight the unequal treatment of foreigners.

Among the essential checks and balances in our system are the different levels of courts, which means mistakes made by judges in the lower courts can be corrected. But here, too, Bush's PMO sought an exception, saying individuals could not appeal to any court – American, foreign or international. Instead, they could appeal within the DOD and the final arbiter would be the Secretary of Defense, who at the time was Donald Rumsfeld, or the President himself.

The sheer audacity of the PMO surprised me, as a lawyer. In a document no more than a couple of pages in length, Bush had thrown out our country's basic rules and procedures, and empowered Rumsfeld or his successors to be judge, jury, executioner *and* appellate court.

Bush's PMO, significant as it was, comprised only an outline of the new system. The order still had to be given the appearance of legal language, and the job of drafting it went to Jim Haynes, the young General Counsel for Rumsfeld's department. A trusted insider for the Republican hierarchy, Haynes had graduated from Harvard Law School in 1983, clerked for a District Court judge, and then served as an Army lawyer. He attained the rank of captain. Within a year of leaving active duty, Haynes was appointed, by the first President Bush, as General Counsel of the Army, a position equal to a two-star Army General. For three years he worked alongside Dick Cheney, then the Secretary of Defense. In May 2001, following a period of employment in corporate America during the Clinton years, Haynes was appointed General Counsel for Rumsfeld, Cheney's mentor back in the Ford administration. When George W. Bush, Cheney and Rumsfeld wanted the legal authority to do whatever they wished with captured enemy combatants from the global War on Terror, Haynes was there to write the rules to suit. On 21 March 2002, Rumsfeld, through Haynes, began to flesh out the PMO with his Military Commission Order (MCO) No. 1.

Under the MCO, Rumsfeld would create the rules of the Military Commissions and select an Appointing Authority (AA), who would approve charges, select the presiding officer and other members of the commission, and approve plea agreements. To sit on the commission, prospective members had to be military officers. Obviously the creators felt they couldn't trust enlisted men to stick to the script.

MCO No. 1 really stacked the deck against the accused. It's a fundamental principle of a legal system in any democracy that the accused is able to see and hear the evidence against him, unless he doesn't want to see it or has behaved disruptively (and even then, he can still see it from a separate area). No US court would allow a criminal trial to proceed without the accused if he wanted to be present and had not been disruptive. Yet these new commissions would have the power to exclude the accused if classified material was presented in evidence. This one rule would lead to the downfall of the system two and a half years later.

In 2002, the media was examining the MCO to some degree, but they missed what was probably its most shocking rule: if a motion arose that could result in a charge being dismissed, the commission had to send it to the Appointing Authority for a decision. It meant that the person who approved charges against an accused would then be in a position to rule on any legal challenge to the charges he had approved. Essentially, this was like letting the District Attorney (or Director of Public Prosecutions) decide on crucial legal points filed by the defence. Obviously, this is absurd: the prosecutor is a player in the trial. If you wanted to view it in a sinister light, it almost betrayed the creators' lack of trust in even the hand-selected commission members to do their bidding.

As I investigated the new system, the question I kept asking myself was, 'Why?' Why resurrect this old system, giving it such bizarre and unconstitutional powers? If the Bush administration wanted a quick criminal process to try those accused of involvement in the 9/11 attacks, why did it not just use the US federal court system? The US has a war crimes statute that permits a federal court trial for '[w]hoever, whether in or outside the United States, commits a war crime'. If found guilty, the accused terrorists could face the death penalty. The US federal courts had been convicting people charged with terrorist offences for years. Certain US attorney offices had become experts in prosecuting terrorist-related cases, and would secure hundreds of convictions in the decade after 2001. If the system had these powers and capabilities already, why was it not being used for the 'terrorists' and 'unlawful combatants' captured in Afghanistan?

I began to dig through the public record into the genesis of the Military Commissions. Shortly after 9/11, William Barr, a former US Attorney-General, had suggested the use of Military Commissions to Timothy Flannigan, a Deputy White House Counsel. It is claimed that this was where it all started. It was taken up by David Addington, the Vice-President's counsel, who had also worked with Dick Cheney when he was Secretary of Defense. Like many others involved in the push for Military Commissions, Addington had no military service (except for dropping out of the US Naval Academy in his first year) or any substantial experience as a criminal trial attorney. It is believed that it was Addington who copied Franklin Roosevelt's order, with a few additions, to be signed by President George W. Bush.

Following the issue of the PMO, the White House Counsel, Alberto Gonzales, began looking at different options for trials. The State Department already had a war crimes ambassador, Pierre-Richard Prosper, but Gonzales is said to have bypassed his office and produced a memorandum on 6 November 2001, authored by Patrick Philbin, a legal officer under Gonzales. Philbin, a Yale and Harvard graduate, also had no real experience either in the military or in criminal trials. His memorandum said the new Military Commissions would be based on the assumption that all potential accused would not be classified as prisoners of war (POWs) or entitled to any of the protections of the Geneva Conventions provided to POWs, thus removing the main hurdle to stripping away their rights.

This was crucial, because enemy POWs are entitled to the same protections as our service personnel if they were ever captured. They had to be treated humanely, and, if charged with a war crime, be tried under the same system we would try our own services members under. Someone would be a prisoner of war if they fell into one of several categories, and the most applicable to the war in Afghanistan were:

1. members of the armed forces of a country including members of militias or volunteer corps forming part of the armed forces;
2. members of other militias and members of other volunteer corps, including those of organised resistance movements, so long as they met four criteria;
3. inhabitants of a country who took up arms to resist an invading force, provided they carried their arms openly and respect the laws and customs of war.

The criteria required for the second category were:
   a. that of being commanded by a person responsible for his subordinates;

b. that of having a fixed distinctive sign recognisable at a
distance;

c. that of carrying arms openly;

d. that of conducting their operations in accordance with the
laws and customs of war.

One important rule came from Article 5 of the Geneva Conventions, stating that if there was any doubt about someone's POW status, a tribunal was required to determine their status based on the facts. Philbin, however, wrote, 'We stress at the outset that determining that the terrorist attacks can be treated under the rubric of the "laws of war" does not mean that terrorists will receive the protections of the Geneva Conventions.' It got a bit *Alice in Wonderland* here. He advised that fighters charged with breaking the laws of war, as defined by the Geneva Conventions, were not to be treated as POWs, because if they were POWs they would be entitled to Geneva's protections. This was something the administration did not want. Why did this really matter, you might ask. Bottom line was, if anyone captured in Afghanistan and shipped to GTMO was determined to be an enemy POW, the newly created Military Commissions could not be used, as this was not the same system we would use for trying one of our own soldiers for a war crime.

The importance of the Geneva Conventions shouldn't need stating, but in these times nothing can be taken for granted. At the end of World War II, the USA was one of the leading countries to create the 1949 Geneva Conventions that governed the treatment and protection of not only civilians, but also anyone captured during a war. Soldiers only need to give their name, rank and serial number, and cannot be tortured or otherwise compelled to give up other information. There are numerous other protections for POWs, made necessary because of the outrages perpetrated by German and Japanese soldiers upon Allied captives in the 1940s.

This major decision to withhold POW status was not as yet based on any facts relating to any particular captured fighter. Those who had carried out the 9/11 attacks were dead. Soon to be captured were some of those who allegedly coordinated or supported the attacks. But what about those who would be captured on the battlefield during the conflict that was brewing in Afghanistan? Were they to be designated as terrorists, on the same legal footing as the men who devised or carried out the 9/11 attacks, before they were even caught? It seemed that they were, because the United States, according to Gonzales, wanted to use 'every tool and weapon' available to win the war. If it wanted to use the law of war, it could, but if it wanted to create some new, fictitious legal basis – denying detainees POW status – it would do that too.

As US forces began capturing people in Afghanistan during Operation Enduring Freedom, how our troops would apply the Geneva Conventions was raised. During the battles from October through to December 2001, thousands of enemy soldiers surrendered, or switched sides, as deals were cut between the Taliban and Northern Alliance commanders. A handful of US troops had to screen and select those to send to the processing centres in Afghanistan, and then, for those the Bush administration had termed the 'worst of the worst', off to the swiftly erected facility at Guantanamo Bay, Cuba. Some enemy fighters were handed over as a result of the US bounty program, where cash was paid for foreigners or alleged Taliban leaders. There were no firm criteria for the screening of detainees, and it was done haphazardly, to say the least. Among those detained was a pathetic foot soldier with half his head blown off, a very old white-bearded man whom the US soldiers would dub 'al-Qaeda Claus', and so many bit players that the first commander of Guantanamo Bay, Major-General Michael Dunleavy, protested at the 'Mickey Mouse' detainees he was getting instead of actual terrorists. An Army lawyer, Lieutenant Colonel Thomas Berg, concluded, 'We had simply gotten the slowest guys on the battlefield.' Of course, we now know that most of the real leadership of the Taliban and al-Qaeda made it out of Afghanistan in late 2001, and most of those who were captured were foot soldiers and people attending the camps who were left behind to fend for themselves. Of the estimated 45000 enemy soldiers in Afghanistan, only some 770 made it to Guantanamo Bay, which undermines the Bush administration's justification for using GTMO as a place to keep the enemy off the battlefield.

No war crimes investigations were conducted in Afghanistan, to see who might have violated the laws of war and if a trial was warranted, before a person was shipped off to Guantanamo Bay. Initially, I believed, perhaps naively, that such investigations were taking place. Not unsurprisingly, at first the US military was following the Geneva Conventions. Military units in Afghanistan, such as Task Force 58 of Operation Enduring Freedom, were processing detainees as presumptive enemy prisoners of war (POWs), and were preparing to conduct tribunals as required under Article 5. A 500-capacity detention centre was set up at Kandahar where such tribunals could have been held. This is the military: we have regulations and orders on everything, including how to treat people who are captured and how to determine who is and who is not a POW. Central Command, the overall authority for Afghanistan based in Tampa, Florida, who was taking these new prisoners, had conducted more than a thousand of these Article 5 tribunals during the first Gulf War. All that was required was a panel of three commissioned officers, at least one of whom had to be a Judge Advocate. It was a simple process. If a military unit held an Article 5 tribunal and determined a captured person was a POW, though, it would have caused enormous problems for the Bush administration's plan, so this had to be stopped.

On 19 January 2002, Rumsfeld issued a memorandum to the Chairman of the Joint Chiefs of Staff, General Richard Myers, stating, 'Al-Qaeda and Taliban individuals under the control of the Department of Defense are not entitled to prisoner of war status for purposes of the Geneva Conventions of 1949.' In five short paragraphs, Rumsfeld, presumably with Bush's approval, was breaking from the Geneva Conventions. Without hesitation, Myers transmitted this order to the commanders two days later. The two commanders with overriding responsibility for captured fighters went right along with ignoring the Geneva Conventions. There was a whimper from Secretary of State Colin Powell, himself a decorated former general, but he was seen as nothing but a speed bump.

On 7 February 2002, Bush sealed the deal, saying the Geneva Conventions would apply to our war in Afghanistan but, unlucky for the Taliban, none of their forces met the criteria entitling them to POW status. (Whether or not this decision was correct for each person is debateable, but it broke from the process required under the Geneva Conventions and set up a strange outcome: the US could invade a country and no one who resisted was entitled to POW status.) Nor would the Geneva Conventions apply to a captured person the administration labeled as 'al-Qaeda' without any analysis of what they might have actually done in the war in Afghanistan. In a few sentences, Bush created out of thin air a 'new' type of war – the global War on Terror – that somehow was not governed by the Geneva Conventions.

As a lawyer preparing for the possibility of representing some of the captives from the war, I felt like I was sinking in quicksand. How could we know if the detainees were legitimate POWs or this new class of 'illegals' from the War on Terror? How could we tell who was a member of al-Qaeda? What were the requirements to be considered part of the Taliban? Or was I asking the question the wrong way around? More Lewis Carroll logic: were they 'illegals', and not entitled to POW status or the protections of the Geneva Conventions, merely *because* they had been captured? I was soon to confront this strange legal quagmire not in the abstract, or on paper, but in the form of a human being.

6

My 'Client'

At Marine Corps Base Hawaii, the Fourth of July weekend was huge. The base opened its gates to the community for its annual carnival, featuring displays of weapons and equipment, the best fireworks display on Oahu, and musicians for three days of fun in the Hawaiian sun. I had married my girlfriend, Dara, in 2002, and we were enjoying Hawaii.

In the aftermath of the holiday weekend, I was preparing for the work arising from the misconduct charges that usually occurred when you mixed thousands of young Sailors and Marines with alcohol, when I received the call from the Military Commission defence office that changed my life for the next four years.

I was enjoying my job as a prosecutor, believing that in that role I could do some good. I appreciated the fact that the junior enlisted Marines, the majority of defendants in court, also did the majority of dying for their country. I had compassion for the stupid mistakes young people make, having made my own share. My sense of what was right or wrong did not change just because I was with the prosecution or defence.

On 9 July 2003, Navy Lieutenant Commander Philip Sundel called to tell me that Colonel Gunn might detail me to David Hicks.

Caught up in the celebration of our independence, I had missed a quiet announcement made by President Bush on 3 July 2003 designating David Hicks, an Australian national, and five other Guantanamo detainees as 'enemy combatants' subject to his PMO of 13 November 2001. Hicks had been captured by Northern Alliance Forces in Afghanistan a few weeks after the PMO was first released.

It seemed that this new 'enemy combatant' term was just a vague umbrella definition that the administration could massage into whatever shape it chose. The PMO gave the President absolute power to arrest any suspected enemy combatants, who were not US citizens, anywhere in the world and detain them without charge, calling them 'enemy combatants', a term without legal definition. It was quite extraordinary.

Sundel said it was expected that Hicks would enter a guilty plea, and Sundel and one other Navy lawyer were being reserved for contested cases. I was puzzled that they could already know which cases were going to be contested and which would end in guilty pleas, even though up to that point Hicks'd had no access to a lawyer. As a lawyer being detailed to the case, I was professionally confused at being presented with what seemed to be a foregone conclusion. I also wondered, with a sense of service rivalry, who this other Navy lawyer was who was supposedly being saved for the contested cases.

Anyway, that could wait. Now that I had a name for a potential client, I began looking for information on David Hicks. I did what anyone would do: I searched the internet. ·

I scanned press photos of the men in the orange jumpsuits in Camp X-Ray at Guantanamo Bay. It was not hard to find Hicks articles in the Australian media. After he was taken into custody in Afghanistan in December 2001, Hicks had been portrayed in the Australian media under headlines such as 'Meet David Hicks, an Ordinary Australian Boy Who Became a Traitor'; 'Australian Terrorist David Hicks'; and 'Journey to the Heart of Darkness: Aussie al-Qaeda Islam Convert Fought in Kosovo with Albanian KLA'. His father, Terry Hicks, had been quoted saying that David had told him he had joined the KLA, but Terry had thought it was an airline. Following 9/11, Terry explained to the media that his son had called him and said he was in Afghanistan heading to the front line, so there was no doubt that he had been there. But the speculation had grown.

There was no shortage of people who claimed to have known Hicks and were happy to speak to the media. I found the infamous photo of Hicks holding what appeared to be a rocket-propelled grenade launcher. The photo, which was actually of Hicks and three others posing with empty weapons in Albania, had reportedly been sold by a 'friend' of his to a media outlet for $1500. Like everyone else, I was unaware that the photo had been cropped to give the impression it was taken in Afghanistan or elsewhere during combat. So it was easy to believe the hype – that he might be truly one of 'the worst of the worst'.

It also seemed the Australian government was washing its hands of him – though this hadn't happened initially. Soon after Hicks's capture, the defence minister Robert Hill had said, 'Ultimately, we want him prosecuted under Australian law in Australia and we believe that the United States will cooperate in that objective.' But nothing had happened, and by mid-2002 the government had changed its tune and it seemed that Hicks had little hope of repatriation. Hill was calling him 'one of the most dangerous people in the world', while Prime Minister John Howard said, 'He's in detention. He knowingly joined the Taliban and al-Qaeda. I don't have any sympathy for any Australian who's done that.' Not only was the Australian government not demanding Hicks's return, they seemed unconcerned with ensuring he was protected by the Geneva Conventions. Attorney-General Daryl Williams said, 'Whether the Geneva Conventions apply to him and the other people detained there is really a matter for the United States.' Which is, of course, legally incorrect – all parties to the Geneva Conventions should respect and uphold them. Williams also said Hicks 'was with Taliban forces, he had previously undergone extensive training with al-Qaeda . . . [and was] among the Taliban and al-Qaeda prisoners who have already engaged in breakouts in Mazar-e-Sharif and in Pakistan'. If this was true, I wondered if Hicks would be implicated in the killing of Johnny 'Mike' Spann, a former Marine and CIA employee who was killed at the Mazar-e-Sharif prison uprising in 2001. This was the first information I received that Hicks might have been involved in a crime, but it would turn out to be completely false. As my Marine friends liked to say, 'The first report is always wrong.' But at this stage, the news reports were all I had to rely on.

In America, President Bush was calling the detainees 'killers' and 'terrorists', while Secretary Rumsfeld described them as 'committed terrorists'. He went on, 'We are keeping them off the street and out of the airlines and out of nuclear power plants and out of ports across this country and across other countries. And it seems to me a perfectly reasonable thing to do.' Rear Admiral John Stufflebeam, the Deputy Director for Global Operations on the Joint Staff, said of the detainees, 'They are bad guys. These are the worst of the worst. And if let out on the street they will go back to the proclivity of trying to kill Americans and others.' From my discussions with other military personnel, these statements represented the common belief about those who were locked up at GTMO. I don't think many within the military questioned whether it was true.

Although I was still working on many cases in Hawaii in July 2003, I got a call from Gunn within days of the initial call from Sundel, asking me to travel immediately to Washington DC to be detailed to Hicks; I might have to travel to Cuba straight on from DC.

I began rushing around MCBH getting my TAD orders (the military funding for my travel) and organising flights from Honolulu to DC. By the end of the next day, Friday, I was able to arrange a flight to DC over the weekend. I was excited about the possible assignment and still idealistic, or naive, enough to believe that the apparent changes to basic legal procedures and rights in the Military Commissions, the newly created status of the Guantanamo Bay inmates, would all be sorted out in due course. The situation was new to everyone. I believed that as it settled down, the legal process would follow established court-martial principles.

After flying into Ronald Reagan National Airport, I tried to catch some sleep at a hotel in Crystal City, which (although I didn't know it at the time) was to become my working home for several years. Crystal City, nestled next to the Reagan airport, was two metro stops from the Pentagon and a few miles from the Capitol. A mini-city of high rises and office buildings, Crystal City was built in the 1960s as an overflow area for the Pentagon and other government offices. While only a few thousand people lived there, more than 60 000 made their way to work there every day.

The next day, Lieutenant Commander Philip Sundel met me at the Pentagon, where I had never been before. I had visited DC as a child and driven through it many times, but had not been stationed any closer than Quantico, Virginia.

Sundel helped me through the maze of security to the CDC office, located on the bottom floor. Construction was still being completed on repairs of the damage done on 9/11. The basement CDC office looked as if it had been abandoned and then haphazardly reoccupied. There were some odds and ends of office furniture and desks divided into spartan cubicles. I finally met Will Gunn, a thin-framed six-foot five-inch Air Force Colonel. After the initial pleasantries and updates, he told me he was going to sign my 'detailing letter'. I was put in a cubicle to read three documents: the draft detailing letter, the target letter and an NCIS (Naval Criminal Investigative Service) statement signed by Hicks.

As I came to grips with representing someone locked up at Guantanamo Bay, my mind was racing with anticipation to see what awful crimes my potential client had committed. I reviewed my draft detailing letter, which was still to be signed, and then got to the target letter and the typed NCIS statement. Target letters were used by prosecutors to brief defence lawyers, to begin pretrial negotiations before charges had been laid. The target letter is a device sometimes used within the Department of Justice but not in courts-martial so I hadn't had experience with them – and this was also a hint as to who might have really been running the prosecution office.

I sat reading the target letter and made a list of queries. A few things disturbed me. Why was the prosecution deciding when defence counsel would be assigned? Surely, after being in GTMO for almost two years and now that President Bush had designated Hicks as someone to face legal proceedings, he should have had a defence counsel. The next red flag was that the letter stated that access to Hicks would be coordinated by the prosecution and would hinge on the conduct of pre-trial negotiations. Why should the prosecution have such power? Surely they couldn't stop an attorney from seeing his client? I hoped that this would be overridden once an attorney–client relationship existed, but nothing in this highly irregular process could be taken for granted.

Impatient to get started, I found Gunn to ask if he had signed my detailing letter yet, officially making me Hicks's attorney.

Gunn told me he would not be detailing me.

My impulse was to ask, 'Why the fuck not?' But Marine Majors don't get to say that to Colonels!

'Why?' I said as calmly as I could manage.

Gunn relayed that the DOD GC, Haynes, had called to ask him not to detail counsel to Hicks. He explained that an Australian delegation will be meeting with the DOD GC's office to discuss Hicks, a discussion in which Gunn would be involved, not me.

It was peculiar, to say the least, that someone who wasn't actually representing Hicks was going to take part in a meeting that could be crucial to his future. If the Australians were open to negotiating for Hicks, this was a moment when he needed an advocate who might point out the flaws in the system. But what could I do? I returned to my cubicle, wondering why I had been brought to DC, and what kind of system I had got myself into.

Most unusual for the defence office to come to terms with was that Gunn's official loyalty was not to the clients but to his superiors. This was not his choice, but how the system had been created. If he knew of information that would stop the commissions against a client, he did not have to tell the defence counsel. The rules were written so that he had no attorney–client relationship or any direct obligation to the clients. And yet he was the one who, in the critical period when the Australian government might still be looking after their citizen, was standing in as Hicks's representative, when his role neither empowered nor required him to do anything on Hicks's behalf.

Equally worrying for me was the NCIS statement itself, signed by Hicks. It had Hicks's initials after every paragraph; intentionally inserted typos or omissions were there for him to correct, so the agents could say he had read it carefully. When I read it, even though I'd never met Hicks, it struck me as odd in terminology, legalistic and technical, as if the words had been put into his mouth. It was at this point, after reading and re-reading it, that I finally focused on what was the most obvious.

'Wait a minute,' I thought. 'What did he *do*?'

Most everything in it had already been reported in the media. No matter how many times I read it, I couldn't figure out what crimes were being confessed to in this NCIS statement. The thought hit me in a blinding flash: *I am getting ripped off.* During the weeks of research and briefings and preparations, I had seen a great deal that concerned me, but my experience, and my basic belief in my country and the people running it, meant that I maintained the optimistic conviction that the process would be fair and the right people would be detained. Despite all I had learnt, I still believed this.

But now, reading the first communication that was supposed to be from David Hicks himself confessing to war crimes, I was faced with the blunt reality. Hicks had not blown up anything, planted any bomb or even hurt anyone. I wasn't getting any terrorist, let alone one of 'the worst of the worst', one of those responsible for 9/11. When I sat down with the NCIS statement, I expected to see all the horrible things that had been done by one of the most dangerous men in the world. Instead, there was not one allegation that a single person had been hurt by Hicks. The first Military Commission in sixty years, I thought, and this is the best they can do. I was utterly confused.

Though I still hadn't been detailed, I decided to be proactive, so I contacted Stephen Kenny, an Australian solicitor from Adelaide, where Hicks's family lived. Once Hicks's detention hit the media back in early 2002, Kenny had phoned Terry Hicks, David's father, offering his help. When I called Kenny, he said he and Terry were coming to New York City later in the month to meet with the lawyers from the Center for Constitutional Rights (CCR) who had been involved in federal court litigation for Hicks. Terry, he said, was planning to raise public awareness of that case. Kenny also told me that they were assisting with a documentary film about Terry retracing David's travels. I couldn't release any detailed information, but merely wanted Kenny to let the Hicks family know that their son might finally be getting a military lawyer. I wondered if that would actually be good news to them, as it also meant he would not be coming home until he had faced a US military trial.

'If I get detailed before you leave the US,' I concluded, 'I'll try to come to New York to meet with you.' That proved sadly optimistic. It would be four months before I was detailed.

7

Limbo

There was nothing for me to do any more in DC, and I didn't feel as if anybody wanted me there. So after only a few days, I headed back to Hawaii, unhappy about what I was getting myself into. But my curiosity had been piqued. What was really going on with these commissions, and with this one Australian man?

While the Howard government had made it clear that it had no intention of intervening on its citizens' behalf, the British government took a much different approach. British Prime Minister Tony Blair was quoted saying, 'Either there will be a proper due process with a Military Commission or alternatively [the British detainees] will return to Britain.' The British government was insisting that if Military Commissions were to proceed against its citizens, then the commissions would have to meet international legal standards of justice. Within weeks, the United States agreed to suspend Military

Commission proceedings against the nine British citizens being held at Guantanamo Bay, pending further discussions with British officials.

The Australian Foreign Minister, Alexander Downer, then said, 'We've got a very similar arrangement out of the Americans to the arrangements that the British have got. And we've also been working very closely with the British.' There was an understanding, at that point, that whatever decisions were made on behalf of the British detainees would also apply to the two Australians (Hicks and Mamdouh Habib).

But when five British citizens were repatriated from Guantanamo Bay in 2004, to be freed within days of returning to Britain as they had not broken any British or international law, nothing happened for the Australians.

In July 2003, Prime Minister John Howard had to admit that Hicks's conduct, as investigated by Australia, did not violate any Australian law. But it was clear that the Prime Minister was content with leaving Hicks in Guantanamo Bay; he said, 'It could well be that if Mr Hicks, for example, were to come back to Australia, it may not be a prosecutable offence, yet if he's retained in the United States there is an offence.' It seemed as if Howard was going to allow the US to do to Hicks what Australia could not do, and what Britain had not permitted. But Hicks had not violated any more American laws than he had Australian. The only place he could be held was this no-man's-land, beyond the laws of any country, in Cuba.

On the day Howard made his statements about Hicks, the United States released twenty-seven detainees from Guantanamo Bay to their countries of origin. The DOD said these detainees 'no longer posed a threat to US security or no longer required detention by the United States'. This seemed, in my opinion, quite possibly a fictitious cover for the fact that mistakes were made in the screening process in the first place, and that these men should never have been sent to Guantanamo Bay. A detainee did not magically cease to be a security threat if he had been one a year earlier. Or, their countries had more pull with the United States than Australia was able, or willing, to exert.

Five days later, it emerged that a compromise of sorts had been reached regarding Hicks. DOD GC Haynes had met with Australian Senator Chris Ellison, and told him that Hicks would not be sent before a Military Commission without further agreement from the Australian government. Unlike the British government with their citizens, however, the Australian government had not even hinted that they would try to bring Hicks home.

Once President Bush had agreed not to commence Military Commission proceedings against Hicks, I calmed down a little bit over not being detailed as his lawyer. It looked like Hicks might not be tried at all. The effect of the decision was to buy time for the Australian and US governments, keeping Hicks in Guantanamo Bay without any trial whatsoever. Indeed, *not* sending him to trial became the justification for keeping him locked up. What an upside-down world we were living in.

Soon after my return to Hawaii, I was disappointed to learn that I was to move duty stations to DC. As I began preparing to leave, I chatted with my colleagues about my new assignment. Many would say the same thing: 'Defend terrorists? They should just be shot.' It gave me a hint that convincing a military jury that someone labelled a terrorist by the President might be innocent would have some challenges.

I moved to Virginia and checked in to Henderson Hall, the administrative support centre for all Marines assigned in the offices throughout the DC region, and the Pentagon. My new workplace was in the basement of that gloomy building. The Chief Defense Counsel's staff included Sundel, Navy Lieutenant Commander Charles Swift and Air Force Lieutenant Colonel Sharon Shaffer, as well as Major Mark Bridges, an Army lawyer I'd known in Hawaii. I respected his legal ability and his determination on his clients' behalf, and it was good to have someone in the office I connected with.

The prosecutor's office was down the hall from us, and had been fully staffed for some time. One of the prosecutors was a Marine, Major Kurt Brubaker, who would end up being the lead prosecutor on the Hicks case for a while. It was bizarre that both the prosecutors and defenders would be working in the same organisational structure, reporting ultimately to the same boss, Jim Haynes, who had created the Military Commissions and had such a vested interest in them. And next to the CDC was the office of the Public Affairs Officer, who was then an Air Force lawyer, Major John Smith (I know it sounds like a fake name, but it is not). Smith would be one of the talking heads telling the world how full and fair the Military Commissions would be, and he earned himself the nickname 'GTMO Gary'. Haynes would also guide some key appointments. The chief legal advisor would be Air Force Brigadier General Thomas Hemingway, and in early 2004 retired Army Major General John D. Altenburg would be named as the Appointing Authority.

By the time I was settled in Washington it was September 2003, almost twenty-two months since the President's Military Order established the Military Commissions, and no one had yet been charged. Every week, there were rumours that charges were imminent. Nothing ever happened. If I had known the first charges against detainees were still nine months away, I might have prepared differently. But settling into my cubicle in the Pentagon, I felt rushed and overwhelmed; there was so much to learn and I was not quite sure where to start.

The first trial to come out of GTMO was about to begin: not for a detainee, but for the Muslim Army Chaplain Captain James Yee, a West Point graduate who was arrested in September 2003 and faced a court-martial for alleged mishandling of classified documents. A few months later, the charges were dropped. If this was any indication of the quality of the cases that were going to come out of GTMO, it was not a good sign for the prosecution.

Everybody I spoke to in the CDC office assumed I was going to be David Hicks's lawyer, but as I had still not been officially detailed, I was not given any of the prosecution evidence that might be used against him. I was in the same position as a member of the general public, gathering what information I could from publicly available sources. It was no secret that Hicks had been in Afghanistan when he was caught. His father Terry was telling the media that the last he heard from David was a phone call in late 2001. Terry was quoted as saying David 'said he was off to defend Kabul against the Northern Alliance'. It was the Northern Alliance who captured him and handed him over to the Americans. It would emerge that Hicks was one of the 86 per cent of Guantanamo detainees who were captured not by Americans, or as a result of US intelligence, but were handed over by Afghan warlords or Pakistani police for a bounty. It was reported that the Northern Alliance earned US$5000 for Hicks's arrest.

I was getting the sense that this case was not going to be a 'who-dunnit' case. Terry Hicks had already confirmed David had been in Afghanistan with the Taliban. Additionally, Hicks had written letters to his family during his travels. The Australian Federal Police (AFP) had seized them when they raided Terry's house in Adelaide soon after David's arrest. Kenny had then provided them to a documentary filmmaker. The letters were filled with rambling militancy and anti-Semitic statements that would be thrown back in Hicks's face for years and sort of removed any possible 'I was not there' defence.

But so what if he was there? My question as a lawyer was, What crime did he commit?

The Howard government was demonising Hicks, making much of his attendance at 'training camps' in Afghanistan where Osama bin Laden supposedly showed up. Hicks had mentioned meeting bin Laden in his letters to his family, although what this amounted to was attending some talks where bin Laden was a speaker. Since 9/11, the context around such encounters had changed, and bin Laden had emerged as a much more sinister figure. When I later met an Australian reporter at Guantanamo Bay, he told me that before 9/11, he hadn't even heard of bin Laden.

Whatever the politics and principles, anyone could feel for Terry Hicks, a suburban father busting his gut to help his son. By this time Terry had travelled to the United States, locking himself into a cage in an orange jumpsuit on the sidewalk of a busy New York street to raise awareness of his son's plight.

Mark Bridges and I had first met when he was stationed in Hawaii at the Army's Schofield Barracks. He once represented a Marine against me in Hawaii and got his client acquitted. He would never let me forget it!

Not long after I started at the Pentagon, Bridges and I ran into the commission chief prosecutor, Colonel Fred Borch, the author of the July 2003 target letter on Hicks. I didn't know Borch, but Bridges knew him from the Army, and he did the introductions. Borch told me that Hicks was going to plead guilty. I asked Borch what sentence Hicks would be offered and what he might agree to. Borch thought twenty years was a starting point.

I was taken aback at that. Borch's guideline for such a sentence offer was the case of John Walker Lindh, who became known as the 'American Taliban' when he was captured in December 2001. Lindh was held as a prisoner in Mazar-e-Sharif at the time Mike Spann was killed in the uprising, and while there was no evidence that Lindh took part, there was little sympathy for him. Initially charged with offences that carried a life sentence, Lindh agreed to a deal under which he would plead guilty to two charges: supplying services to the Taliban and carrying an explosive device (firearm) during the commission of a felony. In July 2002, the federal court sentenced him to twenty years without the possibility of parole.

If Lindh was the benchmark, a twenty-year deal for Hicks seemed extreme. There were some significant differences in their cases. Lindh had actually violated the laws of his country, while there was no evidence that Hicks had violated any law of Australia or the United States, which would not have applied to him in Afghanistan anyway, not in the way that US laws applied to Lindh. Lindh was actually tried, in the US federal court system, whereas Hicks was not being tried. And Lindh was kept out of Guantanamo Bay and the Military Commissions. This deferential treatment left a deep stain: it showed the world that we did not think our Military Commissions were good enough to use on our own citizens.

A more reasonable plea offer for Hicks, and other Guantanamo prisoners, might have saved the US government a lot of problems. Sensible plea deals at the beginning would have got the Military Commissions system up and running, and provided good cooperative witnesses, and might have changed the outcomes of legal challenges in the future. But I suppose the government thought they were operating from a position of strength. They thought they could do as they pleased.

One perfect September day in late 2003, I was coming home from work, walking down the street from the metro station, and a police cruiser with its window down pulled over on my street. I said hello to the officer, who had a military-style haircut. We traded a bit of banter, and he said, 'Oh, what do you do?' He had been in the military before switching to the Fairfax County police.

'Well,' I said, 'you know the people locked up at Guantanamo Bay? I'm one of the military lawyers assigned to defend them.'

I half expected him to say something hostile about the detainees, but he said, with some passion, 'You know, it is wrong, what we're doing. How could they hold someone for two years and not charge him?'

Here was what everybody's gut reaction should, in my view, have been. But people are easily fooled when the office of the President and the media are all preaching one message.

In the CDC office, we all turned up every day to jobs without clients. The prosecutors, meanwhile, were hard at work: two lawyers were already preparing the Hicks case. As Donald Rumsfeld might have put it – in a line he borrowed from the military! – I had a lot of known unknowns in front of me, but even more unknown unknowns.

What I *did* know was that I had a lot to learn about these new Military Commissions, and, while in limbo over the Hicks case, I continued my course of self-education. I ran scenarios of what I would need to do when I did get a client, such as requesting interpreters, law-of-war experts, terrorism experts and an investigator, or at least permission to travel to conduct my own investigation.

But, late in 2003, my office-bound preparations were brought to a halt. The defence office was off to Guantanamo Bay.

8

Guantanamo Bay

The whole CDC office, all seven of us, travelled together on our first trip to Guantanamo Bay. We flew to Miami on a commercial airline, and then transferred to Air Sunshine, a Florida-based commercial operation that serviced many of the smaller Caribbean islands and Guantanamo Bay. In the airport, we showed our DOD security-clearance documents and stood on the luggage scales. There were no other security procedures, although we were told to make sure we used the bathrooms before boarding, as there were none on board the ten-seater plane. In lieu of flight attendants, drinks were left in a self-serve plastic cooler in the aisle.

After a flight over the beautiful blue waters of the Caribbean, Cuba came into view. Around the coastal fringe it was barren and brown. Guantanamo Bay, near the south-eastern tip of Cuba and a short distance from both Haiti and Jamaica, had come under US control during the Spanish–American War in 1898. In boot camp, every Marine learnt of the heroic action at Guantanamo Bay of Sergeant John H. Quick, who was among 650 Marines who had landed at the bay. Sergeant Quick signalled the naval gunfire upon the Spanish forces and, for his bravery in exposing himself to danger while signalling from the crest of a hill, was awarded the Medal of Honor. So it already had significance for me.

A Marine friend of mine had worked at Guantanamo for two years and told me he loved it, despite its infestations of sandflies, banana rats and iguanas. In the settlement on the windward side of the bay, there were DOD schools, a commissary (grocery store), an exchange (like a Kmart), an outdoor movie theatre, a scuba-diving shop, and even a McDonald's. The labour force was mainly Jamaicans and Filipinos brought in via contractors. The permanent Navy personnel had their families with them, while platoons of Marines guarding the fence line rotated in and out. It remained this way until preparations began in December 2001 to give GTMO, as it was called, a new life as a detention and interrogation camp for captives from the global War on Terror.

We flew in to the airstrip, Leeward Point Field, from which we had to travel by ferry (after a long walk to the ferry station if there was no vehicle at the airstrip to meet you) for a half-hour trip across the bay. On arrival, I felt a wave of enveloping Caribbean heat, but as the evening fell, it cooled down rapidly. While Cuba is mostly tropical jungle, Guantanamo Bay is a tropical desert. I noticed the wildlife immediately, especially the olive-green rock iguanas, a protected species at GTMO. As some would argue, the iguanas had more rights than the detainees.

I was conscious that Guantanamo would have seemed like

anything but a Caribbean nature reserve to the detainees when they arrived in January 2002. The first group of captives from the war in Afghanistan were initially held in Camp X-Ray, a primitive facility built upon the site of the old detention camp for Haitian and Cuban refugees. Hicks was held there for three months, wearing an orange jumpsuit and held in a small wire cage no better than a dog kennel, with limited protection from the Caribbean sun and the incessant sandflies. There was little to do in those cages. The metal buckets provided for drinking water and toileting purposes were shocking. I'd seen the photos, and wondered how our country had become so callous. Who was the genius who came up with the idea of using dog kennels for people? In 2002, when Hicks arrived, I suppose no one gave a damn about anyone who had been labelled a terrorist. In the popular mind, treating them worse than dogs might have been seen as better than they deserved.

Donald Rumsfeld was doing his best to entrench this idea in the public opinion when he announced the plan to send detainees to GTMO on 27 December 2001. He said that day, 'I would characterise Guantanamo Bay, Cuba, as the least worst place we could have selected. It has disadvantages, as you suggest. Its disadvantages, however, seem to be modest relative to the alternatives.'

I don't know what alternatives were considered, but I'm pretty sure that creature comforts were not considered at all. Guantanamo Bay was selected simply in the hope that US federal courts would not have jurisdiction, and that any protections afforded under the US Constitution would not reach the detainees. I had to ask myself, as a lawyer entering the site, why would they choose a place beyond the courts' jurisdiction if what they were doing was lawful? As I learnt in the Marines, if what you are doing is correct, you have no fear of being inspected. So what did the Bush administration have to hide?

In my view, holding the detainees in a POW camp in Afghanistan would have been the correct choice. That was where the conflict was, and that was where any intelligence would be of immediate use. The use of Military Commissions in a theatre of war had long been upheld. But GTMO, in the eyes of the Bush administration, had one big advantage over Afghanistan as a place for detaining captives: at GTMO, the government hoped, the detainees would not have the protection of the Geneva Conventions or the oversight of the US federal courts.

Our first visit was just a quick one, for familiarisation. Far from the detainee camps, we went to see the courtroom and our offices. All were still under construction; workers were transforming an antiquated beige building into a modern-day courthouse. It was not going to be easy. On the same hill was the headquarters building for Joint Task Force (JTF) 160, the military authority running the detainee operations. Our 'office' was a single room, windowless so that it could be certified to contain top-secret evidence. Not having a window did not bother me, but I asked Gunn, 'How are multiple defence teams going to work out of one office?' The prosecution had several offices on the floor above us. The lack of defence offices was out of Gunn's control.

Camp Delta was a few miles from our office, very close to the coastline. We were given a quick tour of Delta, where the detainees were held from about April 2002, and of Camp America, where the US guards had their buildings. I remember our drive out, chugging along under the 25 mph speed limit to the detainee camp, set well away from the main part of the base and the US personnel's families. We approached the gate through a set of low hills, and began catching glimpses of the detainee camps. It felt surreal as the camps came into view.

Camp Delta comprised large rectangular segments that had been assembled to make up detention blocks. Cells were created by dividing up these sections. Each cage had a squat toilet and a tap, and a narrow bed on a raised metal platform. I was nervous and intrigued to be getting this close to what I had been reading about in the media, but a part of me was also appalled and I wondered if I would be able to do anything for my potential client.

On this visit, while we saw many detainees, we did not have any interaction with them. There were some 700 of them at that time, being supervised by a camp staff, including interrogators, of about 2800. Camp Delta was not the last or newest accommodation: Camp Echo, a settlement of one- and two-cell huts, would be used for solitary confinement; Camp Iguana would be used for the children of detainees; and, later, Camps Five and Six would be built to more modern, permanent prison specifications.

After inspecting the camps, we were taken to the exchange, where items on sale included GTMO caps and T-shirts with the slogan 'Taliban behaviour modification instructor'.

The visit affected me deeply. It was upsetting to see the awful conditions in the camps, but above all it stimulated my desire for action, to get a case. When we returned to DC, I said to Gunn and the others, 'We really should be stationed at GTMO. Being there would make representing someone locked up there a hell of a lot easier.' Most of them looked at me as if I were crazy. No one wanted to be living down at GTMO.

What struck me was how unready the facilities were for Military Commission hearings. There were no finished offices, no housing, no vehicles, and no computers for the defence. No one from the Military Commission office was at GTMO to organise anything. The place was clearly set up for detention and interrogation, not for legal processes.

Before this visit, Guantanamo had only been represented in the media through blurry photos and news reports. Like most Americans, I had had no concrete connection to the place. Now I did. There were human beings in there, one of whom would become my client.

9

'Significant Assurances'

As the rumours began to build up about the approach of the Military Commissions – there were always rumours – I knew I needed assistance. There were so many areas of the law to get my head around, on top of which was a daunting load of administrative and research work for pre-trial legal motions. I began trying to locate any military reservists, civilian criminal lawyers and law-of-war experts to fill out the team. My ego wasn't going to be hurt by getting another lawyer onboard. I was more than confident enough to represent Hicks if he was charged with a typical felony criminal case, such as drug distribution, theft, assault, rape – all the traditional crimes that criminal lawyers deal with. I had prosecuted or defended this type of case for years. I had also done some law-of-war training the first month I arrived in Hawaii. We went through the Geneva Conventions, the rules of how people and places are protected from attack, how prisoners of war are treated, and how Article 5 tribunals worked to determine who was a POW. Before 9/11, there were no grey areas in the Geneva Conventions, just rules that had to be followed. We watched the Australian movie *Breaker Morant* and learnt not to shoot your prisoners and a little bit about unfair trials. But I was by no means a specialist. The military sent attorneys to study for masters' degrees in international law, and you would think that such a degree might be a requirement to serve as a defence counsel at the first Military Commission in sixty years. Not only did I not have such a qualification, but nobody in the CDC office did. Not one advanced degree in international humanitarian law, international criminal law or just plain old international law between us. Honestly, I probably wasn't qualified to deal with all the issues involved, but at least I knew it and knew I would have to find help to make up for it. To level the playing field, I could only study as hard as I could and get outside help.

One of the main legal issues I was trying to understand was how is it a crime for someone to fight in a war? How is it a crime for a member of the Taliban forces, or someone on their side, to fight against the Americans? Could it really be a crime to fight against a military force that had invaded the country in which you were living?

There were some clues in the second Military Commission Instruction (MCI No. 2), issued on 30 April 2003. I knew that the prosecutions in the global War on Terror weren't the first war-crimes trials since World War II. The United Nations had set up tribunals to prosecute war crimes after the 1990s conflicts in the former Yugoslavia and Rwanda. These two tribunals, and then the International Criminal Court, a permanent war-crimes tribunal set up in The Hague in 2002, all had statutes defining crimes against the laws of war. Although the United States had elected not to be party to the ICC, it had taken the lead in drafting that statute. The American military lawyer who had taken a guiding hand in that drafting process was the same man who now drafted MCI No. 2, and was the first chief prosecutor of the Military Commissions: a Marine Corps Judge Advocate, Lieutenant Colonel William K. Lietzau.

Using what I thought was unassailable logic, I figured that if Lietzau had helped define war crimes for the ICC and also defined them for our Military Commissions, then they would be much the same. So I put MCI No. 2 down on my desk and compared its twenty-seven listed crimes to the crimes listed before the ICC and the Yugoslavia and Rwanda tribunals. Even factoring in a little leeway for wording, several crimes appeared in MCI No. 2 that I could not find in any of those international courts: terrorism; providing material support for terrorism; murder by an unprivileged belligerent; destruction of property by an unprivileged belligerent; aiding the enemy; and conspiracy. I wondered, did Lietzau get it wrong, or was he complicit in making up new crimes in the MCI No. 2? I reached out to Professor George P. Fletcher from Columbia law school, an expert in criminal law and international criminal law. He reassured me that I was on the right track. These crimes that had been created in MCI No. 2 were not valid.

To create a new crime and apply it to conduct that occurred before the crime was created is, unsurprisingly, a problem. In American law, this concept is referred to as *ex post facto*, meaning 'after the fact'. This is not just an American protection; it is contained in Article 15 of the International Covenant on Civil and

Political Rights: 'No one shall be held guilty of any criminal offence on account of any act or omission which did not constitute a criminal offence, under national or international law, at the time when it was committed.' It doesn't take a legal mind to explain or understand it. You can't be charged later for committing a crime that didn't exist when you allegedly did it.

It appeared that the Bush administration turned away from US federal courts and courts-martial, and instead created the Military Commissions so it could make up new war crimes and war criminals, to prosecute *ex post facto*. With a few keystrokes, Lietzau, the drafter, and Haynes, the man who signed the MCI, believed they had solved their problem: the law was whatever they decided it to be, *whenever* they decided. It was disheartening to see such legal action so blatantly contrary to the US Constitution and the founding principles of our country. One of the complaints of the USA's founding fathers in our Declaration of Independence was that the King of Great Britain was 'transporting us beyond seas to be tried for pretended offenses'. It seemed we were now doing the same to others.

I was disconcerted by what I learnt. After all, when you are playing a game and you discover that the rules are being written by the other side to ensure that you can't win, it may be natural to want to walk away. As I would later find out, several prosecutors walked away after realising they were almost guaranteed to win, at the expense of justice. The more I discovered about the unfairness within the Military Commission system, the angrier I got, and the angrier I got, the more determined I became. I was still a relatively young lawyer, and knew I had much to learn, but being young meant I was still innocent enough to believe in ideals of justice and to be outraged by hypocrisy. If they wanted the defence side to feel beaten down by the hopelessness of our task, they were going to be sadly mistaken. It was my opinion that the creators of the Military Commission wanted defence counsel to get in the ring and put up a good fight, make motions (which would be denied), make objections and go down with the ship, all for the sake of putting on a good show of justice.

After treading water for so long, on 1 November 2003, the CDC office was abuzz when they found out that the chief prosecutor, Colonel Fred Borch, had said at an American Bar Association function, 'I think it's safe to say our start is imminent, soon.' This might have been yet another rumour, but things were moving fast all of a sudden.

Nine days later, the Supreme Court ruled that it would hear the case *Rasul v. Bush*. A US civilian lawyer, Joe Margulies, working with the New York–based Center for Constitutional Rights, led by Michael Ratner, had filed this case seeking to review the detention of men at Guantanamo Bay. Hicks was part of this case, which had been started in February 2002 and had finally made it way up to the Supreme Court. The Supreme Court hearing was still some months away, but the announcement that it would hold a hearing seemed to give the Military Commission process a kick in the butt. Within days, 'GTMO Gary' Smith circulated seating priorities and seating charts for the commission. This was surprising, as seating had not come up before, but it was a sign that someone thought the commissions would be starting soon. No one had been charged, no one had been assigned a lawyer, but the seating chart was being organised. I am not sure the commission courtroom had even been completed yet.

10

Getting a Client

As things finally got moving, I was detailed to David Hicks in November 2003. And the dominoes kept falling: as if to appease its critics, the United States staged its first mass release of detainees, announcing it would be letting 140 men out of Guantanamo Bay in the next few months. The Military Commission gave off signs that it was moving, and the Australian government agreed to let its citizens be tried by the commission.

For the past several months, ever since my name had been linked with Hicks's case, I had been impatient to represent an actual client. Many negotiations were conducted during that time that directly affected him; I wondered if there was anything that could have been done better if he'd had an American lawyer, within the military system, advocating for him.

Hicks had clearly been abandoned by his own government,

which conceded that he had not violated any Australian law but was still using his actions as justification for leaving him at Guantanamo Bay. I could not understand the logic. If he had obeyed his country's laws and not committed any war crimes for which Australia could prosecute him, what was the reason for leaving him in Guantanamo Bay? In the end, Australia's reasons for abandoning him were, to my mind, disgracefully vague. The Foreign Minister, Alexander Downer, said, 'I don't know how people in Australia would feel having people who trained with al-Qaeda going to the cinema and in the shopping centre, sitting next to them and knowing these are people who trained with the world's most egregious terrorist organisation.' That is something you might expect to hear in a pub or on talkback radio, but for it to come out of the mouth of a minister, who is meant to uphold the law, was puzzling. The only possible conclusion was that Hicks was being detained at Guantanamo Bay for the political convenience of the Australian government, so they did not have to deal with him coming home.

After finally being detailed, my first thought was to return to Cuba to meet my client. And it looked like I wouldn't go alone. Although Stephen Kenny was experienced in neither military nor criminal law (but within the Military Commission system we were asking the question, Who *was* experienced?), Terry Hicks had written to his son about the help Kenny had already given them, and Hicks replied that he wanted to use Kenny. Almost as soon as I was told I could go to GTMO, I was told the Australian embassy wanted me to wait for Kenny before seeing Hicks; the embassy also wanted Hicks to confirm he wanted Kenny before paying for the Australian lawyer.

While Hicks's letter to his father was good enough for me, it was not good enough for the Australian government, which created a lot of red tape over the exact formulation of Hicks's request before it would agree to fund Kenny's visit. Then the political officer at the Australian embassy called to tell me that Canberra wanted an 'official request' by Hicks for Kenny. I suppose if they were going to pay Kenny's expenses and fees, they wanted to make sure Hicks would see him. They wanted me to go down to GTMO to meet Hicks and obtain this official request from him in person. I said, 'How about if I speak to Hicks on the phone and get his verbal confirmation of wanting to meet Mr Kenny?' They eventually permitted this, and on 4 December 2003, I was able to speak to Hicks on a monitored phone call that lasted less than ten minutes.

His Australian accent came through in a deepish voice, though he sounded cautious. I did the majority of the talking. He only spoke in short sentences; this was his first conversation with anyone from outside GTMO in two years. I let him know that I had been assigned as his military lawyer, and that Kenny would also come down if Hicks wanted. Hicks said yes. I gave him an estimate of when he could expect us and said goodbye. To the Australian government's credit, they paid Kenny's fees and travel expenses.

After speaking with Hicks, I immediately called Terry. I would always try to keep the Hicks family informed, whatever complications were caused by the time difference. There was little I could tell Terry at the time, except to explain my role and provide my contact information to establish a means of communication. I didn't yet know enough to provide any definite answers, but could understand that he might not fully trust me to represent his son's best interests, as I was a member of the US military, the body that was incarcerating him.

As Kenny and I were preparing for our first visit to see Hicks in GTMO, Kenny kept saying, jokingly, 'You're an American. Hicks is not going to trust you.' I wouldn't have blamed Hicks if he did hate Americans, but this played on my mind less than the possibility that he might not trust me because I was military.

There was a common belief among the public that military lawyers would not put up a fight against their own system. The government had imposed a rule on detainees, that even if they had a civilian lawyer they also needed a military one, which gave the impression that we might be on the case as government spies. I was concerned about how to build trust with a client who might not understand that, while I wore the same uniform as those who were detaining and interrogating him, I really was in his corner. Also, I might have to interview other detainees in preparation for his case, so I would be starting that trust-building process anew every time.

Another vexing point, as I prepared to meet Hicks, was how to tell him about the plea negotiations without him thinking that I was trying to persuade him to plead guilty. From the start, it had been put in my head that Hicks was going to do so, but until I met him I couldn't know whether that was the case. For the prosecution or the investigators to suggest his guilty plea was a done deal could have been part of the mind games. So I had to start afresh, telling him about his options on plea negotiations without conveying any impression that I was pushing him one way or the other.

Kenny was coming to DC in early December to meet with me before we travelled together to Guantanamo Bay. Our office had to get him a security clearance for the base; I didn't want him being turned away once we got down there. The DOD General Counsel's office wanted him to sign a similar affidavit to the one

American civilian attorneys signed, but with one interesting additional clause: 'I also understand that any communications I may have with Hicks must be in the presence of the Detailed Defense Counsel, unless otherwise approved by the Appointing Authority.' Why, I wondered, would they restrict Kenny from having a private conversation with Hicks without my being there? From my point of view, it only added to my challenge of building trust and assuring Hicks that I was not a military or government spy.

With Kenny coming over from Australia, I knew hiding from the media was not going to last for long, as Kenny was not shy of journalists who would be on his tail. I was still unknown to the public. For reasons of their own, the DOD fixed this by issuing a press release on 1 December announcing that I was the first military defence counsel to be assigned to a GTMO detainee. (The press release used my first name, Michael, not Dan – short for my middle name, Dante, and the name I went by, beginning years of people asking me if I was related to Michael Mori.) GTMO Gary explained to me how the media would work, and said I should channel all my communications with them through the commission public affairs office.

After Kenny arrived in DC on 8 December, we went to the Australian embassy to meet the Australian Ambassador. The media was waiting for us when we departed. This was my first brush with the press and I was able to get away without saying much, as Kenny did the talking. Leigh Sales from the Australian Broadcasting Corporation reported that my experience was limited, which was not flattering. I knew I was experienced enough in criminal trials, but in the Military Commissions system I had no experience at all. Same as everyone else, but it still had me constantly questioning what I did not know and seeking assistance.

11

Meeting David

As the plane banked to land at Guantanamo Bay, Kenny caught his first glimpse of the detainee camps along the coast from the base. Though I had been to GTMO once before, it still struck me: *What was America doing with this camp?* We were arriving soon after a US congressional delegation had visited. The Republican Senator Lindsey Graham said on his return, 'As a former prosecutor, I have been around some tough people, and I have been around some bad actors . . . But never before have I been around so many people, who, by the look in their eyes, I felt they would love to kill me.' It was not surprising that there was little public sympathy for those locked away after statements like Graham's. I wondered how he was so convinced about what was inside the detainees' heads. Had he spoken to any of them?

Our visits with Hicks would begin the next day. I was told that when I entered the detainee camp I would have to cover my name tape, sewn onto the right breast pocket of my Marine Corps camouflage uniform. I asked why. In listening to the answer, I was unsure if they really believed a detainee who knew a guard's name might one day come back to the United States and attack him, or if it was to make it harder for detainees to identify guards to the Red Cross if they were alleging inappropriate behaviour. Even though Hicks already knew my name, I was not going to argue. There was as little use in challenging this as any other ridiculous policy. I was not there to change GTMO, but to get Hicks out. For the next several years, I kept my little strip of duct tape in my cover (USMC word for hat) to conceal my name every time I entered the camps.

That night, Kenny and I ate at the Cuban Club, a small restaurant run by local contractors, and one of the few alternatives to the chow hall and McDonald's. As we sipped our Red Stripes, we talked about our meeting the next day. He was staying at the Navy Lodge, a hotel-type building across from the commissary and exchange that was used for short-term visitors. I stayed at the CBQ (Combined Bachelors Quarters), where the Filipino staff wore Hawaiian shirts and watched a lot of TV in the lobby, just like in an ordinary tropical hotel. Much of the base had an eerie sense of normality.

In the morning, we drove out to the main gate of the camps and waited on our escort. Meanwhile, the Filipino and Jamaican workers were able to drive past us without any interference. As a defence counsel, you were given plenty of signs to show where you stood in the pecking order. Eventually the escorting stopped, but only after I raised it with the JTF and pointed out how ridiculous it was.

Over the years, I continued to stage my own personal acts of independence. Whenever someone drove through a checkpoint to enter the camps, the guard would salute and say, 'Honour bound.' The other person would return the salute and say, 'To defend freedom,' the motto of the JTF-GTMO. The irony was so rich, and was probably not lost on all of those who worked there. On later trips, I took it upon myself to butt in with my own reply, 'To defend David Hicks,' which was, after all, what I was honour bound to do.

We had to follow a vehicle from the Staff Judge Advocate (SJA)'s office for half a mile to Camp Echo. To leave or go for lunch, we would have to wait again for the escort to arrive and drive us back. To get into Camp Echo, we had to be processed as well as make sure our name tapes were covered. We had to say we were there to see Detainee 002, as David was known by those in the prison bureaucracy. John Walker Lindh had been 001. The numbers were assigned as they fell into the hands of American forces.

The soldiers working at the camp did not quite know what to make of us. Only interrogators and other prison staff had been allowed in before, and now there were defence lawyers. We were thoroughly searched. Over the next few days of visiting, we would bring in food and drinks. When Kenny brought a small jar of Vegemite, the guards had to check it twice and, after some querying and a bit of laughter, let it through.

We parked and walked across a gravel area towards a twelve-foot-high diamond-wire fence covered in green shade cloth. A guard took us through two locked gates into a caged gravelled courtyard surrounded by about ten wooden huts with brown doors.

We were shown to a hut on our right. Outside was the 'recreation area', where the detainees could walk a sum total of four paces in a large chain-linked cage, like you might see in a wrestling cage match. We were required to leave the hut's outside door open so that a junior enlisted soldier could sit on a plastic chair and watch us from a few steps below. The US and Australian governments had previously agreed publicly that there would be no monitoring of conversations between Hicks and his lawyers at GTMO, but so much for that. There would be many hints, over the next four years, that the no-monitoring rule was never followed. Defence lawyers would later complain about listening devices disguised as smoke detectors during visits to Camp Echo.

Inside, the hut was split in two. There were no windows. The ceiling, walls and floor were made of wood. One half of the hut contained an inserted cell with a metal bed, a steel sink and a lidless metal toilet, and a shower area separated from the sleeping area by a metal mesh door. The other half of the hut was a sparse area with a small table for meetings, where the guard usually sat. It was in this room that I first laid eyes on David Hicks, sitting at the table.

He wore a beige-coloured outfit, like hospital scrubs. We introduced ourselves. It was difficult for him to stand up for the formalities: under the table was a bolt with a loop embedded into the floor to which he was chained, as he would be during all of our meetings there. What struck me first, besides his strong Aussie accent, which was even stronger in person, was how small he was. I guess I was still expecting some hard-core soldier-of-fortune type. But he was not like that at all. He spoke softly, smoked incessantly – so the open door did have one benefit! – and did not have horns coming out of his head. It's hard to imagine what Senator Graham would have said if he had met Hicks, but he would have had to work hard to turn this small, quiet, lost-looking man into someone who would love to kill him.

Over the next several days, we visited Hicks. He was in a highly institutionalised and isolated state, which left him more focused on his immediate needs than the bigger picture. He had not been allowed out of his cell in daylight hours since he had been moved from Camp 4 to Camp Echo in about May 2003. Why this was, I couldn't find out. Was it a deliberate condition imposed with approval from the chain of command, or just some practice of the sergeant who ran the daily operations at Camp Echo that his superiors failed to know about, or knew about but did not care to question? Either way, it was wrong.

And the food left something to be desired, to put it politely. In the camps there was detainee food and guard food. The food brought in for Hicks during our visit smelled extremely bad. Whatever it was, it was not acceptable. Apart from an apple or orange for breakfast at 5 a.m., the food was all like this: egg from a can, undercooked rice, disgusting fish. When they had first been in Camp X-Ray, the detainees had been given parts of MREs (meals ready to eat, the rations given to US soldiers). But these had been discontinued, replaced by atrocious stuff. During my first several visits, when Hicks's food was brought, I threw it away, outside of the hut, as the smell was unbearable. I brought him some real food.

There was no doubt that the months of isolation in these conditions had affected his mental and physical heath. The guards were under orders never to speak to him, not even to say hello. His only human contact had been with his interrogators and the occasional merciful guard who would risk punishment by showing him a magazine or passing him some food. He was in great physical discomfort; he was pale and thin. His back was hurting him, and the chain holding him to the table restricted his ability to make himself comfortable. I knew I would have to investigate issues of his physical abuse at the hands of US forces.

After the first meetings, Kenny and I shared our serious concerns about Hicks's wellbeing. His weight, normally around 80 kilograms, had slipped down to 58 kilograms. He was not getting quality food, sunlight or proper exercise. The space he lived in was barely the size of a double bed. Many weeks, he was only allowed outside for a couple of fifteen-minute 'exercise' breaks on his own, at night. He ate every meal alone. On a few of the visits in this trip, Kenny and I brought him steak. Kenny cooked it at the lodge, and we were able to take it to Hicks – as long as we had cut it into bite-sized pieces, as he was not allowed a knife – along with some other food, drink and cigarettes. It was all we could do to take his mind off his conditions and get him to focus on the legal issues. Not that we had many answers.

We talked, paranoia keeping our voices below the sound of the droning exhaust fan in the ceiling. We told him about the activism his father had undertaken on his behalf, and David was tearful to see photos of Terry protesting in an orange jumpsuit in a cage on the streets of New York City. He was also overwhelmed to hear how Bronwyn, Terry's first wife, had set up the Fair Go for David group to lobby for him. We told him about the case the CCR was running in the US courts and tried to explain what it meant.

Not surprisingly, Hicks was very confused about his future, and also about what had happened in the months before I met him. In early 2003, when his interrogators were softening him up to sign his NCIS statement, he had been taken each week to a hut called the 'Love Shack', where he could have his chains taken off, sit on a couch, watch a DVD, eat normal food and smoke cigarettes. This was a reward for cooperation. He was told that signing the NCIS statement was the first step in getting home to Australia. He signed the statement, and was shipped off to isolation in Camp Echo. He had pinned all his hopes on being released by August 2003, the date mentioned by his interrogators, but then he had to deal with the disappointment when August came and went.

Now he expected us to be able to give him a date for his release. We struggled to explain the workings of a system that was so arbitrary and illogical that we didn't understand it ourselves. In response to any questions about how the Military Commissions system would operate, I had to be honest and say, 'I don't know.' I explained how things worked in courts-martial, but knew they were not the same.

Kenny provided him with a much-needed update on what was transpiring politically in Australia. The division between the Liberal–National government and the Labor Opposition was strong. Clearly, the detention of people at GTMO, the harsh interrogation techniques and the use of Military Commissions, and the war in Iraq were political issues that divided Australians as deeply as Americans. The facet of the Australian situation that was hardest to explain to Hicks was that the Howard government's justification for leaving him at GTMO was that he had *not* violated any Australian laws. Kenny and I did not pull any punches on the unfairness of the system he was facing. But I am not sure he was even in a state to understand the unfairness of the system.

We met on each of the five days we spent in Cuba, giving us a chance to get to know each other. I discovered that I didn't need to worry about him not trusting me because I was American and military. Hicks never had any animosity towards Americans. I would not have blamed him if he did, yet he didn't. He viewed himself as having been a soldier, not a terrorist. If only he had been able to join the Australian military when he tried years before, his life would have been so different. He would have been given the direction and purpose that so many of us find when we join the military as young men. His initial reaction when I told him I was a Marine was, 'I'm glad I got a Marine. Marines are the best.'

Although I was instructed to be in their presence at all times, I felt it was important to provide Kenny with some alone time with Hicks. I left the hut and half-closed the door, so that none of the guards would get angry. It was enough to allow Kenny a short private chat with Hicks. I was not sure why the guards thought my supervision was necessary, or even if they thought Hicks was dangerous. But at that time, as we were the first people allowed to see a detainee, suspicion was rife. I suspect everyone working at GTMO was paranoid about outsiders.

During our downtime, it was difficult to be productive, as the still-unfinished defence office had no working computers or phones. I was able to borrow some technology from the Marine detachment, without which we would have been cut off. And I made the first of many complaints about Hicks's conditions and the breaking of agreements, such as the monitoring of our visits by guards. (Over the following days, the guard would move further and further from the door, and eventually left altogether.)

As we were leaving Hicks for the last time, he kept asking when someone would be back. He was extremely upset. Having got used to our visits, he thought we would be with him every day until the whole thing was resolved and he was let out. I promised I would come back before the end of the month, and we would try to get his American civilian lawyer, once chosen, to visit as soon as possible. Kenny also promised to come back as soon as he could. As we said goodbye, I was saddened by what a lonely and depressed sight Hicks made.

The next morning, Kenny and I dropped off our bags to be inspected, got the ferry to the leeward side, and boarded a flight for our onward trip to New York. Once we got back to the mainland and my phone started to work, I found out that approval had been granted for a media conference Kenny wanted to have in New York. No permission had been granted for me to speak to the media. I was not disappointed by this, as I had yet to decide if I should even speak to the media. Maybe, I thought, I should just leave it to the civilian lawyers. But one thing had become clear to me. Now that I had met Hicks, the sense that we were definitely not holding the 'worst of the worst' magnified. He needed to get out of GTMO. I just had to figure out how to do it.

12

Meet the Press

On our return from Cuba, Stephen Kenny and I travelled to New York on 17 December to meet with members of the CCR, and Eric M. Freedman, a constitutional law professor from Hofstra Law School who had been advising on the federal court challenges. Besides updating them on our visit to the man they had been fighting for over the previous two years but had never met, our main goal was to finalise a civilian lawyer.

The brief to the Supreme Court was due after the New Year, which was keeping Joe Margulies and the CCR team busy. One of the civilian lawyer candidates, Joshua Dratel, made the decision easy with his willingness and experience. He had represented Wadih El-Hage, one of the conspirators involved in the bombing of the US embassy in Kenya in 1998, so he had experience in government cases against al-Qaeda. We expected the evidence produced by the Military Commission prosecutor to follow some aspects of the embassy case. Additionally, after spending time with Kenny, I could tell it was going to help having Dratel, an older lawyer, with us. Kenny, understandably, didn't like the fact that he was not Hicks's lead lawyer, and had to work under a 'young' 37-year-old military lawyer. Personally, I felt that having Dratel on the case would remove some of the pressure from me. He was the right man to bring onto the team because he was a good sounding board, but the reality was he had a finite amount of time to devote to the case. So we had to use it wisely. The military could order me down to GTMO anytime they wanted; they couldn't order the civilian lawyer down there. They could order me to do something and I would then have to deal with how to either follow or challenge their order, whereas Dratel was not bound in the same way. Bringing him on gave us some leverage.

During our initial meeting, I tried to lay out my ideas on what might happen. As Dratel knew, this new system was hard to predict. There was no guarantee this case would be over in a year or two. Dratel was more than willing to take the case pro bono, even though it might last for several years. This was no small commitment, as he had a thriving criminal law practice. With Dratel came his paralegal, Elisabeth Besobrasow, who became a valued member of our team and probably got sick of my numerous phone calls, but never let on.

In our meeting and throughout the case, individuals asked if Hicks would have any problem with a Jewish lawyer. It's funny, the assumptions people made just because someone has studied Islam. It was never an issue.

I wanted to make it as easy as possible on Dratel, so he could continue serving his paying clients at his office on Wall Street, where I am sure the rent was not cheap. We divided the casework to reflect Dratel's knowledge of the federal criminal system and my experience of the courts-martial and law of war. When it came to the maze of Military Commissions, we would muddle through together. I was so grateful to have Dratel working with us.

We had to interrupt our meeting so Kenny could do the planned press conference, which was to be held in the same building. As someone from the outside had finally met with a detainee inside GTMO, the media was hungry for details, so a lot of reporters turned out for Kenny's press conference. As it kicked off, I watched from the back of the room.

The media wanted to know if there was going to be a plea deal. Playing it very straight, Kenny said, 'If a deal is struck that is reasonable and acceptable, then I presume we will go to a Military Commission.' He and I had discussed raising our concerns about Hicks's treatment, but here too our present strategy was for restraint, as we realised that any improvements for Hicks would have to come from the good graces of the powers-that-be at GTMO. Hicks, Kenny said, 'has not been ill-treated since his arrival in Guantanamo Bay, if you ignore the isolation, his lack of access to the outside world and the denial of his basic human rights'.

I was trying to stay out of sight, as I wasn't in uniform and had been told I couldn't appear on camera without it. I was not unhappy that I could not speak to the media, as I didn't feel properly prepared. I had no media experience; I'd talked to reporters only once or twice in my whole career. I didn't want to jump off the cliff that dealing with the media might be.

But as Kenny was finishing up, Leigh Sales, the Australian

Broadcasting Corporation reporter, saw me and started coming after me, with her cameraman in tow, while I was walking towards the elevator. To shield me, some of the other lawyers blocked the cameraman and held up a jacket and some documents to block the camera, but I was filmed, looking for all the world like a dodgy person trying to avoid the media.

As we waited for the elevator, the other lawyer I was with cried out to the cameraman, 'No, no, you can't do that! You're going to get the poor guy fired from his job if you keep taking pictures.'

'Who are you with?' Sales asked him.

'I'm helping him,' said my friend.

'Are you with the Pentagon?' she asked.

'No!' my friend said. 'God help us!'

'Major Mori,' Sales addressed me, 'can you say anything?'

I could have said a few things, but luckily the elevator arrived and I was inside before the conversation could continue. It was comical, really: the government did not want to give me permission to talk to the media, but this only made it a bigger story. When I returned to DC, GTMO Gary harassed me, claiming I had staged the whole 'paparazzi chase'. I said, 'Well, you were the ones who said I had to avoid the cameras while out of uniform.'

Kenny returned to Australia, and I to DC, but I was very keen to get back to Cuba, to agitate to improve Hicks's conditions, particularly the matters of access to sunlight and food. I flew down the day after Christmas. In a three-day visit, I pushed as hard as I could. I wanted some results to show Hicks I was fighting for him.

I met with him on each of the three days I was there. The good news was the meals had improved. To get anything accomplished for Hicks's living conditions seemed to involve the Australian consular staff, the prosecutor, the legal office for the Joint Task Force, and sometimes the Appointing Authority's office. The food had been addressed quickly, so I turned to getting him something more interesting to drink than water. I worked at getting approval to bring in Gatorade powder – they gave him one bottle of the weight-gaining drink Ensure a day – and then to bring in protein bars, before expanding to personal hygiene products such as shampoo, deodorant and a toothbrush. After a Red Cross campaign, 'windows' were installed in the Camp Echo huts: a narrow slit of frosted glass. He had been living without a lot of what civilian prisoners take for granted. The complete isolation from the outside world was immense.

One success was to get him a phone call with Terry. Hicks and I were taken to the shipping containers at Camp Delta, where he sat in front of an old-fashioned telephone. He was given a long list of what not to say: nothing about the camp, his treatment, food, daily routines, *anything* concerning Guantanamo Bay. I was listening in, along with the staff, and had to shake my head at Hicks to tell him not to answer his father's questions or else they would cut him off. He spent the whole call sadly saying, 'Sorry, Dad, I can't talk about that.' I suspect Terry and his son came out of the call with mixed feelings: joy at hearing each other's voice and depression at how constricted the whole exercise was.

Some other requests never got anywhere. Throughout my career, I was always allowed to meet clients in pre-trial detention in my defence office to prepare for their trial. Accused rapists and violent offenders, trained Marines who were considered dangerous – they were all cleared – but not our five-foot two-inch Australian who was not even accused of hurting anyone. Major

General Miller, Commander of the Joint Task Force at GTMO, shot that one down. I thought, if I can't meet him in an office, can we at least have his chains removed during our meetings? The interrogators could have Hicks unchained, so why couldn't I? For whatever reason, this was denied as well. The artificial safety rules were relaxed for interrogators, but not military defence counsel.

There wasn't much to do at Guantanamo, but in an odd way I was beginning to quite like the base. There was a little library, a video store, a few shops and an outdoor theatre named the Lyceum. There wasn't enough time to go scuba diving, but the base had a nice feeling of being a world unto itself. While you needed a car to get anything done or to get around the base, as it was so hot most of the time, the proximity of facilities was very convenient. But it has to be said, your experience of the place depended entirely on which side of the bars you were on.

I returned to DC and updated the Australian consul. The consul was an experienced employee of the Department of Foreign Affairs and Trade (DFAT) who had genuine concern for his country-man and was willing to assist in any way he could, but a lot would depend on the actual jailers at GTMO: JTF, led by the recalcitrant Miller. I was also trying to obtain from the Australian embassy and Appointing Authority's office the exact agreement between the United States and Australia in relation to Hicks going before a Military Commission, but I was brushed off and told that their press release covered it all. I was suspicious that this was not accurate.

Even as the commissions looked like they were getting closer to reality, the picture on the ground showed we still had a long way to go. Our defence office was still only nine strong – six lawyers and three enlisted support staff. Only two of us, myself and Swift, had been detailed to actual clients. The prosecution office had fifteen staff, and even the Appointing Authority's almost dormant office had more staff than we had. The Criminal Investigative Task Force, the investigative body assigned to uncover evidence against the detainees, had 180 staff spread between the USA, Guantanamo Bay and Afghanistan.

The prosecution, meanwhile, was nudging us on plea deal negotiations. They were still talking twenty years. I informed them I could not give any answer until a civilian lawyer got down to see Hicks.

Then, on the first day of the new year – a presidential election year – I discovered everything was liable to sudden and unpredictable change. Someone from the prosecutor's office called me and said, 'Hicks has tried to escape.' I sat tight until they provided me with more information. I reassured myself with the old saying from the Marines: 'The first report is always wrong.'

The saying turned out to be true in this case. Hicks hadn't tried to escape. All he had done was show a guard how he could open a door in his cell. Not that it would have done him any good! Nevertheless, for his audacity, he lost all the privileges I had just obtained for him, and went back to the bottom of the queue when it came to several other 'good behaviour' privileges. It would take him thirty days on each level to climb back up – it was very structured. However, there were always ways and means. I would take a lot of time, and dispense a lot of Krispy Kreme doughnuts at GTMO, to claw Hicks's privileges back. The 'escape' story was so pathetic it never made the news.

On 14 January 2004, the CCR's written brief was filed with

the Supreme Court. Our office (along with many other bodies, national and international) filed our amicus brief alongside it, alerting the Supreme Court to those that might face a Military Commission (like Hicks's) special circumstances. Hicks was part of the central *Rasul vs Bush* case, but we wanted the court to recognise that a detainee who had been designated for prosecution in the Military Commission had an even stronger claim than the other detainees to be under federal jurisdiction.

As these documents were being filed, I was finally successful in getting a civilian lawyer down to visit with Hicks. Dratel, Master Sergeant Pierre (our Air Force paralegal) and I were in GTMO with Hicks for three days.

Upon my return, I had four days to prepare for a media conference. The Appointing Authority's office had given me limited permission to provide the media with the defence's opinion on the rules and procedures of the Military Commissions. I still wasn't sure if it was best for Hicks that I talk publicly, but there were a few arguments swaying me towards going public. At this point, Hicks had been locked up for two years, with the Australian and US governments labelling him a terrorist and saying the Military Commissions would provide him with a fair trial. It wasn't my choice to make this a media cause célèbre – Bush and Howard had already done that. It seemed that Hicks needed credible people to speak up for him, as he had no voice of his own.

But would it be tactically beneficial? My job was to either get Hicks a fair trial in a real system or get him back to Australia as soon as possible. It was clear that Hicks was not going to get a fair trial with the way the commissions had been structured. Had he been facing trial in a US federal court or within a court-martial, I would have had nothing to complain about. But not only was the commission unfairly structured, but those running the commissions were out there briefing the press on how fair the system was. When my boss, Colonel Will Gunn, was included in press conferences, he never provided any criticism of the system, so it gave the impression that the defence had no issues.

And waiting to complain about the system after the fact would be futile. Imagine if Hicks were sentenced to forty years, and I then went public saying how unfair the commission system was. It would come across as sour grapes. I had to put our complaints on record before the trial, before he was even charged. Having seen the British stance, and how their government had stopped commissions against their citizens in GTMO, it was clear that this was a political process, not an independent judicial process, so the only way to effect real change was by exposing the absurdity of the system in the only arena that mattered to politicians: the court of public opinion in Australia.

There was a final persuasive reason to go public. The commission had its vocal critics, such as Human Rights Watch and Amnesty International. In Australia, there had been Kenny and Terry leading the way. It was clear that many Australians could feel for Terry and sympathise with this father, but Kenny was too easily ignored by the government. Always, those who criticised the process were attacked by the Bush administration as being unpatriotic and wanting to weaken America. As a serving military officer, in uniform, my patriotism would be harder to attack, or so I thought.

On the day of the media conference, I was praying I didn't mess it up by saying something stupid or losing control of my emotions.

I'd had several sleepless nights since returning from GTMO and was feeling some stress. I knew the media would be unforgiving if I screwed it up. The press conference was held in the only conference room we had access to, right next to the prosecutor's office. As I re-read and rehearsed my media statement for the umpteenth time in my office, I was begging my body not to sweat through my uniform. Sure enough, my body did its own thing and I was sweating buckets. Colonel Gunn came in and said, 'Are you sure you want to do this?' Although he declined to publicly criticise the system, he did not stop me from going ahead. I'd already made the decision, and there was no time to call it off, even though inside I would have loved to. As I left my office, the other CDC lawyers lined the passageway and murmured such helpful advice as 'This is a bad idea', which echoed in my head as I headed to the elevators.

The conference room was packed, at least in my mind. Staff from the prosecutor's and Appointing Authority's offices were taking up seats for the media. GTMO Gary was there, of course.

In terms as simple as possible, I made an initial statement about the system the Bush administration was holding out as 'full and fair'. I explained that 'the Military Commissions will not provide a full and fair trial. The commission process has been created by those with a vested interest in conviction.' I detailed the problem with the lack of rules of evidence and the improper procedure of the Appointing Authority ruling on defence motions. I fielded questions, and then the reporters left. I thought it had all gone fairly well.

Little did I know what a hornets' nest I had stirred up. It only took the one sentence: 'One of the concerns is that this is a system that has been created by individuals only with a vested interest in convictions.' Once that got out, I went through an onslaught of phone calls at all hours from numerous news organisations, major and minor, American, Australian and international. I did not feel that, having started it, I could ignore them. I knew I would need them in the future, and I always tried to return everyone's call as soon as I could without playing favourites. I certainly backed up what I'd said. The incompetence of the Military Commissions system provided me with a lot to say. I could not lie about it. People had to know, and we were coming from a position of strength – legally, logically and morally.

The backlash wasn't slow in coming. The Australian government responded by saying that my comments were just the type of thing a defence lawyer would say. Philip Ruddock, the Attorney-General, said I was just doing the normal pre-trial jockeying. When Maxine McKew of the ABC's *7.30 Report* put that to me, I replied:

> That's criticism that's very hard to address in this sense because I am a defence counsel and that's usually what the government says whenever the defence counsel points out that something's wrong. But let me go back to, first, to the rule that I cited to you, the rule where the Appointing Authority decides motions raised by the defence. Can anybody sit back and objectively say that that is an independent system, to have the person who initiated the charges and approved the prosecution be the one to rule just on specific defence motions? Everyone out there, your viewers, can make their own determination. They don't need to believe me. Look at that situation and think, is it fair?

In Washington, the DOD responded by rolling out Altenburg and Hemingway to talk about how fair the process was. Reporters, under the influence of the Armed Force Press Service, would passively report their statements as truth. GTMO Gary was not happy, claiming that I was overstating things in the media. He accused me, falsely, of being an unnamed 'military lawyer' cited in some previous articles. That criticism probably revealed a lot more about GTMO Gary's way of going about things than it did about mine.

Within the military, disapproval filtered back to me. 'Why is he doing this?'; 'Why is he bashing the President?'; 'Is he just looking for the limelight?' And so on. I expected this to happen. Complaining to the media was something you just did not do in the military, and those who did were usually ostracised. But inside the CDC office, once I came back alive the next day and proved that the black vans had not shown up at my house and taken me away, it emboldened the rest of the defence lawyers to interact with the media. Those who were shaking their heads as I headed up to my press conference were now fielding media calls. Swift came in one day with a framed article about himself; he was so proud.

I'd helped open up the discussion about the fairness of the commission process, but one thing I never wanted to do was make it about me. I wasn't doing anything wonderful; I was just doing my job. My friends in Iraq and Afghanistan were the ones at risk. Reporters would ask, 'How does it feel to challenge Rumsfeld in federal court?' or 'How do you feel?' or 'What does your family think?' A heroic lawyer fighting against Rumsfeld might appeal to them, but I wanted the focus to be on the unfairness of the process and the plight of an Australian. Speaking up for due process seemed to me nothing unusual: due process is part of what America stands for. We don't treat people differently based on their race. We don't treat people differently based on their nationality.

We don't make up crimes arbitrarily, regardless of what a person is accused of.

I was often asked if this was a new kind of war that required a new system of justice. My response was that our justice system had always tried to move away from unfairness. When I raised issues of unfairness in the process, I was embracing the values I had been taught in scouts, sports, high school, college, law school and the Marines. The White House had changed the moral compass. My sense of fairness, right and wrong, didn't change whether I was a defence counsel or prosecutor in the Marine Corps.

13

Retaliation

I was under no illusion that Hicks was going to get a fair trial at the Military Commission. I was convinced the charges were not valid, but we were not going to get an Appointing Authority who approved charges only to rule them invalid later. That is why the system was set up in the way it was. In my opinion, there was not a chance Hicks was going to be acquitted.

In representing him, I was not out to stop the commissions or take on the Bush or Howard administrations. It was not a cause, but a client. I just wanted to get Hicks out.

While there had been some talk in the press that the Australian government was looking at whether or not Hicks could be prosecuted in Australia, it did not seem likely that Howard would back down from his bizarre position that Australia was leaving Hicks in GTMO because he did not break any Australian laws. This left us in the unusual position for defence lawyers of trying to find a way for our client to be prosecuted under Australian law – then he might be taken home, albeit to an Australian jail.

The strangely sobering reality was that the Australian government had actually investigated Hicks (more than the United States ever did) and did not find any violation of Australian law. Even under the Taliban, Afghanistan was not off limits to Australians. A 1999 executive order signed by President Clinton prohibited US citizens from providing benefits to the Taliban, and this had swept up some Americans who had been in training camps there, but it did not apply to Hicks. It wasn't until 2002 and 2003, long after Hicks was captured, that Australia enacted laws prohibiting association with the Taliban or al-Qaeda. Australia did have a Foreign Incursions Act that made it illegal for Australians to go to foreign countries to use force to overthrow the government of a foreign state. Even under this law, ironically, Hicks would have been innocent, as he was with the Taliban, Afghanistan's government. If only he had been with the US ally, the Northern Alliance forces, fighting the Taliban – then he might have broken an Australian law and been allowed to go back home! It's hard to understand the logic now, and it was almost impossible to convey it to a person in Hicks's situation then.

As Hicks languished, the world's attention drifted. As we got back from our eight-day visit with him, in February 2004, the New England Patriots defeated the Carolina Panthers at Super Bowl XXXVIII, but more importantly, Janet Jackson's wardrobe 'malfunctioned' with the help of Justin Timberlake's hand. You had to keep things in perspective.

Three weeks later, as we were still waiting for Hicks to be charged, two GTMO detainees, Ibrahim Al-Qosi from Sudan and Ali Al-Bahlul from Yemen, were charged with offences before a Military Commission. From our office, Shaffer (Al-Qosi) and Bridges and Sundel (Al-Bahlul) were detailed to represent them. Now five of us had clients and could get to work.

Being detailed to Hicks meant having more of a public profile, and there were aspects of having my head above the parapet that I wasn't prepared for. After I got back to DC, I got a call from a military friend wanting to meet for a meal. As we were chatting, my friend said, 'Look, I gotta tell you something. Do you know you're, you're being investigated?'

'What are you talking about?' I was puzzled. Investigated for what? By whom?

All he knew was that there was an ethics board looking at what I had said in the media. He did not know specifics, but thought he should warn me. He thought it strange that I had not been told as, under the Navy ethics regulations, when the board is looking into someone they are supposed to be notified.

I didn't know what to think, but I was getting suspicious. Soon after, another friend told me they knew who was investigating me. I was confident I had done nothing wrong, but as a precaution I started reaching out to fellow lawyers, in case I was notified that I was being investigated. My media statements at this time were being heavily scrutinised by the DOD public affairs office and GTMO Gary; if someone thought I had overstated something or was incorrect, I was quite used to getting an email about it, either directly or through Gunn. Being investigated was something else entirely.

This was my first taste of the subtle type of retaliation that would be used against me, and not the last. I would not find out I was 'officially' being investigated until February, when Gunn slipped up in a conversation. He approached me about some German article that GTMO Gary was upset with. It appeared to me that Gunn was irritated at having to deal with this kind of thing, and he said, 'This is why you're being investigated.'

I played innocent. 'What do you mean, investigated?' Gunn looked frustrated that he had let it slip and brushed me off, but I could not understand why he had not told me. I was trying not to be worried, but at the same time, the US government was in the middle of prosecuting a civilian defence lawyer, Lynne Stewart, for allegedly providing material support to a terrorist activity by assisting to pass messages for her client, Sheik Omar Abdel Rahman, while he was in prison serving a life sentence for his part in the 1993 plot to blow up landmarks in New York City.

It would be almost two months before I was formally told that, yes, I was being investigated. Even with it hanging over me, I was not going to let it deter me from exposing problems with the system to the public. If anything, it drove me harder, as I knew I had not violated any rule.

In mid-February, I headed back to GTMO for my fifth visit with Hicks. I was getting the hang of the logistics. We were able to fly on six-seater propeller planes, staffed by Reserve or National Guard crews, out of Davidson airfield, about 15 miles from my house in Northern Virginia. If we planned it right, we could get to GTMO the same day. Of course, those planes had no fancy bathroom, so you had to hold it in until the refuelling stop in Florida. For males, there was a 'piss tube', a plastic tube with a funnel on the end that was built into the plane, but I felt sorry for the females on the team on many of the trips. On one of these flights, there was some disagreement between the tower at GTMO and the National Guard pilots as we approached to land. The tower thought the pilots had not executed some radio procedure correctly, and called out the Marine Security force as we touched down. The plane was ordered to the end of the runway as the Marine Security raced up in Humvees. We left the plane with our hands in the air as Marines spread out, weapons aimed at us; there were even snipers in the back of the Humvees. I don't think one of my fellow passengers, a civilian contractor on his first visit to GTMO, found it as humorous as I did.

But on this visit in February, I appreciated the help of the JTF-SJA office, the prosecutors and the Australian embassy in getting Hicks back on the same food as the guards, which he had briefly been denied after the 'escape' attempt. Improving his daily conditions was one thing I could actually do for him, and it was still his preoccupation. I couldn't help him with the noise of woodpeckers hammering at the outside walls, his headaches or his back pain, which resulted mostly from the lack of any real physical exercise, except, when his back was particularly painful, to meet him in his cell so he could lie down and change positions. Since moving to Camp Echo in May 2003, he had only been out of his cell for thirty minutes to an hour at night – when he was taken into a large chain-linked cage, about the size of a small bedroom, with a concrete floor.

During that trip, I noticed a conspicuous change underway at GTMO. Kellogg, Brown and Root, the construction firm owned by Vice-President Cheney's former company, Halliburton, was building Camp 5. Designed along the lines of a US maximum security prison, it would hold 100 detainees on two storeys of cells in five spokes leading into a central observation office. The GTMO commander was describing it as an 'interrogation facility' that would 'accelerate and help us in the interrogation process'. Next to the ramshackle existing camps, it had a vastness and modernity that made it loom forebodingly. I'm sure that was the impression they were aiming to create, too. This was not a place I wanted Hicks to end up in.

14

Why Was He There?

To gather information on Hicks's case, I needed to retrace the path he had taken from Australia through Kosovo, Pakistan and Afghanistan. As a starting point, I was anxious to get my hands on an interview between Hicks and Australian government officials in GTMO, the only interview, we were told, that had been recorded.

This was strange, to say the least. Having been interrogated repeatedly through the process, from Afghanistan to GTMO, Hicks had surely been recorded. Police record the most basic suburban interviews. If the US military were interrogating someone who might have valuable information about the location of weapons of mass destruction, or how al-Qaeda operated, of course it would be recorded. The art of interrogation is a science. Nuances of language, when interpreters are involved, are complex, and make the recording of such interrogations even more essential. So were they recording detainees' interviews and hiding these recordings, or were they deliberately not recording them because they might document what a poor job they were doing, or for some other nefarious reason?

There was one clue to what might have been happening. At one point, an interpreter for the US Air Force was accused of spying. The government said it was going to go back and review all the recordings and transcripts of interrogations he was involved in, to see if he had done anything wrong. Shortly afterwards, his case was abruptly dropped. Several months later, General Miller, the commander of JTF GTMO and a classic case, in my view, of someone promoted beyond his capabilities, contradicted the government's prior claims that there were recording of the interrogations. Miller explained to a *Washington Post* reporter that the interrogations were not videotaped or tape-recorded. Miller said the interrogations were designed primarily to yield intelligence, not evidence for a court. Miller added that taping 'causes us legal problems'. Detainees might gain access to tapes through court proceedings. 'Then, it becomes exculpatory,' Miller said. I asked myself, then as now, *What system am I in?*

A possible wrinkle for my planned trip to Australia was hearing that the documentary Terry Hicks and Stephen Kenny had been cooperating with, *The President Versus David Hicks*, was going to be aired on 15 March, when I was scheduled to be in Australia. I knew I would get questioned about it, but I hadn't seen it. Curtis Levy, the director, was kind enough to get me a rough copy.

I was worried about how it would portray Hicks, particularly in its use of letters he had written to his family at a time when he was exploring a world of which he had, as yet, no experience. I expected some of what he had written to be thrown back in his face, to justify the Bush administration's treatment of him. It was obvious to me that his writing was just a regurgitation of what he was hearing from people on his travels in Pakistan and Afghanistan, but I was concerned about a backlash.

A positive aspect of the documentary was that Terry was someone people could identify with. What he went through for his son was very moving. In the end, the screening was out of my control, and I resolved to highlight the positives and publicise the unfairness of what was happening to Hicks.

On a later trip to Hawaii, I showed the documentary to some Marine colleagues of mine; I wanted to use them as a kind of military test jury. As I'd suspected, it increased nobody's sympathy towards Hicks, confirming my suspicions that any military panel who had been swallowing the Bush administration's propaganda, already believed that all these people were war criminals. Convincing them otherwise was going to be a hard sell, to say the least. Their reaction worried me greatly. In the War on Terror, there was no great leap, in the military mind, from someone being a Muslim to their being an Islamic extremist. It was an insurmountable barrier. Even though Hicks was not a terrorist, the perception of the Guantanamo Bay detainees was fully entrenched in the military psyche in 2004.

As I was preparing to leave for my trip Down Under, the Australian embassy in DC and the US embassy in Canberra were calling Hemingway to ask why I was going. To Hemingway's credit, I got no resistance. The US embassy would track my travels, but not obstruct me.

Just before I left for Australia, the US released five British citizens held at GTMO: four British men still remained in Cuba, two of them having been designated for Military Commissions along with Hicks. But it looked like the UK was not backing down on its scepticism about the commissions. I thought the contrast between their activism and Australia's passivity was worth telling the public about.

As I flew to Australia, I was clear on the message I wanted to put out. I was not saying Hicks should just be released; I was saying he deserved a fair trial. I was nervous that some Australians might take offence at some Yankee coming over and telling them what to do, and so I would steer clear of getting involved in Australian politics – although that would become harder over time.

On 8 March 2004, I arrived in Sydney and went to stay with Bruno and Jane, relatives of my sister's Australian husband, to have a shower and relax. Speaking to them, I tried to get a sense of what people thought about Hicks in Australia. They had the same question that I think people still ask today: *Why was he there?* I couldn't answer this to anyone's satisfaction, and possibly still can't.

I was again struck by the beauty of Sydney Harbour, which I remembered from my rugby trip in 1988. This time, however, I didn't have much time to enjoy the sights.

Master Sergeant Pierre was flying in the day after me. She had lived in Canberra during a tour of duty attached to the embassy, and I would need her help getting around. We would spend the next two weeks travelling back and forth between Sydney, Canberra and Adelaide while I tried to duck the media.

In Canberra, I established contacts with the Attorney-General's department and the AFP. Throughout the case, everyone at the

AFP was helpful, including the National Manager for Counter Terrorism, Graham Ashton, the lead agent on the Hicks case, Ramzi Jabbour, and David Gourge, a seconded South Australian police officer. As far as I could tell, they helped the prosecution and defence equally. Jabbour was always available for my calls. (It's true: I'm not saying nice things about the AFP just because I now live in Australia and don't want to get arrested!)

While it seemed that anyone who had ever met Hicks had been interviewed by either the AFP or the media, I still needed to track them all down and interview them myself. The AFP had been seizing any computers that Hicks may have used, including those belonging to family and friends. The terrorist bombing of the Madrid subway occurred just after I arrived in Australia, and sensitivities were high.

When in Canberra on those cool mornings, I would jog around Lake Burley Griffin. I came across a memorial on which there was a bronze plaque commemorating 'Australians in the Spanish Civil War 1936 to 1939'. The memorial recognised the seventy Australians, among around 50 000 people from fifty-three different countries including the USA, who had fought the fascists. It struck me that in the new Bush war, those heroes would be 'unlawful enemy combatants'. I wondered about all the armed conflicts of the past 150 years that Australians fought in. There were Australians on both sides of the US Civil War. Why were people so shocked that an Australian might have been fighting in another war? Was it just because Hicks found himself on the wrong side?

When we got to Adelaide, I was finally able to meet Terry, along with his wife, Bev. Meeting Terry was like meeting an older version of Hicks, they looked so much alike. I was very nervous, but

Bev made me feel right at home. Aside from Stephen Kenny, I was the only person they knew who had seen their son. As I'd seen him more often and more recently than Kenny, they were hungry for whatever I could tell them about his conditions and his state of mind. I told them what I could about the process and possible outcomes, from a plea to how we could fight the case in a commission as well as in federal court. I wanted them to know they could send me books, mail or even emails, which I would print off and get to Hicks; I would try to get his mail back to them as soon as possible. As with Hicks, they had many urgent questions that I could not answer.

I met Hicks's sister Stephanie Mewitt, his uncle Chris Hicks and his stepbrother Steve, as well as Karl and Kerry Cripps, who had been Hicks's friends for years. His parents had divorced when he was young, and I also met with his mother. I observed that this time of hardship had pulled the family together. Bronwyn Mewitt, Terry's ex-wife, had founded and organised the 'Fair Go for Hicks' group. Bronwyn poured her heart into fighting for Hicks, as did some seventeen other people, for almost six years. I attended a meeting and saw a dedicated group of people fighting for Hicks in the face of public indifference. My connection to Hicks must have offered them hope, but at the same time disappointment, as I could not give them what they really wanted, which was certainty of when he could come home.

Terry's neighbours from across the street, Ian and Annette Knevitt, had known Hicks well for many years, and he even lived with them when he split from his ex-girlfriend Jodie, the mother of his children. I met with Jodie and the kids at their home. I felt bad for the kids. It's tough enough having your parents split up, as I knew, but when your life falls under the public microscope and the media is thrust upon you, in these unique circumstances, it must be so incredibly difficult. Getting photos of the kids and everyone else back home to be able to show Hicks was a priority for me. I knew that these would be even more nourishing for him than protein bars and Gatorade.

I also arranged high-school coursework through an open-access college in Adelaide, so that Hicks had something productive he could do with all his time in the cell. It took a month to get the Australian government to agree, but it got through with a little pushing by the South Australian Labor Party Senator Linda Kirk. Over the next two years, I picked up Hicks's assignments and schoolwork from GTMO and shuttled them back to Adelaide and then back again to him. He had not finished Year Nine, but while he was at GTMO he continued his studies. At times, it felt like helping him with this was the one useful thing I was actually accomplishing.

The media's persistence in Australia made it hard for me to keep as low a profile as I'd have liked. When I landed in Adelaide, the camera almost followed me into the airport bathroom. Somehow a reporter, Ray Bonner, ended up in my car for one of my drives from Sydney to Canberra. He was a former Marine and claimed to have needed a lift. Once he was there, I took the opportunity to try to explain the unfairness in the system. He might have thought he had me trapped, but I think I had him! Like many other reporters, in a US election year, he wanted to know whether I was politically a Republican or Democrat. Since I had spoken publicly against the system, everyone assumed I was a Democrat. I told him, 'I don't care if there's four more years of President Bush followed by eight years of Jeb Bush, or if John Kerry wins the election. Honestly, I have never voted. I've been in the military since I was eighteen and will follow whoever the citizenry votes in.'

Dealing with the media on that first trip was challenging. I was trying not to offend anyone, but – although I know Australians speak English – there were a lot of subtle differences in the language and tone. I needed a good sports analogy to explain the unfairness of the Military Commissions system, but my baseball version – it's like letting the pitcher call his own balls and strikes – was not going to work in Australia. One evening, I was sitting in a hotel bar getting something to eat. Cricket was on the television, and I was asking the bartender about the rules. He explained the leg-before-wicket rule, and I thought, *Eureka!* The Military Commission was like allowing the bowler to decide LBWs. I had my sports analogy that Australians would understand. Cricket was going to free David Hicks!

While I was in Sydney getting ready to make my second trip to Adelaide to conduct some interviews, I arranged to stop over in Melbourne to talk to a gathering of the Victorian Bar Association. Sarah Hinchey, of the association, explained it was during the afternoon and organised at short notice, so there might only be a handful of lawyers there. She picked me up at the airport, and when we got to the meeting, it was packed with 250 people inside and outside. I was sweating bullets. The biggest group I'd ever addressed had been a class of Marine recruits. I didn't realise it then, but this was the start of a way to encourage the legal community's mobilisation for a fair trial for Hicks. Until then Australians hadn't shown as much interest in the system's problems as in the personality of Hicks, but now I could explain that there was an important principle at stake.

In my PowerPoint folder, I had about six different shots of GTMO. This presentation would grow over the years to an hour-long road show with close to seventy-three slides outlining the problems with the system and illustrating how unfairly Hicks was being treated.

From Melbourne I headed back to Adelaide, where Amnesty International Australia and Stephen Kenny had organised a small public event. It was great to see about 150 people interested enough to hear what was happening to Hicks. It was clear that most of the audience were liberals (small-l liberals, not Australian Liberals), and I realised that one of the big challenges was going to be to get Australians from across the political spectrum to listen. Linda Kirk and Robert McClelland from the Labor Party were interested, but the conservatives were in power and it was hard to get through to them or their constituencies. The Howard government's bizarre position on Hicks, that he had committed no Australian crime and therefore had to stay in Guantanamo Bay, was entrenched. Some of what I was saying in public was filtering back home, and I got a message via one of the CDC staff that the chief prosecutor said I needed to watch what I was saying.

One of the effects of appearing in the media, though, was that people were starting to recognise me. The Marine haircut and big nose and ears made me easily identifiable. On one trip – not this first one – a friend took me to a casino, and we were playing Texas hold 'em poker. The guy next to me started looking at me closely.

'Where do I know you from, mate? I know you from somewhere,' he said.

I said, 'No, I don't think so.'

He kept at it. So I finally said, 'You must have seen me on the world poker tour.'

He started to tell the next guy and it went around the table. Some of them began leaving the table, so I had to do the right thing.

'I'm the military guy defending David Hicks,' I admitted.

Then the light bulb went on and I was glad to see a positive reaction – at least some poker fans felt that what was happening to Hicks was wrong. They would have known the truth anyway, when I lost all my money a few hands later. But it dawned on me that I no longer had the anonymity I used to take for granted.

People would approach me and tell me what they thought about Hicks, most of it not good. 'I hope he rots,' they said. 'What was he doing in Afghanistan?' 'He got himself into this mess, what was he doing with the Taliban?' It was not hostile, just an expression of what they felt. The worst thing I would hear was, 'Hey, are you that Army guy defending the traitor Hicks?' (The Army part was kind of an insult, but I let it slide.) This was everyday Australians saying what they felt, and I didn't object. I was glad people felt free to approach me, and it was good for me to know how they felt. Kenny felt, optimistically, that almost everyone supported Hicks, but in March 2004, I got the sense that the majority did not. Those people who came up to me were proud Australians who felt that Hicks had sided with the enemy. It did not shock me. This was what the government and much of the media had been telling them since he was captured. It let me know that we needed to get people to look beyond Hicks being 'over there', and step back to see how he, an Australian, was being treated. It was not going to be an easy task, but the failures of the system would provide us with enough evidence and time to start changing hearts and minds.

My two busy, jet-lagged weeks in Australia flew by, and then I flew from there to a two-day legal conference in London organised by the prominent attorney Clive Stafford Smith. I proudly used my cricket analogy at a press conference: 'The Appointing Authority, who approves the charges, is the same person who gets to rule on defence motions . . . He is basically reviewing his own decisions . . . It's like letting the bowler call LBW.' They seemed quite impressed that an American would talk about cricket, and it got the message across.

15

Charged

I finally got back to the USA on 27 March 2004, and had one night in my own bed before heading back down to Guantanamo Bay. Joshua Dratel was accompanying me and his paralegal, Elisabeth Besobrasow, was coming a few days later, but I desperately needed another full-time military lawyer. My pleas to Gunn were still being denied.

Since my last visit to GTMO, Army Major General Jay Hood had taken over command, inheriting the problems caused by Miller. It was claimed that detainees were still being treated inhumanely, such as, in one case, being moved from cell to cell 112 times between 7 May and 20 May 2004, shackled and unshackled every move, an average of once every three hours. Though it was on his watch, Hood claimed to be unaware of this. He certainly had a more accommodating manner than Miller. During our first visit, Hood approached us and said, 'Hey, look, you guys have got a duty, you've got a mission to do. I fully support it. If you ever think you're getting caught up in red tape, you come see me.' He had a background as a convening authority, overseeing real military courts-martial, and was a fair man. During the next two years, Hood's tenure, Hicks's conditions improved and I think there was a change overall as well. While Miller had denied Hicks's request to work on his education, Hood approved it. Things would decline again, however, when Hood left in 2006.

Our top priority on that visit was to consider if we were going to seriously explore a plea option. The prosecutors had provided me with their draft charges, and wanted to know if we were going to work out a deal. Additionally, the Australian parliament had recently amended the *International Transfer of Prisoners Amendment Act 2004*, which 'enable[d] any Australian citizen detained at Guantanamo Bay who is convicted and sentenced to a term of imprisonment by a US military tribunal to be transferred back to Australia to serve their sentence'. While this was a positive change, it also meant that the Australian parliament was supporting the legitimacy of the Military Commissions. I saw this as an indication of the Howard government's unyielding desire for Hicks to be dealt with in a commission. But it did improve his chances of getting out of GTMO and back to Australia.

Dratel and I felt we had to at least test the waters. If we could get a deal that got him home to Australia before the US election campaign heated up, even if that was to serve out a sentence, it might be worth it. We knew there was no real chance if he came before a Military Commission, and the Supreme Court process still had an indefinite time to run, even if it went the detainees' way.

Bush might lose the 2004 election, the Military Commission system might be stopped; anything could happen, and Hicks would be in a better position to benefit from change if he was in Australia rather than GTMO.

Between Dratel and me, we hashed out an offer over a few days: a ten-year sentence, with five years suspended, meaning five years incarcerated, starting from when Bush designated Hicks for the Military Commissions, on 3 July 2003. Two years after sentencing, according to our offer, he would be repatriated to Australia. That meant he could go to an Australian prison, at best, in May 2006, and be free on 3 July 2008. It could be even better, if he became eligible for parole in Australia earlier than 2008. A crucial benefit of doing this was that if the Military Commission system was found to be unlawful by a court in another case, Hicks would likely be freed in Australia.

After we settled on this, Dratel and Besobrasow returned to New York – I was still amazed that Dratel was doing all this for free; he was clearly passionate about the issues at stake – while I spent a few more days with Hicks, bringing him family news, showing him the photos, passing on mail and educational materials, and making sure he was well stocked with chewing tobacco and protein bars. On this, my sixth trip to GTMO, I was still trying to get our office phones turned on.

When I returned to Virginia in April, the major thing weighing on me personally was the investigation into my press statements, as I had received no official word on the investigation's progress. Unbeknown to me, it had already been completed. A fellow defence lawyer had to work a contact to get a copy of the report that had been sent to the Navy Judge Advocate General, Admiral Lohr. The opinion was couched in such a way that I would not have to be notified because – get this – the investigation was not into *me*, but my *statements*:

> Media sources reported that [Mori] stated that the Military Commissions will not provide a full and fair trial and have been created by those with a vested interest only in convictions. While these statements triggered the questions presented, we note that this opinion does not attempt to judge, in any way, the propriety of such remarks under applicable professional responsibility rules.

Then why do an investigation at all? This was clearly not what I had heard from my sources at the time. Years later, I met a military lawyer who had been specifically ordered to look at my conduct in the media and told to find an ethics violation. Shamefaced, he told me that he initially reported back that he could find no ethical violation. He was told to 'go back and check again'. When he reported back the second time, that he could still find no violation, he was told to keep looking until he found something. I suspected that initially I was in their sights, but once it became clear no ethics rule was violated, the focus shifted to the vague version I read in the report. Once the entire ethics panel of seven senior Navy and Marine officers looked at it, they did not find any violation by me. Hearing this was one weight off my shoulders. No matter that I knew I'd done nothing wrong: I had been around the military long enough to know that whether you did something wrong is not always the most important factor.

Back from GTMO, I took our deal offer to the prosecutors. They would not support the five-year sentence, but they did not have the final say. The Appointing Authority, retired Major General John D. Altenburg, who was in charge of approving charges and plea agreements, did. When we met him, he had only been in the job for a few months and was still getting up to speed, so he would not give an immediate answer. Days after our meeting, I finally got a response: five years was not an acceptable sentence.

So that was that. We had to continue to prepare for a full trial.

Our resources were always being stretched – not a problem the prosecution generally had to deal with. The Appointing Authority staff was now nineteen, the prosecutor's was fourteen, and ours was still nine. The prosecution had two to three lawyers on every case, and we had one lawyer on each except for the one detainee who did not want a military lawyer:he had two. We did not even have a mailbox; all of our mail had to be siphoned through the Pentagon for security screening, which by now was moving at a glacial pace due to the recent anthrax and ricin terrorist scares, when biological agents were sent through the mail to some congressional office buildings. But whether or not it was through overzealous or incompetent security processes, mail would disappear or not make it to us. I started to have our case mail sent to my home.

To illustrate what we were fighting, resources-wise, here is a to-do list I wrote a few months into 2004:

- Research and develop an understanding of all prior Military Commissions and international tribunals.
- Interview all the people who have interacted with and/or interviewed Mr Hicks.
- Review all documentary evidence and follow-up leads discovered.
- Interview all individuals who have provided statements in this

case (this includes various persons across the United States; review several federal trial transcripts, each of which contains over 3000 pages and follow-up leads discovered).

- Complete (potential) sentencing preparation.
- Research the history, operations and make-up of Lashkar-e-Tayyiba.
- Research the history, operations and make-up of al-Qaeda.
- Research the history, operations and workings of the Taliban.
- Research the military operations conducted during the invasion of Afghanistan.
- Identify, research and draft motions necessary to challenge the charges before the commission.
- Identify, research and draft motions necessary to challenge the rules and procedures of the commission.
- Identify, research and draft motions necessary to challenge the commission itself.
- Identify, interview and prepare expert witnesses for the defence.
- Identify, research and prepare cross-examination for any government expert witnesses.
- Interview several foreign defence witnesses.
- Identify, research and prepare all issues for submission to the review panel as well as the typical trial preparation of directs, crosses, exhibits and arguments; and other issues that will arise during the completion of these tasks.

And still Gunn turned me down when I asked for a second lawyer. The Australian embassy showed more concern about the inadequacy of resources behind Hicks's representation, but their response was to raise it with the Pentagon, who assured them that I had not requested a second lawyer. This was not true, but a formal response from some faceless official at the Pentagon usually managed to appease the Australians.

In the Supreme Court, Hicks's case's legal argument finished on 20 April and we expected a decision by the end of June. We put a lot of thought into how to use the civil courts to challenge the validity of the Military Commissions system. The only knockout blow that could free Hicks was if the federal courts ruled that the charges against him were invalid. But until he was charged, we couldn't use this avenue. For many reasons, we were growing beyond impatient to see the actual charges against him.

On 28 April 2004, during argument in the Supreme Court case involving 'enemy combatant' Jose Padilla, the Deputy Solicitor-General Paul Clement denied that torture would ever be used by the US military to extract information from prisoners. Within days, Seymour M. Hersh broke the Abu Ghraib story in the *New Yorker*, and *60 Minutes* showed the photos of the abuse of prisoners at Abu Ghraib. The outrage at pictures of US soldiers maltreating inmates was universal. In the United States and the Western world, the perpetrators were condemned. In the Middle East, it confirmed all the worst suspicions of American forces, and was a persuasive recruitment tool for insurgent organisations fighting us in Iraq. There was a link to GTMO in the person of Miller, the former commander of JTF GTMO and advisor for interrogations in Iraq, whose name had been mentioned in connection with the abuse of prisoners. Another official, speaking anonymously to the *Washington Post*, put the matter more plainly: 'If you don't violate someone's human rights some of the time, you probably aren't doing your job.'

I went down to GTMO in mid-May to see Hicks. Part of my job was to act as postman, making sure his mail was getting in and out. The little things always helped. He hadn't had a chair in his cell in which he could sit to do his reading and schoolwork, and the Australian consular officer helped us secure a small plastic table and chair. The Australian consul had a similar job to mine, in trying to build relationships with the JTF staff to help Hicks's welfare, and I found him caring and hard-working.

Kenny had been keen to go public about the abuse Hicks had suffered, and with the wave of disgust at the Abu Ghraib revelations, he thought it was the right moment to highlight what had happened to our client. Dratel and I wanted to gather more concrete evidence. The matter was taken out of our hands when, on 20 May, *The Australian* newspaper broke a story about Hicks being beaten by US forces in Afghanistan, which unleashed a flurry of reactions. The reporter had actually been to Afghanistan and talked to former detainees.

We had been trying to get Hicks's allegations of abuse investigated. Hemingway asked me to disclose specific facts and circumstances about the abuse, which he said he would forward to appropriate investigators. I wanted it to go to the Australians first and I requested authorisation to provide the information to the Australian embassy without DOD staff being present. It seemed obvious that Hemingway was trying to see the information before we disclosed it to the Australians, so he could try to control the situation. He had a power of censorship; the Military Commission system had invented a classification of information relating to cases as 'Protected', meaning it was not classified, but this was just another mechanism to control the defence counsel, and to keep embarrassing information from getting out. Colonel Gunn, in a welcome show of resistance, said Hemingway did not have the authority to order me to release the abuse information to him. So I didn't. I wanted to provide it directly to the Australian government. Our position was rewarded: a week later, permission came through for me to speak to the Australian embassy.

I suspected, based on their past performance, that the Australian embassy might just pass the information straight on to Hemingway anyway. However, I was determined to not set a precedent of having to pass everything to the Australian government through the Appointing Authority's office.

As I prepared to release information about Hicks's abuse to the Australian diplomats – and tried to work out how to get it investigated objectively, not under the sway of political controllers – the Military Commission cranked into gear on getting Hicks charged. They always seemed to move forward when they were under pressure, or when they needed to create a distraction. We had been waiting many months for these charges, and now that news of Hicks's abuse had gone public – hey presto! – the charges materialised.

The charges, publicly released on 10 June, did not surprise me. But it was good to have the waiting over, and to have something official to fight. We could attack the validity of the charges, now that we had them, in federal court. There were three: conspiracy, attempted murder by an unprivileged belligerent, and aiding the enemy.

The charge sheet began with a background section detailing that

Hicks had 'engaged in hostiles' with the Kosovo Liberation Army (KLA) in Kosovo in May 1999, even though he was not charged with a crime for this. Hicks's past experience training in Albania with the KLA was being used as a negative, implying he showed a tendency to aid America's enemies. But I remembered that many more Americans also fought for the KLA in the late 1990s. Senator Joseph Lieberman, the 2000 Democrat vice-presidential candidate, said the KLA stood for 'the same human values and principles' as the United States. Unless I was mistaken, the United States, as part of NATO, participated in bombing the KLA's enemy, Serbia. It was hypocritical that Hicks's participation in the KLA was now being held up as a sign of criminality.

The background section mentioned that Hicks had converted to Islam, as if that was some crime in and of itself. It asserted that he travelled to Pakistan and joined Lashkar-e-Tayyiba (LET), 'a terrorist organisation'. Of course, this was not a crime either, as neither the US nor Australia had designated LET as a terrorist organisation until after Hicks was captured. It was alleged that Hicks attended training camps and then travelled to the Line of Control between Pakistan and India-controlled Kashmir, where he 'engaged in hostile action'. Again there was a little overstatement here. Marvin Weinbaum, who had been the US State Department's analyst for Pakistan and Afghanistan from 1999 to 2003, explained that LET was an organisation that operated openly within Pakistan, with the support of the Pakistani government, through the Pakistani Intelligence Service and Pakistani army. It was somehow evil for Hicks to be involved with an organisation run by one of the US's allies in the War on Terror.

Then followed nine background paragraphs on the history of

al-Qaeda, including events dating back to 1989, when Hicks was fifteen years old and at school in Adelaide.

When it finally got to the actual charges, it started with conspiracy, claiming that Hicks conspired with Osama bin Laden and others to commit crimes, including terrorism. In twelve paragraphs, it detailed Hicks's attendance at camps in Afghanistan culminating, after the United States invaded Afghanistan, with Hicks guarding a Taliban tank and alleging that he engaged in combat against coalition forces. What was missing from this crime of conspiracy to commit terrorism was any claim that Hicks had built or planted any bombs or was even willing to carry out any attack against a civilian target. One of the paragraphs describing Hicks's training claimed he conducted surveillance of the US and British embassies in Kabul, and then filed reports. However, as one Australian reporter asked me, 'Weren't the embassies in Kabul closed at the time?' I guess Hicks's 'reports' were not very long!

I am not making light of Hicks being over in Afghanistan, and I think that the hardest thing for Australians to understand was why he would go over there in the first place. But from a legal mindset, I still could not find a crime, and it seemed that the prosecution was stretching in its shading of the facts. The crime of conspiracy did not exist in the international law of war. At the Nuremberg trials for the Nazi leadership, the US prosecutor, Robert H. Jackson, had attempted to use the US version of conspiracy in relation to war crimes, but the tribunal rejected this. Now sixty years later, the United States was trying it again.

As for the crime of terrorism, this was a new crime invented by MCI No. 2. US courts had been prosecuting terrorism-related offences for years. Internationally, there were multilateral treaties aimed at certain 'terrorist' conduct, such as airline hijacking, hostage taking and bombing. But there was no international crime or war crime of 'terrorism'. The practical problem with defining terrorism is that one country's terrorist might not be seen as a terrorist by other countries – for example, Nelson Mandela was convicted of terrorist activities and was on the US terrorist watch list until 2008.

The second charge against Hicks was 'attempted murder by unprivileged combatant'. The charge stated that in Afghanistan between 11 September and 1 December 2001, Hicks, as a perpetrator and co-conspirator, attempted murder by directing small-arms fire, explosives and other means intended to kill American, British, Canadian, Australian, Afghan and other coalition forces, and civilians. My initial reaction was, *Attempted murder? Who did he try to kill?* I had not been provided any evidence Hicks had shot at anyone or planted any bomb. It would take another two years before the prosecution would admit Hicks had not done any of these things. Even assuming that Hicks had shot at a US soldier, it was my view, after speaking with the international law experts, that the charge was not a valid law-of-war offence.

The laws of war do not make it a crime to shoot a soldier in battle. (It would kind of defeat the whole purpose of a war.) However, the laws of war do make it a crime to shoot certain people such as medical personnel, and soldiers who have surrendered or are wounded. The law of war is written to protect certain people from being shot, not everyone.

The evil genius of the Bush administration and its minions, including Lietzau, was to create the crime in MCI No. 2 of 'murder by an unprivileged belligerent', in an attempt to criminalise shooting at a soldier in a war when the person doing the shooting would not have been entitled to POW status, if captured. Bush wanted to focus not on who was being shot but on who was doing the shooting.

Under the Bush administration's newly proclaimed law of war, those detained at GTMO were without POW status and were labelled 'unlawful enemy combatants' or 'unprivileged belligerents' and any act they took in a war was deemed to be a war crime.

While Hicks was not accused of using any illegal weapon or shooting a wounded soldier, he was being charged solely for participating. They were trying to criminalise merely being in the war, especially if the combatant wasn't wearing a uniform. Never mind that our Central Intelligence Agency, Special Forces and Northern Alliance allies might also, by those rules, not qualify for POW status. Simply put, it was not a crime against the law of war to fight out of uniform in a war.

The charge listed several countries' armed forces as 'victims', including Australian, Canadian and British. This raised my curiosity. Were these countries' forces even in Afghanistan at the time, or near where Hicks was? Surely the prosecutors would not charge Hicks with attempting to murder people who were not in the general area of where he was? Or would they?

The charge of 'aiding the enemy' was actually a crime that a Military Commission could hear, according to an act of Congress. What made absolutely no sense was how he could be both part of the enemy and aiding the enemy. This would be akin to charging every German soldier fighting in World War II with aiding the enemy. If this really was a valid offence, everyone who was resisting the Northern Alliance was guilty. That would mean that a lot of people the United States worked with to build the new Afghanistan were also war criminals.

In reality, the 'aiding the enemy' charge was only valid if the accused was violating their allegiance to the United States. This was how the charge had been used in the Korean and Vietnam wars, when US prisoners of war had cooperated with their captors. But an Australian in Afghanistan had no duty of allegiance to the United States. Being Australian didn't automatically mean an allegiance to the United States.

Australia might have been able to charge him with an aiding-the-enemy violation, but no enemy had been officially proclaimed. To be honest, the charge of aiding the enemy would never even pass the straight-face test. You didn't have to be a lawyer to understand how ridiculous it was. The United States had supplied more than $20 million in aid to the Taliban to eradicate opium, money that probably ended up in armaments; if this could be proven, was the United States aiding the enemy too? The Taliban's biggest international ally and supporter was the government of Pakistan. Had it been aiding the enemy? I couldn't believe the hypocrisy of charging Hicks, for a minuscule role, while the Bush administration welcomed the Taliban's main sponsor into our coalition of the willing.

I kept half-expecting something more, but eventually realised there was never going to be anything more. There was an air of naked desperation in the charges against Hicks. They had been holding people at GTMO for more than two years without charge. They had interrogated and mistreated them. And they had screwed up. Unable to admit it, they cooked up an almost unbelievably weak set of charges.

I attended a US Naval War College conference in Newport, Rhode Island, in June, trying to locate a new expert in the law of war to be assigned to our team. Lucky for us, we were able to meet with Michael Schmitt and get him assigned to our team. Schmitt, a retired Air Force lawyer, had taught international law and was then serving on the staff at the George C. Marshall European Center for Security Studies in Garmisch, Germany. We wanted the best legal experts who were going to be unassailable, independent and honest. By the time we were to argue our motions in November 2004, we had lined up an impressive group of legal experts whom we wanted to testify at GTMO.

From within the United States, we had Professor M. Cherif Bassiouni, of the DePaul University College of Law, a distinguished diplomat and academic and the chair of the drafting committee for the International Criminal Court, for which he had been nominated for the Nobel Peace Prize. Professor Jordan Paust from the University of Houston taught international law, international criminal law, and law of war. Paust had been writing on war-crimes jurisdiction and due process since the early seventies. Additionally, we had Professor George E. Edwards, a Harvard Law graduate, of Indiana University McKinney School of Law. Professor Edwards was a highly renowned expert on international human rights law, and had worked on high-profile international criminal law and international humanitarian law cases in international and domestic tribunals around the globe. Edwards focused on whether the Military Commissions violated the fair trial rights under international law and US law. Ultimately, he would produce and tender a hundred-page affidavit on the fair trial standards applicable in Hicks's case.

From outside the United States, we used Tim McCormack, a law-of-war expert from the University of Melbourne in Australia. McCormack was the Australian Red Cross Professor of International Humanitarian Law and Director of the Asia Pacific Centre for Military Law. McCormack had practical expertise and experience with international war-crimes trials at the International Criminal Tribunal for the former Yugoslavia for the trial of Slobodan Milošević. From Italy, we were fortunate to obtain the assistance of Antonio Cassese, who had been a judge with the United Nations International Criminal Tribunal for the former Yugoslavia, and was the author of some of the premier textbooks on international criminal law. He had the international reputation that would make it difficult for the prosecutors to undermine his opinions. Especially because, at the time, he was Chairman of the UN International Commission of Inquiry into Genocide in Darfur, Sudan. It would also provide credibility to our arguments to have them considered historically.

It was important to have strong experts, because one thing we did know was that the case would be reviewed by the US federal courts, and the same experts could be used in the review. After putting the building blocks of Hicks's defence into place, I felt confident. My biggest fear was that he would be unfairly convicted and railroaded to some thirty- or forty-year sentence. The only thing that would be looked at years later on appeal would be the transcript, and we needed to be correct on all our legal arguments, even if we had no chance of the commission agreeing. All of our experts would provide testimony of invalidity of the offences used, as well as the commission system itself. The only challenge was getting them to GTMO.

As the conference ended in Rhode Island, I was informed that Altenburg had referred the charges against Hicks to a commission and had selected officers to sit on it. This was the final step in initiating proceedings. We would finally learn who would decide Hicks's fate.

16

Cracks Appearing

On the plane out of Jacksonville, Florida, bound for another GTMO trip, the young sailor next to me began chatting. He had no idea who I was, as we were in civilian clothes. He was returning to GTMO for duty after a period of leave.

'What do you do at GTMO?' he asked.

'I'm one of the lawyers for the detainees at the commission.'

'Which one?' He knew some of the detainees from his duties.

'Hicks,' I said.

'I haven't met him,' he said, explaining that he didn't work in Camp Echo. Yet he knew Hicks was 'the detainee who had a bow-flex in his cell'.

I tried not to laugh, as he was serious. I shook my head and said, 'No, not true.' The idea of Rumsfeld having provided body-building equipment to detainees was comical. I would hear other rumours about Hicks, such as that he had threatened to kill guards, was a karate expert who could kick the ceiling of his cell, and had slipped out of his handcuffs on the flight into GTMO. All of which, of course, were untrue.

These would have been easy to laugh off, except that in preparing Hicks's sentencing case, his behaviour during confinement could be relevant. Unlike civilian criminal trials, where there is a break of time between the trial and sentencing, in courts-martial, sentencing occurs right after the verdict, so we had to be prepared since no commission was going to simply let him go free. I was hoping that the military officers who would one day sentence Hicks would listen to the opinions US service members had of him. Hicks reminded me of many of the young enlisted men I had met over my career: someone seeking adventure, a better life, or an escape from small-town aimlessness. I believed that the JTF guards who saw him day in, day out might have come to see him the same way.

Some of his guards saw him for only an hour a day, five days a week, while others spent several hours a day with him for months. Some were active (regular) Army while others were National Guard, from all across America, and their experience ranged from very little to more than fifteen years of active service. Their tours to GTMO varied, with only one short leave pass every six months, and the best thing some had to say about the place was that it wasn't Iraq. Some had never been involved with law enforcement while others had been military police, civilian prison guards or seasoned cops from major metropolitan cities. Most guards completed a one-year tour at GTMO; they would have been exposed to hundreds of detainees, so there was a wide basis for comparison between Hicks and others.

I found them to be decent young men and women who could see through all the BS that higher-ups pushed down. Many were kind to detainees, while some were not. When I spoke to the guards who had interacted with Hicks, I was not surprised to hear what they thought. They said he was cooperative and treated them with respect. While other detainees caused problems and threw things at them, Hicks did not. If they could have chosen to guard one detainee at GTMO, it would be Hicks. One senior sergeant commented that Hicks treated him 'like I'm his Platoon Sergeant'.

Almost all the feedback I received, on that and later trips, was positive and helpful. Some guards were even willing to testify before the commission about Hicks's behaviour.

Back in the United States, I had a different type of suit to think about. I asked for money to get Hicks something other than his detainee uniform to wear at his commission hearing. The orange jumpsuits had been replaced by equally inappropriate tan outfits that resembled medical scrubs.

Hicks had never owned a suit, so we could not get one from Australia. Master Sergeant Pierre and I went to the mall with Hicks's measurements. We needed to get the suit, shirts, socks, shoes and even underwear (which detainees were not provided with). One of my challenges on my most recent trip to GTMO was getting Hicks's feet unchained so I could get his in-seam measurements. Years later, when one of the commission prosecutors wrote a book, she claimed that Hicks had demanded and been provided with Brooks Brothers suits. He wouldn't know what Brooks Brothers was and certainly was not provided with any, but that lie went out into the public domain and took the place of truth.

Nobody transformed rumour into accepted truth more power-
fully than George Bush and John Howard. A week before Hicks was
charged in June 2004, Bush hosted his good friend from Australia
at the White House. After their meeting, they held a press conference at which Hicks was discussed. Bush said:

> The United States and Australia are committed to the principles of
> human dignity. Today I assured the Prime Minister that my nation
> will conduct a full accounting of the cruel and disgraceful abuse
> of Iraqi detainees. He strongly reflected his government's and the
> Australian people's desires to make sure that the Australians being
> held in Guantanamo are not only treated fairly but their cases are
> brought to finality. And I appreciate your candid discussion, Mr
> Prime Minister.

Howard replied, 'I've welcomed the assurances the President has
given me regarding the proper treatment of the two Australian
detainees in Guantanamo Bay.' That limp sentence was all he said.
Even after all that time, Australia was not going to rush to take any
action on Hicks's behalf.

Asked by a reporter whether he could guarantee that Hicks
hadn't been mistreated, and when a decision would be made on
when Hicks would face trial, Bush said, 'It is my understanding
that Hicks — the Hicks case will be referred to the military shortly
and that the other case [Mamdouh Habib] is proceeding as well.
And we are — the military is fully investigating any allegations as
to whether or not they have been mistreated.'

The stories of abuse had reached the highest level of government. They had to deal with it now. And yet, this was all Bush and
Howard would say. A handful of words, and all was well with the

world. But because the President had been forced to at least address it, I felt confident that an investigation might actually take place.

On 28 June, we finally got what we had been waiting for in the civil process: the Supreme Court ruled in Hicks's case that US federal courts did have jurisdiction to review the legality of the detention of non-US citizens held at Guantanamo Bay. It was a 6–3 decision. Justice John Paul Stevens, who wrote the majority opinion, emphasised, 'Executive imprisonment has been considered oppressive and lawless' and harked back to the Magna Carta, quoting King John I's pledge that 'no free man should be imprisoned, dispossessed, outlawed, or exiled save by the judgement of his peers or the law of the land'. No man, in other words, can be above the law, not even – or least of all – the president.

In the dissenting opinion, Justice Antonin Scalia, a judge appointed by George Bush, Senior, who had given his vote to George W. Bush after the disputed 2000 presidential election, wrote that Justice Stevens's decision 'springs a trap on the Executive' by subjecting it to review.

I was very happy for Joe Margulies and the CCR people who had put such hard work into a difficult and unpopular case. While there was cause for some celebration, it was just the beginning. The decision only allowed detainees to file cases in the Federal District Court. After two and a half years of detention, not one judge directly ordered the release of anyone.

Hicks's case was not the only Supreme Court decision that day involving war-on-terror detainees. There was also the case of Yaser Hamdi, who had been taken to GTMO in January 2002. Three months later, it was discovered that Hamdi was a US citizen. He was transported back to the naval brig in Norfolk, Virginia, as an 'enemy combatant'. The majority of the US Supreme Court determined that a detained US citizen must be given notice of why he is classified as an 'enemy combatant' and provided with an opportunity to challenge it before a neutral decision-maker. The Bush administration didn't want to have to face Hamdi in a federal court, and found another way to disregard this problem. After almost three years in custody, Hamdi was released to Saudi Arabia on the condition that he renounce his US citizenship and not leave Saudi Arabia for five years. It was a good result for him, perhaps, but it excused the government from having to justify its detention system in a civil court. The frustrating thing was that the allegations against Hamdi – that he had been caught fighting against the Northern Alliance in Kunduz in late 2001 – were no different from those against Hicks, who was no closer to release. The hypocrisy really got under my skin.

While I was not a loyal watcher of *The Daily Show with Jon Stewart*, I did catch an episode following the Hamdi decision where he mocked Justice Clarence Thomas. An appointee of George Bush, Senior, and another veteran of the Bush v. Gore 2000 decision that had given Bush, Junior, the presidency, Justice Clarence Thomas was the only justice who wanted to uphold what the Bush administration had done in detaining Hamdi. In his dissenting judgement, Thomas wrote that the Supreme Court 'lack[s] the expertise and capacity to second guess' the President. On *The Daily Show*, Jon Stewart pondered who might be responsible for second-guessing a president in the American government. Stewart wondered aloud: 'If only there was a group of people whose job it was to judge such things. It wouldn't take many people, I don't know, eight to ten?' Is it really possible that Justice Thomas did not know that a Supreme Court justice's role in our government was to review the legality of the executive branch's decisions and actions?

The other 'enemy combatant' case was that of Jose Padilla, who had been arrested in May 2002 in Chicago's O'Hare Airport after arriving from Pakistan allegedly carrying more than $10 000 in cash and was labelled in the media as the 'the dirty bomber'. When his lawyer, Andrew Patel, challenged this, President Bush designated Padilla an enemy combatant and sent him to the naval brig at Charleston, South Carolina. Padilla's lawyer filed a 'next friend' Federal District Court challenge in New York. The administration countered that the case should have been filed in the federal court district that had jurisdiction over the Commander of the Naval Brig. The Supreme Court agreed and the case had to start again. Padilla's lawyers spent the next two years fighting their way back to the US Supreme Court, challenging Padilla's military detention, only for the Bush administration, in January 2006, to transfer Padilla back to civilian authorities and have him tried in a US federal court for charges that had nothing to do with the alleged 'dirty bomb' threat that had been the justification for holding him for several years. Padilla would eventually be convicted. He received a seventeen-year sentence in 2008. Watching this unfold, I had to wonder why he was treated so differently from Hamdi, both US citizens. Maybe it was good to be a Saudi.

Once we got over the euphoria of having won the hearing that pertained to Hicks, a more sobering reality dawned. A pattern was emerging that would continue for years. Supreme Court cases hailed as blows against the Bush administration resulted in no GTMO detainee being freed. For Hicks, it meant we would be able to challenge his detention and the invalid charges being used against him at the Military Commission, but we needed to write a new petition adding new arguments that were not part of his case in 2002 when it started. It would be another two years before the

Supreme Court would weigh in again on a case of a detainee.

These Supreme Court decisions were not an effective blow against the Bush administration. It was an effective way for the administration to waste money and time, but they had plenty of both of those. It appeared that delay was their main legal tactic in the federal litigation. Was it chicanery, or just incompetence? I couldn't work out whether the Bush administration was the Inspector Clouseau government that bumbled about with things just working out, or whether it really was clever planning.

The Bush administration and the DOD quickly responded to the Supreme Court's decision to open the doors of federal court to the detainees by creating a Combatant Status Review Tribunal (CSRT) to validate its 'enemy combatant' designation. In typical style, the CSRT was to be made up of military officers. They were to review the labels that had been put on the detainees by higher authorities. The detainees would get not a lawyer but a military officer to act as a 'personal representative'. Communications with the personal representative would not be confidential. The detainees were not given access to the classified evidence against them, or told what it contained. The definition of 'enemy combatant' did not even require that they be involved in 9/11 or the conflict in Afghanistan. Nor was the CSRT going to decide the detainees' status under the Geneva Conventions.

As I watched the Fourth of July fireworks over the Capitol, on the other side of the globe Terry Hicks was fighting on, holding a protest with Amnesty International Australia outside the US embassy in Canberra. Dick Cheney appeared in the Australian media, asserting, 'Hicks will be given a fair trial.' Meanwhile, Bush designated nine more individuals for trial by Military Commission.

With Hicks's charges referred to a commission, but no start date announced yet, I went down to GTMO with Stephen Kenny and Josh Dratel in mid-July, alongside a media contingent the government was allowing into the camps for the first time. We had the difficult task of explaining to Hicks that he had won in the US Supreme Court, but that this was not going to change anything.

Finally we received a date for the commissions to start. The first step would be an arraignment for Hicks and the other three pending cases in the middle of August. As the end of July approached, the Democrat convention in Boston was selecting John Kerry as Bush's challenger in the November election, and I was flying to Chicago to meet with Gary Isaac from the law firm Mayer Brown. Gary had been helping to identify a law firm to assist with Hicks's federal court case for free. We met with Andrew Jacobson and Andrew Vail, from Jenner & Block's Chicago office. With little fanfare, a team from their DC office, led by Mark A. Goldman, did great work for Hicks over the next three years. For every step forward, however, there were two steps back. In the same month, Gunn finally offered me two military lawyers to interview as possible assistant detailed defence counsel. One was a brand new Navy lawyer without any experience at all, and the other was an Army major and an experienced trial attorney, Jeffrey Lippert. He looked promising – except he was stationed in Germany. But it was not really a choice. Lippert would come out to D.C. a week or so before the hearing in August.

As we got nearer to a Military Commission trial, the foolishness of using the outdated commissions system was exposed. The Bush administration's abandonment of the criminal-trial structure created for courts-martial meant there were large holes in the commission process. The United States had done no investigation into Hicks, nor I suspect into any of the GTMO detainees; they just detained them on the battlefield and shipped them to GTMO for interrogation. In August, I began preparing to follow Hicks's footsteps through his travels in Albania, Pakistan and Afghanistan to conduct my own investigation.

The Australian Federal Police (AFP) had done a partial investigation into Hicks's travels, starting in Kosovo and interviewing people he had met in Pakistan. The prosecution – who had not yet been to eeither Pakistan or Afghanistan to do any interviewing themselves – were hoping to use the written statements gathered by the AFP without calling the witnesses to the commission. The AFP hadn't gone to Afghanistan. I knew I had to go into both countries and find the witnesses myself.

I was hoping to find a witness who saw Hicks in Afghanistan in a camouflage uniform. I also wanted to find the battlefields, and to locate some Northern Alliance forces who could tell us, from a non-Western viewpoint, what the Taliban had been doing. Did they carry arms openly? Did they wear a distinctive emblem, distinguished from the population? Did they obey the laws of war? Did the group he was with have a chain of command? If the answer to these questions was yes, then such evidence could have him designated a prisoner of war. If he was a prisoner of war, he would be entitled to Geneva Convention protections and the legitimate trial of a court-martial.

Realising how crucial this evidence could be to Hicks's defence, I planned my trip for the end of 2004.

17

The Commissions Start – and Stop

With the initial session approaching, our focus was on getting prepared. There was so much to do: preparing to question the commission members; preparing written legal motions; preparing the federal court briefs; attending to the ongoing NCIS investigation into Hicks's allegations of abuse; preparing our expert witness requests; coordinating Dratel's and Kenny's travel to GTMO; and making sure we met what felt like hundreds of deadlines.

On 21 August we flew down to Guantanamo Bay. There was an obvious increase in security, with extra boats and roving foot patrols, barriers and new security checkpoints. Even during the hearing, two security staff would be sitting directly behind Hicks, within arm's reach. In every court-martial I had ever seen or acted in, even with large and violent defendants, there had never been security like this. We asked for a normal arrangement, which was for guards to sit in the public area. Hicks stood five-foot two-inches in his socks, and very obviously posed no threat to anyone. The security was to be so close that we couldn't have a private conversation with him, as legal staff are entitled to in any court proceedings. There seemed little reason for all this except to impress the media, and any spectators.

The reporters were mostly pushed out of the way, staying on the leeward side of the bay except when hearings were happening. A media centre was set up less than a mile away from the commission building. A strange social life would develop on GTMO when hearings were in session, whether it was Mongolian BBQ night at the Officers' Club or drinks at the Tiki Bar. The few places to eat would have everyone mixing: prosecution, defence, Appointing Authority and presiding officer's staff, JTF personnel, and even, occasionally, the media: whoever was about. I think a rule developed of 'What happens at GTMO stays at GTMO'. Sorry, Vegas.

Our biggest challenge during this stage, administratively, was that our office, with all the paper files and documentation we were finding and generating, was 1300 miles away in Washington DC. When we travelled to Guantanamo Bay for the hearings, we had to box everything up; the boxes would fly down and back with us. Initially, there was only one office shared by four defence teams, in an area where you could barely fit four desks. Whenever one team had to discuss anything privileged, everybody else had to leave the office.

Access to computers was controlled and restricted by the JTF. Our computers in DC were controlled through the Department of Defence's General Counsel's Office, so there were no secrets to begin with. The challenge of operating on two separate computer systems only compounded the problem. We couldn't just bring the files on a portable USB or hard drive without a tortuous approval process.

Using the JTF system raise one important question: who exactly is monitoring it? There were also problems with electronic data disappearing. The American agreement with Australia meant that there was not to be any monitoring of Hicks's communications with his legal team, but we had no guarantee of this.

Luckily for me and Hicks's team, there were Marines at Guantanamo who were not part of the JTF: the Marine Corps Security Force that guarded the perimeter of the base. They controlled their own computer system, separate from the JTF, and also had access to their own vehicles. Some great Marines helped me out of a fix now and then.

For the commission, they had converted some old command buildings above the old airstrip. There were two main buildings over the runway. One was the JTF Headquarters, for whom there would ultimately be a brand-new building constructed closer to the camps, and the other was going to be the commission building. It was a two-floor building, and part of the ground floor had been renovated into the commission's courtroom. The other part had been converted into prison detention cells and one little office for the defence. The entire top floor had been given to the prosecution and the Appointing Authority.

We could work in our housing. On that trip, I checked into the 'permanent' house, in the area called Windward Loop, a street of old duplexes that had been used to house Sailors and Marines years before. Making a phone call from GTMO meant taking a trip to the main office. The phones in the houses could only be used for local calls. When the line from the office was finally set up, it could be relied on to disconnect randomly. The fax machine was no better. Often I felt I was spending more time trying to get phone, housing, vehicle and administrative issues resolved than actually working on the case.

During the next four days, I visited Hicks. I knew this would be an emotional time for him, as he would be seeing his family for the first time in years. On 24 August, Terry and Bev Hicks and Stephen Kenny arrived, taking up residence at the Navy Lodge. The next day, Hicks dressed and showered in his hut, and was brought in from the camps, wearing his new suit and chains on his wrists and ankles, to the commission building where we were waiting. He was allowed to meet with Terry and Bev before the hearing, but was still chained to the floor. This would be their first reunion in over five years.

The defence team was Dratel, Lippert and me. The prosecution consisted of Lieutenant Colonel Brubaker and Major Ron Sullivan. The commission started at 9.30 a.m. with five military officers making up the commission along with one alternate member. The first and only substantial task was to question all the members to determine if there was any reason why they should or should not sit.

In courts-martial, there are clear legal standards to be applied for someone to sit as a jury member or judge, such as whether there are facts that would create an appearance of bias or partiality. In the commission, they had forgotten to create this rule – whoops! Additionally, the commission did not have the power to rule on any challenges. They had to go to the Appointing Authority. So nothing was going to be accomplished at this session except the questioning.

Aside from the presiding officer, former Army colonel Peter

Brownback, who had retired in 1999, all of the members had been involved in the war in Afghanistan or 9/11 in some way, either directly participating or having friends who had lost their lives. Many of the areas we wanted to question them about might stray into classified material, which would require a closed session that Hicks could not attend. This was the complete opposite of any court-martial and would be a substantial fact upon which the Supreme Court would find the Military Commissions unlawful.

The questioning of Brownback would establish that he shared a significant personal relationship with the Appointing Authority, Altenburg, whom he had known since around 1978. Their careers had intersected many times, and Brownback's wife had worked for Altenburg in the 1990s. When Brownback had retired, Altenburg presided at his retirement ceremony and was the primary speaker at the dinner. Brownback attended Altenburg's retirement and was also one of the speakers. Brownback attended Altenburg's son's wedding in 2002. Then, out of thirty-three applicants, Altenburg had miraculously selected Brownback to head the Military Commissions. Brownback tried to assert that it was his performance as a military judge that qualified him, even though he had been retired for almost five years.

The members were sitting on all four hearings during the week. How could they sustain objectivity in this most irregular situation? In reply, they went away and then came back to assert that they could keep the legal and factual issues separate.

For formality's sake, we had to put our challenges in writing and send them to Altenburg to decide at his leisure. Hicks entered a plea of not guilty. The next session, to address legal motions, was set for the beginning of November 2004. The hearing, purely procedural in nature and something of an anticlimax, was over by 3.19 p.m. We then went to the press hall for a scheduled conference. GTMO Gary stood up and said how 'full and fair' the commission was. I said something like, 'Hicks is facing an unfair justice system that's not tolerated anywhere else in the world.' The NGOs and Law Council of Australia observers would add some unflattering comments about the commission.

On the one hand, being able to hold press conferences like this is what is great about America. Only in America would a president create these sham trials and then permit a press conference that would slam everything he had created. In a funny way, I was proud of my country for at least letting the world see most – not all, of course – of the shambles they had constructed, and that were slowly unravelling before their eyes.

The next morning Dratel, Kenny and I visited Hicks to update him on what was happening next with the commission, and Terry and Bev left on the ferry. Over the next two days, the two following hearings, for Ali al-Bahlul and Ibrahim al-Qosi, proceeded in much the same procedural way as Hicks's. Al-Bahlul caused a little bit of excitement, first by dismissing his two military lawyers and requesting to represent himself or have a Yemeni lawyer. But the real havoc ensued when he started talking about al-Qaeda before Brownback could stop him. The media had a field day, reporting the detainee 'admits to being al-Qaeda'. As all this discussion was going through an interpreter, and with the difficulty in translations, the admission might not have been exactly accurate. Some translators not working for the commissions believed Al-Bahlul was trying to say, 'I might be part of al-Qaeda but I was not involved in 9/11,' before Brownback cut him off.

I visited Hicks once more before I left Cuba. After so much build-up, it was hard not to feel that the whole experience had been anticlimactic. The first experience of an actual Military Commission confirmed, for me, that whoever created this system was incompetent. I wondered if they even really wanted the commissions to go ahead. That same month, NCIS, with an Australian government representative present, interviewed Hicks in relation to the physical abuse he had suffered. It would be almost a year before we heard the results.

As August came to a close, Goldman and the Jenner team filed the new federal court petition that addressed the specific challenges to the Military Commission system and the charges against Hicks. We wanted a speedy hearing as the commission was progressing, but you don't always get what you want.

The incompetence had started at the very top, and over the next two months the American public would have their chance to decide whether to entrust President Bush with another four years. On 1 September, less than a week after Hicks's hearing, the John Kerry campaign revealed its position on Military Commissions. Senator John Edwards, Kerry's running mate, indicated that the commissions would be dropped for courts-martial. 'The Bush administration has ignored the model of the military courts-martial,' he said. 'We will use that model as a basis for future trials of detainees.'

Common sense ruled for a day! Or at least a promise of common sense. For the first time, a presidential election could have a direct bearing on a matter that was central to my professional life. If the Democrats were going to drop the commissions, a result of the election could be to free Hicks from this ineffective system and get him in front of a proper court.

On the Australian side, Alexander Downer was still making public statements about what a fair trial Hicks was going to get. But the facts would become known in Australia, which had two observer bodies at the commissions in the form of DFAT staff and the lawyer Lex Lasry from the Law Council of Australia, whose report the following month would be less than glowing.

From DFAT, Peter Baxter, Australia's Deputy Chief of Mission, was invited to meetings with the prosecutors and the Appointing Authority's office. A press release went out saying Australia was looking at 'a number of concerns involving operational and procedural aspects of the conduct of the Military Commissions process'. As 'procedural aspects' involved the defence as much as the prosecution, I thought I would be informed of what their concerns were, and asked for any information. I assumed, naively, that the Australian government was interested in hearing both sides. I certainly wanted our concerns on the record. The staff within the Attorney-General's department were always willing to listen, even if they were helpless to do anything. The Australian government made media statements putting up a show of concern, but it was no more interested in a fair system than the Bush administration.

Our next step was to write to Altenburg asking that all commission members be replaced, posing as a possible solution that legal professionals with extensive experience in international criminal law and/or the law of war be appointed. He was the only authority with the power to do this. We received a quick response from Hemingway, who, as Altenburg's legal advisor, said no. We could bring it up at the commission's next hearing. I was sure the commission wasn't going to agree to replace itself!

Hicks's Combatant Status Review Tribunal hearing was coming up, but we did not know exactly when. We had asked to be able to participate, but our request was ignored. The JTF still sent in its 'personal representative' to question Hicks several times, but he refused and maintained that he wanted his lawyers present before he would participate.

Master Sergeant Pierre was on her way to Guantanamo Bay for a visit, but when she got to Florida she was told that all travel to GTMO had been stopped, due to the 'outbound travel of detainees', a handful of whom were being released back to Afghanistan. That may have been true, but it was the only time in three and a half years of my travels to GTMO that anyone from the defence was stopped, and it just happened to be when Hicks's CSRT hearing was to be held. The CSRT confirmed his status as 'enemy combatant'.

The government finally published its reasons for releasing Yaser Hamdi, one of the US citizen enemy combatants, to Saudi Arabia. This provided an interesting contrast to its treatment of Hicks. It said that Hamdi no longer presented a danger to the United States, and that his intelligence value had been exhausted. How, then, did Hicks remain a danger to the United States? What further intelligence value did he have after more than two years of untrammelled interrogation? The truth was that the United States released Hamdi because it could not risk trying him in a US court that would have afforded him due process and Geneva Convention rights. The only venue it felt safe in was the kangaroo court of the CSRT and the Military Commissions. It was so terrified of a legitimate court hearing, which Hamdi, as an American, would have been entitled to, that it released him. It was now out in the open: the US government simply did not trust its own legal system or the form of justice created by the Constitution, or even, fundamentally, the American form of government that balances power between the judicial and executive branches. That was decidedly *un-American*, and dangerously undermined the core American values the government professed to respect and protect.

It was an absolute and continuing disgrace that the Australian government did not demand the same result for Hicks as Hamdi had received. That the Saudi government would do more for Hamdi, a US citizen who took up arms against the United States, than the Australian government would do for its own citizen who did not fire a shot or harm a single soul, was hard for me to understand, and rather disappointing.

Once the farcical nature of the commissions was revealed at their first sittings in August, Rumsfeld had to try to do something to give them some semblance of legitimacy. On 22 September 2004, a month after the first commissions, the Department of Defense made a big splash in the media about the review panel for the Military Commissions taking their oath of office. These men were to play the role of an appellate court for the Military Commissions. They had been selected back in December 2003, but for some reason had not taken their oath yet. The review panellists were civilian legal figures with what appeared to be the proper pedigree; the DOD hoped that would allay fears that the military was running the show without any oversight. In typical style, this was a move to give the system some semblance of legitimacy, but, also in typical style, it soon backfired when the backgrounds of the panel members became known.

Griffin Bell, age eighty-seven, had been President Jimmy Carter's

ABOVE LEFT: In the Color Guard for the local Marine Corps Ball as a young Private First Class (1984).
ABOVE RIGHT: In Yokosuka, Japan, in 1999, with my commanding officer, Captain Wedan.
BELOW: Running over an opposition rugby player at Marine Corps Air Station Cherry Point.

ABOVE: David Hicks in the infamous photo from Albania that was splashed all over the media.
BELOW: After Hicks's release from Yatala Prison at the end of his sentence – finally a free man.

ABOVE: My first press conference, trying to convince the Australian and American people of the injustice of what was happening to Hicks.

BELOW LEFT: The first legal team with Hicks's family. (L-R) Me, Stephen Kenny, Terry Hicks, Jeff Lippert, Josh Dratel, MSgt Pierre, Elizabeth Besobrasow, Bev Hicks.

BELOW RIGHT: The second legal team. (L-R) Tim McCormack, George Edwards, me, Sarah Finnin, Rebecca Snyder, Michael Griffin. Sgt Rios, David McLeod.

Key players in the US and Australian governments at the time.

CLOCKWISE FROM TOP LEFT: Australian attorney-general Philip Ruddock; US secretary of defense Donald Rumsfeld; Australian prime minister John Howard and US president George W. Bush; Australian foreign minister Alexander Downer; US vice president Dick Cheney.

Australian attitudes start to shift.

ABOVE: GetUp! petitions in support of Hicks are delivered to John Howard's office in 2005;

BELOW LEFT: Talking with the Australian state attorneys-general in Fremantle, 2006. (L-R) Steve Kons (Tasmania), Jim McGinty (WA), Kerry Shine (QLD), me, Bob Debus (NSW) and Michael Atkinson (SA).

BELOW RIGHT: St Paul's Cathedral in Melbourne displays a huge 'Justice for David Hicks' banner in 2007.

ABOVE: A shot of the Military Commission Building at Guantanamo Bay.

BELOW: Me at the gate between the US base and Cuba.

Travelling the world in the search for justice.

ABOVE: In Adelaide in 2004 with Terry and Bev Hicks and Stephen Kenny.

BELOW: In Afghanistan in 2004 searching for people who had met Hicks when he was there.

A permanent Australian: in Melbourne in 2012 with two of my three sons, Enrico (far left) and Dante, who were born during the Hicks case.

Attorney-General, which gave him a bipartisan gloss. Bell had advised Jim Haynes on setting up the Military Commissions, as was discovered through documents obtained through the Freedom of Information Act. But that didn't rule Bell out from appointment to the panel to review what he had helped create.

Edward Biester, a 75-year-old former congressman, had become a state judge in 1980. He had been close friends with Rumsfeld since their time serving in Congress, and had bought property from him in 1985. They enjoyed vacation homes near each other in Taos, New Mexico.

William T. Coleman, aged eighty-six, had been the Republican President Gerald Ford's transportation secretary and, like Bell, had been involved as an advisor to Haynes in setting up the Military Commissions. He had even been briefed by the prosecution on the 'prosecution effort and strategy'.

The final judge, 66-year-old Frank Williams, Chief Justice of the Rhode Island Supreme Court, had served as an Army captain in Vietnam. We didn't need to guess what his opinion on the detainees was as he had already published an article in the *Providence Journal* in which he wrote, 'It is clear that the September 11 terrorists and detainees, whether apprehended in the United States or abroad, are protected neither under our criminal-justice system nor under the international law of war.'

So much for independent civilian review. An article published on the website In These Times aptly described them as the 'Court of Cronies'. Each was connected in some way with Rumsfeld personally or with the creation of the Military Commissions, and one had publicly stated that the detainees didn't deserve protection under international law. This was the appeals court, hand-picked by Rumsfeld without any confirmation by the Senate; they were going to be made two-star generals.

I would've laughed if it wasn't so serious. But the joke hadn't stopped there. In the DOD press releases, the photo showed the four review panellists raising their right hands swearing to something, even though at that stage they were not actually appointed. That's right. Someone had worked out that if they were appointed – a two-year limit would be imposed from when they were officially appointed as two-star generals – and if the commissions continued to grind along slowly, then their appointments might expire before they were needed. So a big media show was created, to simulate a 'swearing in', but they were never actually appointed.

Once again, I felt that everyone was in on the joke, except us.

18

A New Path

At the beginning of October, we had about a month before the next hearing before the Military Commission. We were still waiting to see when our federal court hearing was going to happen. Altenburg, meanwhile, published his decision on our challenges to the members of the commission. He upheld our challenge against three of them (coincidentally, the same three had been challenged by the prosecution). Those three were removed. The other three we had challenged (but whom the prosecution had not) remained in place. Nor did Altenburg replace the alternate. This cut the size of the commission down to three members. No US criminal court that could impose a life sentence ever had a jury of only three members. A court-martial required a minimum of five members. It was another motion that needed to be filed in our argument to have the Military Commissions declared improperly constituted.

We had submitted our request to the prosecutors to bring our expert witnesses to GTMO to testify during the next hearing. When the prosecutors saw the experts we had lined up, I think they shit themselves. They had no experienced legal expert who would testify under oath in support of any of the Bush administration's legal positions or the structure of the commissions. They knew the backgrounds of our experts, and knew that they would completely undercut the validity of the charges and commission structure. They could not have our experts see the inside of a public courtroom.

Faced with this clear imbalance, they had to keep our experts off the stand, and denied every request we submitted to bring our experts to the upcoming hearing. Brownback, the Presiding Officer, showing his bias for the prosecution, rubber-stamped the rejection of our expert witnesses. Our only recourse was to raise the issue at the hearing with all the commission members, which placed them in the position of either denying our experts or delaying the hearing so our experts could get to GTMO. After 100 people were all flown to GTMO for the hearing, a delay was not going to be permitted.

The only way around it, and to preserve what they would testify to on the record, was to have written statements prepared by our experts. Whether the commission would accept them or even read them, we didn't know.

I was on my way to Germany to meet up with Jeffrey Lippert, as we were going to try to track down people Hicks had met during his less than one month's training with the Kosovo Liberation Army. Many of the other trainees Hicks had met had since moved back to Pristina in Kosovo. The US Army had Camp Bondsteel outside of Pristina, and Lippert's Army contacts were going to come in handy.

The prosecution had included in the charges that Hicks had been 'fighting on behalf of Albanian Muslims' and 'engaged in hostile actions' after completing the basic training for the KLA. The prosecution always liked to highlight any association with Muslims, as if that in itself was a crime. There was no other purpose for including the religious reference. And the AFP, at least, knew there was no truth to the stories about Hicks fighting, as they'd tracked down and interviewed several people Hicks had met at the KLA training camp in Albania.

I linked up with Lippert in Germany and off we flew to Pristina, Kosovo. Master Sergeant Pierre and Sarah Finnin manned the office in DC. Finnin was a Melbourne University law student who gave her own time to come over and help us with the preparation of motions. She would return two more times, helping when we most needed it. Lippert had our housing, transportation and even an interpreter locked in through the defence legal office at Camp Bondsteel. The next day we headed off into Pristina with a list of names and several years-old addresses. Pristina is a beautiful city, but the neighbourhoods had small winding streets that were not as well organised as I was used to, coming from the United States. Our interpreter was not from Pristina, so he had no local knowledge. As we got to the general area of the first person on the list, we became lost. I saw a post office and said, 'Let's ask in there.' The postmaster found our first witness, who was then able to locate all the rest within an afternoon.

The witnesses' comments to us were all consistent with their AFP statements: Hicks had never participated in any 'hostile action', only basic military training. They had all been at the ceremony where they had saluted the NATO flag with Hicks. Two of these young men had been in the infamous 'rocket launcher' photo with Hicks, and explained that this was from one of the first days of training when all the recruits went to look at unloaded weapons and take photos. I doubted the prosecution would allow us to bring these witnesses to GTMO for the actual trial, but their statements might force them to remove one blatant falsehood from the charges. The fact that the prosecution could keep any witness from coming to GTMO, though, would limit any real defence in the commission system.

From Pristina, Lippert and I went to Garmisch, Germany, to work with Schmitt on preparing our motions. Even though we were busy, I took a two-day trip into Florence late one night to meet with Antonio Cassese to collect his affidavit. Cassese, who'd been a judge with the International Criminal Tribunal for the former Yugoslavia, was a wonderful man, and it was a great experience to sit down and talk with him in an Italian restaurant up on a hillside overlooking Florence. My old Italian blood came to the surface: I loved it there, even if everyone in the office was giving me a hard time for travelling to all these exotic places. If only I actually had time to enjoy them! Then it was back to Garmisch to finish our motions and on to DC to get the document boxes packed up to go to GTMO.

By the beginning of November, the 100-plus horde of prosecutors, defence, media and staff from the Appointing Authority's office were back at GTMO for the motions hearing. This would be my fourteenth trip there in less than a year. It would have been so much easier had we been stationed there. Terry Hicks had come again, bringing David's sister Stephanie. Through the good graces of the staff, Terry and Steph were able to sit and have more time with Hicks. I had been there so many times now, it took the arrival of a new person to remind me how arriving at GTMO was like stepping onto another planet, especially for those who were not military. Stephanie was impressed with the professionalism of the military staff assigned to assist her on the visit.

Under the hum of all the air-conditioners, the Military Commission was called to order to address our eighteen-plus motions attacking the charges and commission structure. We would spend the next three days arguing back and forth on motions that, at the time, we did not know would never be decided. Every motion we argued about, had the commission granted it, would have brought the hearing to a stop, and the commission was not going to do that with the US presidential election just two days away.

We challenged the commission structure; the failure to allow our experts; Altenburg's ruling to not remove certain members, and his failure to appoint an alternate member; the denial of legal representation to Hicks for two years until 2003; how Haynes's office stacked the Military Commission by only permitting the services to nominate service members with the rank of Major or above, and not permitting any enlisted person; the denial of a speedy trial; and the absence of any rules of evidence complying with the Geneva Conventions. We argued that the commissions could only be used during a real war, not Bush's invented 'War on Terror'. We raised the issue that none of the charges were valid law-of-war offences. Arguing these legal motions before two members of the commission with no legal training was difficult, as if I was speaking a language they did not understand.

We didn't necessarily believe we would make much headway, but it was important to get every last problem with this system onto the legal record. Also, the NGO observers, a member of the Australian Attorney-General's department, and the Law Council of Australia's trial observer, Lex Lasry, were witnessing this travesty of justice. Lasry's report would sum up the situation from an Australian perspective: 'This is much less about Hicks than it is about a grossly unfair process, and in many ways Australia's own moral authority is at risk if it continues to condone this process as "fair or just".'

On the second day of the three-day hearing, the presidential election was taking place as we were arguing our motions. By that evening, Bush had defeated Kerry. I was disappointed; I felt Kerry would make better decisions about sending US troops off to die, given his actual service in Vietnam. With the Bush administration continuing for another four years, it was only going to reward those who helped craft the commission system, an incompetent system that only worked to the benefit of those who might have actually violated the laws of war, while victimising hapless bit players such as Hicks.

The commission was not empowered to rule on our motions but had to send them to the Appointing Authority. The middle of January was set as the next hearing date for us to argue about the admissibility of evidence. We all flew out of GTMO. Just as the gloom continued to sink in, there was a ray of light. In the case of *Hamdan v. Rumsfeld* in the DC District Court, Judge James Robertson (a former Navy JAG) finally *got* it, ruling that the detainee, Hamdan, had to be treated as a prisoner of war until a valid Article 5 tribunal determined otherwise. It did not free Hamdan, but it threw a wrinkle into the commissions. But it also played into the Bush administration's strategy of delay. There was now a federal court decision that could be appealed, so the detainees would still languish in GTMO. This was the heartbreaking reality of the US justice system: even a win strung out the appeals process and ensured that Hicks stayed behind bars longer.

Judge Robertson's ruling did help in one area. The isolation in Camp Echo was taking its toll on Hicks. The minimal human contact with the guards who used to sit in the hut outside the cell and check on him had been replaced by cameras so, except for guards bringing in meals or taking him out for his thirty minutes of exercise, Hicks was alone. He had gone eight months without access to sunlight. With Judge Robertson ruling that a detainee facing a commission had to be treated under the conditions of a POW, isolation was prohibited. Additionally, the FBI reported its concerns at the use of 'intense isolation' on GTMO detainees. Thankfully, Hicks was moved back to Camp Delta, with its open-air cells and access to sunlight. The mundane environment of Camp Delta was not up to Geneva Convention standards, but it was better than being constantly alone and without natural light.

I appreciated any help I could get from the lawyers working in the Staff Judge Advocate's office for JTF GTMO. They understood we had a job to do. We wouldn't always agree, but I followed the maxim that you get more through sugar than salt. The JTF staff would rotate in and out every six to twelve months, and I would run into people I knew from previous trips. Sometimes I would have dinner with them, or socialise during the periods I was not allowed access to Hicks. One person I ran into during late 2004 was Lieutenant Commander Matt Diaz, whom I'd first known when he was the SJA at Diego Garcia while I was stationed in Japan. In 2006, he would be charged at a court-martial for espionage, for providing a list of the detainees' names to the Center for Constitutional Rights. While Diaz was motivated to make sure all the detainees had legal representation, the CCR thought they were being set up and turned the list over to law enforcement. In May 2007, as Hicks was leaving GTMO, Diaz was ultimately convicted and sentenced to six months in the brig and discharged from the service, losing a nineteen-year career. Ironically, the government publicly released the entire list of the detainees shortly before Diaz's trial.

As I returned to DC and Lippert to Germany, I was trying to get organised. Our evidentiary motions hearing was supposed to be in January, so motions would be due soon. I still had to travel to Pakistan and Afghanistan. First, though, I went back to a key task that I knew I would have to complete: I wanted to interview about forty detainees whose interrogations might be used in the case or had information on the abuse Hicks suffered. I submitted my request on 12 November 2004. Then I needed to organise interpreters – no easy task – for every language the prospective detainee witnesses spoke. As only JTF-GTMO had that information, I had to request it from them. It took weeks just to get the language list, of which there turned out to be twelve. Once that was accomplished, I had to request the actual interpreters from Altenburg. Here is an illustration of how 'helpful' his office was: I requested interpreters on 26 January 2005; Gunn forwarded them with his recommended approval on 1 February. This request was never answered. I put in another request on 15 April, highlighting that I had made the same request sixty-five days earlier; it was finally approved on 5 May 2005. I could finally start *looking* for interpreters, more than six months later. The commission system had a habit of slowing down and speeding up when it wanted.

Now all I had to do was work through the government contracting system to obtain interpreters who had the required clearance, had not already worked for GTMO, and were willing to go there. With the help of Chief Warrant Officer Jennifer Young, one of the competent people in Altenburg's office, and Master Sergeant Pierre, I would finally be able to begin interviews in September 2005, just in time for the commission to start again. All I had to do was convince some detainees who had been held at GTMO for nearly four years to talk to me! Of course, I was not allowed to use the same technique as the interrogators, and by then some of those I wanted to talk to had been released.

If the prosecution wanted to speak to a detainee, on the other hand, they just went down, used a staff interpreter, and did it more or less the day they thought of it.

In December 2004, I was finally approved to go to Pakistan and Afghanistan. After picking up my helmet, flak gear, holster, malaria pills and other necessities at Quantico, I flew into Islamabad along with two prosecutors, to interview two individuals who had met Hicks on his travels through Pakistan. Islamabad was an interesting city but what I remember most were the colourfully painted trucks. There were incredibly detailed paintings all over dump trucks. After conducting the interviews, I flew on to Kabul.

Investigating at this time was always going to be hard for me. For a start, my wife was pregnant and our twins were due in March 2005. So I had a lot on my plate and Dara was not too happy that I was flying off around the world. When the prosecution needed to gain evidence from Afghanistan to document some destroyed camps, they had the resources of the Criminal Investigation Task

Force, the FBI and military units support. What did I have? Nothing. I had to scrounge up what I could in Afghanistan.

I had to figure out how to move around Afghanistan without the national government knowing what I was doing. The Marines I knew in Afghanistan were not in Kabul, but Lippert was able to connect me with the Army SJA office in Kabul. I made contact with Lieutenant Colonel Turner Rouse, who was extremely helpful with getting me organised and connected to the two-man US Army trainers up in Kunduz. Rouse had been sitting in the office for a long time, and was happy to come along on the adventure. They put me up until I could get a flight to Kunduz, a city 330 kilometres further north, where it was claimed that Hicks 'had engaged in combat against coalition forces'. I was also lucky to reconnect with Larry Kitchen, the US police advisor who had helped the AFP in Kosovo. He was now a police trainer in Kabul. His boss was more than happy to send him along. I now had a two-man security detail to accompany me. We packed our gear and MREs (meals ready to eat) and waited for a flight.

My objective was both crystal clear and extremely difficult. I had to find the people who had known Hicks. The US government called him a terrorist, but his version was that he was a wannabe soldier who found Islam as a means to travel the world. It must have barely seemed possible for a poor kid from Adelaide. The AFP had traced Hicks's travels with the help of the letters provided by his family and their interview with him at GTMO in May 2002, before he had access to a lawyer. AFP officers travelled throughout Australia, Kosovo and Pakistan, locating people who had contact with him, but didn't follow the trail to Afghanistan. This was why it was so important for me to discover what evidence might exist there.

Kitchen, Rouse and I, after a few days delayed by bad weather, were able to get a C-130 flight to one of the 'Stan' countries that bordered northern Afghanistan, and then a German helicopter into Kunduz. The German military was in charge of the Provisional Reconstruction Team (PRT) at Kunduz as part of the International Security Assistance Force. They provided us with a place to put our gear and a rack to sleep on. A two-man US Army training team met us at the Kunduz airport and arranged a Toyota Land Cruiser and interpreter. They had also arranged a five-man team from the Afghan National Army (ANA) to help with searching for whatever we wanted. One of the ANA wore the rank of Sergeant Major and was very helpful to have along. He had fought with the Northern Alliance and was able to take us to the battlefields, and explain that the Northern Alliance knew who the Taliban forces were from their distinctive dress, that they carried their arms openly and had removed civilians from the battle areas, all of which went towards supporting Hicks's qualifications for POW status. I guess Rumsfeld was not getting the same information I was. The PRT compound was spartan, but there was a nice bar and restaurant. I sat back that night in Kunduz, amazed we had made it so far. Would I be lucky enough to actually find anyone who had met Hicks three years before?

We spent the next several days driving all over the Kunduz area, looking at the battlefields still littered with the wrecks of armoured vehicles. We avoided any areas that might have landmines, and we met the locals. With the help of the Sergeant Major, I felt that I might find the man who had potentially saved Hicks's life by taking him in while the Northern Alliance invaded Kunduz in 2001. As we returned from one battlefield, we headed into the centre of

Kunduz. It was lunchtime and I wanted to take the ANA guys out for a local meal to thank them for their help. The Sergeant Major chose a local restaurant and we all headed in for skewers of some kind of meat. I wasn't sure what we would be eating, but there was a man sitting near the back of the restaurant shoving bits of raw meat onto long skewers, somehow using his toes to do it. I did not want to think about it. When the skewers came, Kitchen, Rouse and I all looked for the ones that were the most well done.

Following the meal, the Sergeant Major, through the interpreter, said he knew of the business where Hicks had been. Sure enough, there was a young man inside a shop who said he had met the white fighter from Australia named Hicks. He had taken him to his uncle's business down the street, where they had kept him safe from the Northern Alliance, until one day Hicks wanted to try to go back to Australia. The young man took me and the whole entourage to his uncle's shop. We were getting some strange looks. I kept seeing women in burqas; I thought the United States had freed Afghan women from this oppressive clothing that supposedly had been imposed by the Taliban. When I asked the Sergeant Major, he said it was just tradition. I wondered what had really changed.

The uncle remembered Hicks and said he wished he had not left. He explained how Hicks was very scared when he met him, and when the Northern Alliance had come to try to take him, the uncle would not let it happen, as Hicks was his guest. The most important legal question I had was about what Hicks was wearing. After my question was translated, he did not hesitate. He reached and grabbed hold of my cammies and stated that Hicks was wearing what I was wearing. It might be a long shot, but I wanted the uncle to come to the commission and testify. He was more than willing. How I was going to get this gentleman to GTMO, I did not know, but in relation to Hicks's POW status and the attempted murder charge by an unprivileged belligerent, he was relevant. At the time, I had no idea that we would never bring witnesses to GTMO.

It was a successful trip all around. I did not get food poisoning, first off. And I'd learnt that the Northern Alliance knew exactly who the Taliban fighters were. Although the signs might not have been clear to the US soldiers, among the Northern Alliance soldiers, the enemy force was clearly identifiable.

I asked if civilians had been abused during the battle, and was told that the Taliban had done what a normal army would do, which was to get as many civilians as possible out of the area. There was no evidence of war crimes, but rather of a conventional battle having taken place. Hicks had been wearing camouflage and acting like any soldier.

As we waited at the Kunduz airport for our flight back to Kabul, among the rotting Russian aircraft from so many years before, I pondered that, in a strange way, Hicks was lucky he met this young man and his uncle. Had they not taken him in, he may well have been sent to the prison at Mazar-e-Sharif, where several hundred prisoners from Kunduz were sent and the subsequent uprising occurred. Even worse, thousands of prisoners who surrendered at Kunduz were boxed up in shipping containers and driven for days to Sheberghan prison by the Northern Alliance. During the trip, it has been reported, hundreds died from suffocation or were shot by members of the Northern Alliance, while US service personnel may have been present. Yet this alleged mass war crime has not led to a single person being charged. And Hicks would spend five years in GTMO for not hurting a single person.

By the time I returned from my trip, both the commission and the federal court case had been stopped. Altenburg had ordered that all commissions be stopped as he waited for Judge Robertson's POW ruling to be appealed. Australia would unjustly blame Hicks for this delay in the media, when it was Altenburg who stopped the commission and the DOJ asking for the delay in our federal court case. All the new evidence I had found would have to wait. I had no idea yet that it was all a waste of time.

19

Hicks's 'Dear John' Letter

As 2005 began, I had no idea how long it would take before the Military Commissions would recommence. In the delay, we had to take the time to prepare Hicks's case and apply pressure on the Howard government to take some action. Dratel and I had to make progress on interviewing detainees in Guantanamo Bay.

Then, out of the blue, on 11 January, the US government announced that the four remaining British citizens in GTMO and the other Australian citizen, Mamdouh Habib, were to be released. Was Hicks really going to be left behind? I was waiting, half-expecting to hear that he was to be released as well, but that message never came. I did not know the real evidence against these other men, but I couldn't help but compare the allegations levelled at them with those against Hicks. All had been through the Combatant Status Review Tribunal and found to be 'enemy combatants', and all had been personally selected by President Bush for a Military Commission. Australia was going to take Habib back, but there had to be a political reason beyond what was claimed publicly. Its press release said, '[T]he United States has now advised us that it does not intend to bring charges against Mr Habib. In these circumstances, we have requested Mr Habib's repatriation to Australia. The United States has agreed to that request.'

Why, then, had Australia done nothing for Hicks? When questioned, Attorney-General Philip Ruddock said Hicks would not be brought back to Australia as he 'faced three terrorism-related charges under American law'. Hicks faced no such thing. The Military Commissions had been stopped, the federal court action had been stopped, and the charges against him were invalid; Ruddock's department must have informed him of this. I could only conclude that the Australian government was leaving him in GTMO out of stubborn adherence to its old position: for political reasons, pure and simple.

What could we do? I felt like I was screaming to the media, who were happy to report our complaints, but there was no court to go to. We wrote to Ruddock, raising the unfairness of the others being released – and three of them were supposed to be witnesses against Hicks – but I was foolish to even think it would work. In such times, you try everything. I was still thinking logic would prevail. This was the rude awakening: even with the commission system stopped and flaws being exposed, it was all political. Our only hope seemed to be to get the charges invalidated by a court. Then Hicks would be in the same category as Habib, and could be released. Maybe.

My next visit to Hicks was five days away. I dreaded it. How was I going to explain what was happening? It was a tough time, as he was bewildered and disappointed, while I had trouble answering his questions. The allegations against Habib were potentially more serious than those against Hicks, but Habib had been released. The *New York Times* would report that an Australian official who investigated the Hicks and Habib cases described Hicks as 'a bit of a fool, naive', while another official described him as a 'young kid looking for adventure' and less of a potential threat than Habib. But on the other hand, there were reports that Habib had been tortured while held in Egypt; maybe containing that story was the US and Australian governments' priority. There was no satisfying logic behind it.

My typical visit to Hicks involved matters large and small. This time the battle was getting Hicks the calculator I had brought him for his schoolwork two months earlier. In two months, the hierarchy at GTMO still hadn't decided whether it was just a calculator, or some weapon of mass destruction. They wouldn't give it to him, and the consular staff was not having any luck.

When I arrived, Hicks was brought from Camp Delta to Echo. As usual, he was blindfolded and put in a 'three-piece suit', the shackles joining his hands to his ankles and putting him in a bent shuffle to move. When he was put in his van at Camp Delta, the guards held him horizontally and threw him into the door like a battering ram. At Echo, he was thrown out onto the gravel. I saw the marks on him and complained, but to no avail.

Hicks was distressed, to say the least. He said that when he had heard the British and Australians were leaving, he had got extremely excited, and when a guard told him that Habib was going but not him, he threw up. I suspect this was his lowest point so far.

I did my best to give him hope, but it was hard. What I could tell him was that in Australia, the announcement of Habib's release seemed to galvanise fresh support for his case. The Law Council of Australia, headed at that time by John North, was still taking an active role, and a letter had gone out signed by many Australian legal bodies calling for fair treatment. Amnesty International Australia, Terry Hicks and the Fair Go for David group in Adelaide were receiving positive feedback as the injustice of leaving Hicks locked up in Cuba became better known.

The main audience for our case was now Australia. The British government, by acting vigorously for its citizens, had shamed the Australians. The Bush administration's concession to the British showed that it was willing to cooperate with its allies, so what about Australia? How could it justify *not* asking for Hicks's return? I wondered who in the Australian government agreed to stick it out with the Military Commissions. The more the Australian public understood about the unfair process, the better, I thought.

On that visit, Hicks drafted a letter to Prime Minister John Howard, dated 21 January 2005. In it he explained his confusion and increasing hopelessness at being stuck in GTMO while other detainees were freed. He described his love of Australia and his determination to fit into society when he was able to return, and he explained how he'd tried to better himself through education while incarcerated. And he finished by pleading with Howard to ask the US government for his release and help him return to his family and his home.

I left Guantanamo Bay the next day, and emailed a copy of the letter to Kenny and Dratel. We had a conference call, during which we discussed whether it might be in Hicks's interest, as the commissions had stopped, to bring on a new Australian lawyer.

Kenny's assistance to Terry and David began when no one else was helping. He connected with the CCR, and he was very close and very helpful to Terry. Camatta Lempens, the Adelaide law firm Kenny worked at, had supported his long absences during his trips to the United States and GTMO. Kenny and Terry had been close from the beginning, from when Kenny had first read about Hicks in 2002 and called Terry to say, 'I want to represent you.' It was through Terry's letters that Hicks learnt about Kenny, whom he hadn't known, and through Terry's information that Hicks initially requested that Kenny be his lawyer.

Yet, with the stoppage of the commission, there was an opportunity to reassess where we were going and how best to move forward for Hicks. The change in Australian lawyers was not meant to have any negative implications about Kenny, but the media wanted drama. When the media found out that Kenny was being replaced, headlines of 'Hicks lawyer sacked' and 'Mori sacked Hicks's lawyer' were run. The media kept calling, wanting to know what the problem was: were there personality clashes or differences in tactics?

In reality, Kenny's media advocacy did not have any problem winning over those people who did not like Australia's involvement in the Iraq war and were anti-Howard and Bush, but he was making little headway persuading middle Australia or those on the right to listen, and they were the ones who could really put pressure on Howard. The government in Australia, and many other people, dismissed Kenny as a voice of the left. We needed to try to sway those in the coalition government and the majority of the Australian public. The reality was there was little hope of changing the US government, and nobody in the United States cared about GTMO detainees after the Bush re-election. But we could work on gaining traction in

Australia. There might have been no hope of swaying Howard but there were a lot more people in Australia than just Howard.

While some reporters claimed I was 'sacking' Kenny for being too aggressive, this was untrue, as we only increased the public campaign throughout 2005 and 2006.

While I'd like to say the decision to remove Kenny was Hicks's, I think I can honestly say that Hicks, or anyone held under those conditions for years, would never be able to make any real decision of his own while at GTMO. I was extremely sensitive to the accusation that I had manipulated Hicks, because that was the fine line I was walking: being the sole consistent source of information and unduly influencing him. When I was the only one there, I would run to and fro between Hicks and the office, to get a response from Dratel or Kenny or someone else on every little point, without injecting my own views, but I cannot deny that my voice might have been controlling, if only because I was the only person consistently seeing him. Hicks had no real choices, no ability to seek advice from anyone else.

In my opinion, we needed something different, lawyers with experience in the military who could not be brushed off as lefties. We reached out to the Law Council of Australia and senior barristers within Australia to find the right match to help. There was no shortage of distinguished and qualified volunteers. We were also working on expanding the US-based defence team; I felt it was important for Hicks to hear a variety of voices. He needed to hear what was going on outside from others besides me.

Five days after I visited with Hicks at that time, Mamdouh Habib was released to Australia. It was a bitter pill. The same day, we sent Hicks's letter to Prime Minister Howard.

20

Twists and Turns

The fallout in Australia from the release of Mamdouh Habib was growing. The businessman Dick Smith was publicly calling for Hicks to receive a fair trial and adding his reputation to the Hicks family's cause. I was asked to go on Bill O'Reilly's show on Fox News, the Republican Party's cable channel of choice, but making Hicks a cause in the US conservative media was not going to help, and there was little hope of pricking the conscience of President Bush or Vice-President Cheney. They were sending Americans to their deaths in Iraq; the fate of an Australian they had put in GTMO was hardly going to disturb their sleep or be a cause that Americans would take up. Our focus had to be on the decision-makers in Australia, not the United States.

We had a chance to reset now, and ask who was the best Australian lawyer we could get. I spoke to many different prospective lawyers, and went back to Hicks with a list. He chose David McLeod, a commander in the Australian Air Force Reserve, and Mick Griffin, a reserve Army Colonel. McLeod had a postgraduate degree in public and international law from the University of Melbourne. Griffin, who began his military career as an enlisted infantryman, finished his law degree and moved to the legal corps, completing twenty-two years in the regular army before transferring to the Reserves. McLeod would do the upfront public work, speaking to the media, while Griffin worked behind the scenes.

The Australian government agreed to fund one Australian lawyer's expenses, as a straight replacement for Kenny. McLeod and Griffin were keen to formalise their relationship, so I started the process of getting them authorised to travel to GTMO. As they both were military officers, they already had Australian security clearances, which made everything very easy and quick. A few weeks later, David Walters from Jenner & Block was authorised to act as an American civilian attorney, which would give him access to GTMO.

My work as a postman for Hicks was not slowing down. Mail rolled into my house from his family, friends and supporters. Bronwyn, lead organiser of Fair Go for David, was a wonderful source of books for me to take to him. I always felt I was useful if I could keep him busy and distracted from the depressing reality of his situation. I was able to give him plenty of novels and Australian history books, which he enjoyed, but GTMO wouldn't allow – for reasons they never gave us – Scott Turow's crime novel *Presumed Innocent*, the American classic *To Kill a Mockingbird* by Harper Lee, or Robert Hughes' work about the early Australian settlement,

The Fatal Shore. I might have been pushing it when I tried to bring Hicks *Papillon*, which I guess was understandable as it involved an escape from a remote island prison. I wasn't trying to be cheeky, though. I thought reading about the main character's endurance of long-term incarceration and isolation while sustaining hope in the future might inspire Hicks.

In GTMO, the material was screened by the intelligence section and was either accepted or rejected. During General Hood's time in charge, nearly everything was accepted and went through smoothly. There was always the redaction of Hicks's letters going out, much of it randomly and without my understanding of the justification. They took out any mention of love and affection. They took out a reference to the actual number of teeth his baby niece had lost. I was always sad to see his expressions of love and affection being blacked out for no reason.

With McLeod and Griffin onboard, there was new impetus in our preparation of the case, even if we were stalled by waiting for the Hamdan appeal. I had wanted to interview the British Guantanamo inmates, but was prevented from doing so before they left, and was still working through the tangle of finding interpreters for the interviews with non-English-speaking detainees. A junior officer in the Appointing Authority's office suggested I use the same interpreters who had been at the interrogations. I said, 'What detainee is going to speak to me if he has the same interpreter as when he was interrogated?' They didn't get it.

McLeod and Griffin had been officially detailed to Hicks and were ready to visit him at GTMO. It was essential that they have this face-to-face contact, as we were in the unique position of representing a client with whom we could have no phone or email conversations. Having become Hicks's only avenue of contact with the outside world, I felt the weight of responsibility.

We travelled down via Fort Lauderdale and spent several days meeting with Hicks. He was really trying hard on his high-school work, and we brought him new books. He was better read than he'd ever been in his life. Someone brought meals in, but that was the only human contact he had apart from us. I felt that he was getting humane treatment from the guards under Hood's command. Compared with the majority of the other inmates, he at least had something in common with the members of the US military: he spoke English.

Being military men, McLeod and Griffin weren't shocked by GTMO, but even for them seeing the detainee camps was a foreign experience.

We returned to Washington DC to review a few classified documents, which McLeod and Griffin were able to do for the first time. They agreed that very little of what I ever saw was actually deserving of 'classified' status. One of the commission's tendencies was to call something 'classified' for no reason other than to prohibit the defence from talking about embarrassing facts in public. There was also, as usual, a fair amount of incompetence involved. One agency would claim a document was classified, whereas another would not. Having Australian military experience, I hate to say it, but such over-classification might not have surprised them.

In July 2005, I travelled to the Netherlands, where I met with members of the defence office for the International Criminal Tribunal for the former Yugoslavia, and then on to Bali to attend a conference of the Criminal Law Association of the Northern Territory. While I was there, suicide bombers in London killed fifty-two people and injured more than 700: not a good news story when we were trying to get Australia to bring Hicks home. Quite rightly, politicians and the public would harden their views against terrorists after such an event. Quite wrongly, they would misdirect these views against Hicks. It was poignant being in Bali, where 202 people, including eighty-eight Australians, had been killed in the terrorist bombings three years earlier. If only the Bush administration had put the same resources into prosecuting those responsible for that as they were wasting on Hicks.

At around the same time, in mid-2005, the NCIS investigation into Hicks's allegations of abuse petered out, as usually happens when the Department of Defense investigates itself. Hicks had documented his abusive treatment before Guantanamo during the interview with NCIS. He described physical assaults when US forces first interrogated him, days after his capture by the Northern Alliance. I was most interested in two events that occurred when Hicks was being detained on a naval ship shortly after he was captured. Twice, he and a group of other detainees were flown from the ship, hooded and cuffed, to a base somewhere and held for several hours. During these times at the base, he and the other detainees were physically assaulted with weapons and fists, kicked and spat on. What I could not figure out was whether this was some form of organised abuse to soften them up for interrogations or just random US service personnel letting their emotions, so soon after 9/11, override their training.

Regarding these incidents, the DOD told the Australian government, 'The Naval Criminal Investigative Service found no information that substantiates or corroborates these allegations of abuse.' Even a cursory review of the investigation revealed ample substantiating and corroborative evidence. NCIS agents had interviewed other detainees held with Hicks onboard Navy ships, and all described similar incidents: being taken to an unknown area and assaulted. Many described hearing others being hit and screaming. Their evidence was discounted because they were wearing hoods at the time, and could not see other detainees being abused.

NCIS also uncovered US service personnel who provided corroborating information. One sailor had seen Hicks return to the ship with a footprint in his back. It seemed to me that this substantiated that Hicks had been stepped on and kicked but somehow was discounted. As an American, I could understand why, in the months following 9/11, young military men who came into contact with those whom their superiors were telling them were responsible for 9/11 might have got a little heavy-handed. But those emotions, while understandable, don't condone the acts.

For my own investigation, the NCIS report enabled me to identify the other detainees and to find more evidence on which to possibly exclude Hicks's interrogations at GTMO. This could become important again, as the commissions looked like they were going to resume after the pivotal event of late July 2005: the overturning of the Hamdan judgement in the appeals court.

In November 2004, in the DC District Court, Judge Robertson had ruled in Hamdan's favour, saying the United States could not hold a Military Commission unless it had proven that the detainee was not a prisoner of war. Now, in July 2005, the DC Circuit Appeals Court upheld the use of Military Commissions because they had been approved by Congress (something we already knew), and the detainees had neither POW status nor protection by the

Geneva Conventions because he had not been fighting for a foreign power but for al-Qaeda. There went Judge Robertson's ruling. One of the judges who made this ruling, interestingly, was John G. Roberts, soon to be Bush's appointee as Chief Justice of the Supreme Court.

While I did not agree with the POW status part of the judgement, it wasn't all bad. It validated the Military Commissions, for the moment anyway, but left open the possibility that we could seek, within the system, POW status for Hicks, as he had not been with al-Qaeda. It made establishing that Hicks had fought in uniform, for the Taliban government forces, even more imperative. The most direct benefit was that the Appeals Court disagreed with the government's argument that courts had no supervisory role over the Military Commissions. It said there was a 'compelling historical precedent for the power of civilian courts to entertain challenges that seek to interrupt the processes of Military Commissions'. This meant Hicks's federal court challenge against the charges should go forward.

Hamdan's lawyers would begin the process of seeking an appeal to the Supreme Court, but the Military Commission system might also be turned back. Rumsfeld said, 'This circuit court of appeals ruled unanimously . . . in favour of the President's Military Commission policy, and we've announced that we're going to push forward as fast as possible.' He forecast the commissions starting within thirty to forty days. It was nice for me to be able to read this in the news, as I had received no information from the presiding officer myself. But the commissions were about to hit a new hurdle, this one entirely of their own making.

21

A New Briton

In the second half of 2005, Colonel Gunn was preparing to depart the CDC and retire from the military. On his initial appointment back in 2003, his job had been structured so that he was answerable to the commission first and foremost. He never interfered with anything; he was always just looking on. Not an active impediment, but not an active help either. Unfortunately, the rules confined him from actively representing or advocating on behalf of any of our clients. Later, President Barack Obama would appoint him General Counsel to the Department of Veterans' Affairs. I expect he was freer to fight more doggedly for veterans' rights than he had been under the restrictive rules set for the CDC.

One of his last acts was, however, decisive. As he was preparing to turn the defence office over, he called a meeting at which he silently passed around a printout. It contained emails saying how unfair and even rigged the commission system was. That was not news. But then we saw who had written them: the *prosecutors*. I didn't immediately understand the repercussions, trying to skim over the pages as Gunn told us when he had received them. I was amazed at what the emails contained. I realised that they dated from 2004 and that Gunn had held them for some time, without giving them to us until he was leaving.

The emails revealed allegations that prosecutors misrepresented facts, and they acknowledged the system was rigged to ensure convictions. Investigators and prosecutors withheld evidence of abuse and exculpatory evidence from the defence. Military Commission panels were chosen with the expectation that those selected would not acquit any defendant. The systematic destruction of detainee interview records was happening, and was condoned. Notes about abuse of detainees were removed. Three Air Force attorneys, Major Robert Preston, Captain John Carr and Captain Carrie Wolf, were standing up against the process from within the prosecution office. It took a great deal of courage to do what they did. They did not go to the media and expose the flaws, but went up the chain of command and asked to leave the commissions. I don't think it is any secret that, in the military and outside, there are those who place personal career advancement above their integrity. Clearly, Preston, Carr and Wolf valued doing the right thing, whatever the personal cost.

Carr wrote, 'We have invested substantial time and effort to conceal our deficiencies and mislead not only each other, but also those outside our office either directly responsible for, or asked to endorse, our efforts . . . [T]he inadequate preparation of the cases and misrepresentation related thereto may constitute dereliction of duty, false official statements, or other criminal conduct.' He found the commission process to be 'a half-hearted and disorganized effort by a skeleton group of relatively inexperienced attorneys to prosecute fairly low-level accused in a process that appears to be rigged'.

Preston said, 'writing a motion saying that the process will be full and fair when you don't really believe it is kind of hard – particularly when you want to call yourself an officer and a lawyer'.

Whichever way you looked at them, the emails were explosive. Everything I'd come to believe about the commissions was *also* believed by members of the prosecution office. All our worst suspicions were confirmed. We were very excited by the emails, and began discussing what we were going to do with them. They were not classified so there was no restriction on providing them to the media.

At the CDC office, we discussed our options. Al-Bahlul's team didn't really care. Their client didn't even want a lawyer, so they were limited to advocating for the right of self-representation. Hamdan's counsel wanted to hold the emails back, and release them when the Supreme Court would be considering Hamdan's appeal, hoping that a news report would sway Supreme Court Justices. As Hicks's representative, I felt they needed to become part of the public debate in Australia now. Hicks had been sitting in limbo for almost nine months, and the public debate on the treatment of an Australian citizen was starting to gain traction.

I contacted an Australian reporter to release the emails to generate media interest, thinking that they could be used to maximum effect there. I informed Charles Swift, Hamdan's lawyer, so he would be aware and could work with his US media contacts on having the story released in the US media in a coordinated manner.

Within thirty minutes of my informing Swift, he came into my office smiling, saying, 'The story's going to come out tomorrow in the *New York Times*.' This release would beat the Australian reporter's story, spoiling the exclusivity I had promised.

'What do you mean? Why are you doing this?' I asked.

'Well,' he grinned, 'you didn't want to follow our plans, so we're not following yours.'

I immediately regretted telling Swift. As if we didn't have enough problems, now we had in-fighting within our own office. I asked Swift, since he thought the release of the emails would help Hamdan, why he would want to undermine the release in Australia. His response was fairly typical. He rambled on, saying a lot but without any substance. In our office meetings, Swift's ramblings had finally made Gunn implement a rule that allowed Swift to only talk for one minute. He would do strange things, like walk up to a paralegal who was eating a candy bar, grab the bar, take a bite and put it down and walk away like nothing happened. He was very strange, but he had a surface charisma that initially impressed people. He and I were well past that, though.

When I could figure out what he was saying, Swift indicated that he was more interested in sabotaging me and burning my bridge with the Australian reporter I had contacted. That's how our office was operating. I ended up having to talk to the *New York Times* reporter, who agreed to time his publication so that the Australian and US articles came out on the same day.

It was dispiriting, to say the least, that we were fighting internally as well as externally. We still had to work together and share information, though. I was sharing our legal motions and information with all the teams. It was not about personal glory, not for me anyway. There was only one measure of success: getting my client out of GTMO.

It was in that same year that five of us from the CDC office were honoured with the Roger M. Baldwin Medal of Liberty Award from the America Civil Liberties Union. It came with a cash prize of $5000 for each lawyer. I put mine in trust for Hicks's children. It was not much, but it was something. I believed I didn't deserve anything more than my friends who were risking their lives in Afghanistan and Iraq.

The prosecutor email story broke in Australia, and I was pleased that for once it wasn't me, the usual suspect, saying these damaging things about the Military Commissions, but the prosecutors. I hoped that it might be the last straw that woke John Howard up, or prompted Philip Ruddock to make a principled stand. The former High Court Justice Mary Gaudron made a strong statement, saying:

> It's clear that [Hicks] has not committed an offence under American law, or he would have been dealt with in American courts with American law. The rule of law, normal civilised behaviour, says you are not deprived of your liberty, you are not exposed to punishment, if you haven't broken the law. That's the very essence of a civilised, free, democratic country.'

A few weeks later, the Law Council of Australia issued an open letter to Howard advocating for either the trial of Hicks in a 'properly constituted court' or his return to Australia. 'The Australian government's inaction over David Hicks can no longer be ignored or accepted,' the council said. 'They have dismissed the concerns of the legal profession and denied the application of the rule of law – a principle upon which the entire legal system is based.'

Frustratingly, however, it all seemed to wash over Howard, Downer and Ruddock. Downer responded only by saying, 'Whatever these emails might say we, as of now, are satisfied.'

Almost as if in response to the prosecutors' views finding their way into the public, the commission system was coming alive again. Within weeks, I began getting more calls from the media asking what I knew of the Military Commissions starting again. The DOD was saying September, though I had been given no official information. The first I heard of it in person was on 5 August during a conference with the federal judge focused on how Hicks's civil case would proceed, and an attorney from the Department of Justice mentioned it. The government was seeking a delay, as the Military Commission against Hicks was about to start. That was the first I'd heard of it! The judge indicated the civil proceedings were to move forward and it was ordered that we should file our arguments by 17 August with the government replying soon thereafter.

This raised our spirits, as it looked like we were finally going to get the validity of the charges ruled on. Even though Hamdan had lost his appeal, the Appeals Court had made it clear that the type of issues we were raising could and should be heard before a Military Commission took place. We wanted to move forward quickly in the civil case.

Griffin and I visited Hicks at GTMO in August to update him. During this visit, Griffin and Hicks were talking about cricket. At the time, Australia was playing England in the Ashes, and Griffin asked Hicks whom he was barracking for. Hicks said, 'Well, it's hard because, you know, I'm from Australia but my mum is British.'

I knew this already, and had even discussed it with Stephen Kenny sometime earlier, but he had said that the citizenship issue was a dead end, and so I'd left it at that. But Griffin was very interested. Hicks's mother was British? The British detainees had all been released, and the commission had been deemed unacceptable for British citizens. We looked at each other, and I asked, 'Is there something we can do with this?'

We were still talking about it as we were leaving Camp Echo when, coincidentally, we ran into Clive Stafford Smith, the British lawyer, who had a client there. We asked him about the issues and he said he thought the law had been changed in 2003 to allow British citizenship to be passed from a mother to a child born overseas, even retroactively. So Griffin and I dashed back to the office in GTMO and started searching the internet excitedly. Sure enough, there was information on the website of the British embassy in Australia that looked promising, and we decided we couldn't leave without a signed application for a British passport from Hicks. Hicks was surprised, as we had been down this road with Kenny, but he became more excited as we explained the possibilities to him. We took his application back to DC, where I called Hicks's mother to get supporting documents. I wasn't able to get Hicks's passport from GTMO, but we had a copy from the discovery process of the legal case. Having got the paperwork together, I called the British embassy.

'I would like to talk to the person in the embassy who's dealing with the detainees,' I said, 'the British detainees in Guantanamo.'

A guy named Simon came on, and I introduced myself and

explained, 'There's still a British citizen in Guantanamo that you may not know about. So can I come and meet with you?' He was certain that all the British citizens were out of GTMO, but we set up an appointment. I have to admit, I took a little pleasure in knowing that the phone might be ringing at 10 Downing Street that evening.

After we had returned to DC, Griffin and I took a cab to the British embassy, having a chuckle at the commotion this might be causing in London. I presented Hicks's application for citizenship. 'His mother is a British citizen, born in Croydon,' I said. 'His grandfather fought in the British army.' In a deadpan voice I said, 'We believe he's the missing Earl of Croydon, fifth in line to the throne.'

Simon didn't look in the mood for jokes about royalty. As he flipped through the application, he looked like I had just dropped a large pile of shit on his lap. He had plans for a round of golf that afternoon, which had to be cancelled. He took the application. My supporting letter said:

> I make three requests of the British authorities on behalf of David Hicks:
>
> – Consular assistance in confirming and formalizing David's entitlement to British citizenship as a matter of urgency;
> – A statement of the British government's position on the continued detention of David Hicks as a British citizen and his subjection to the Military Commission process; and
> – Diplomatic action to ensure that the current stay of Military Commission proceedings against David Hicks is not lifted. In the circumstances, I ask that you expedite these requests as a matter of extreme urgency and communicate a written response to me by Friday August 19, 2005.

So began a new line of attack and hope for Hicks. His application was with the British, but we were uncertain as to where it would lead. I was sure the British didn't want Hicks, as it would cause too much of a stir.

I was worried that Hicks applying for British citizenship risked rubbing some Australians the wrong way, but at this point the Australian government had abandoned him. And Hicks was not giving up his Australian citizenship; rather he was formalising his British citizenship, which he had not known he was entitled to. The hypocrisy really pissed me off. US citizens and British citizens, even German citizens, got pulled out of GTMO and the Military Commission system. But an Australian citizen was left there – he was just a kid from a working-class family in Salisbury, South Australia. I couldn't help wondering, if Hicks had been from a well-to-do family from the right suburbs around Sydney, would the Howard government's response have been a little different?

We were pushing for the judge to hear our federal court challenge to the validity of the charges. The Department of Justice opposed us, as they had the previous year. The big picture was that we wanted the federal courts to decide on the validity of the commission before the commission convened again. The government wanted the commission to start before the ruling on its validity.

Whenever there was a reason, the government was mysteriously able to accelerate their side of the process. While we were writing our final brief for the federal court, we heard rumours that there might be changes to MCO No. 1, the initial order establishing the Military Commission. On 31 August, MCO No. 1 was revised and reissued. It changed the structure of the commissions to a judge-jury structure. On 20 September, the Appointing Authority lifted the stay on Hicks's case only, and did away with all the legal motions we had already argued. Altenburg restarted the whole system and effectively gave the government a chance for a do-over. All of our old motions had to be modified and new motions written. It was back to square one. Luckily, Sarah Finnin was able to travel back to assist through the generosity of an Australian supporter.

With the commission about to restart, we were finally given what Dratel and I had been denied for more than ten months: access to interview GTMO detainees. This was the first time a defence lawyer had been allowed to interview a detainee other than his own client. None of the detainees I wanted to interview had been assigned a lawyer that I was aware of. I was allowed one-hour blocks, enough for those few who were willing to speak to me. Most were reluctant, unsurprisingly, as in the previous four years their only interaction had been with guards, interrogators and some Red Cross workers. I was dressed in my Marine camouflage uniform and had taken off the stupid piece of duct tape covering my name, but they had no idea if Mori was my real name or not. Some might have thought I was an interrogator, and that my claim to be a defence lawyer was just another interrogation technique. This was certainly not unreasonable, as I had to conduct my interviews in the same trailer where interrogations took place. Even when Dratel was present in his civilian clothes, I am not sure this put any of the detainees at ease as many of the interrogators wore civilian clothes.

I was monitored by audiovisual equipment during my interviews. I could accept that there was a safety factor, but what struck me as odd was that this trailer, filled with all this recording equipment, was where interrogations took place – and yet Miller had denied that interrogations were recorded!

Some detainees said they would speak to me, but wanted it to be private, like when they met with the Red Cross. One detainee refused to speak to me because his interrogator, he said, told him not to talk to anyone else. Another impediment was that many of the detainees had been conditioned to gain something in return for talking to an interrogator, which I could not offer them. I was allowed to bring drinks and snacks, which some took, but most were very suspicious of me.

One detainee had to be carried in on a stretcher. He was in a bad state, as he was on a hunger strike. All he could say in answer to my questions was, 'I just want to die.' And then they took him out.

All of this was in preparation for the restart of the commission in two months. Altenburg unilaterally removed two commission members and added *eight* new ones to what was effectively a jury panel. With a stroke of his pen, he vacated all prior decisions by the commission and provided a 'fresh opportunity' for the prosecution. Nowhere in the rules was Altenburg empowered to remove members who had already begun sitting on a commission hearing, but that was the beauty of this system. If it wasn't working, the prosecution could just change the rules.

From the outside, more voices were joining the clamour against the commission. Brigadier Gerard Fogarty, who was awarded an AM for his leadership of the Australian contingent in East Timor, said the trials should be scrapped because of the damage they were doing to the reputation of the United States and its allies. David McLeod gave our reaction in Australia, saying, 'Brigadier Fogarty's article highlights the sad reality of Australia standing alone as the only Western nation that is prepared to stick with a discredited process which is not only counterproductive to the very terror that Australia and the US rightly seek to suppress but against the very ideals held by their own citizens.'

On 11 October 2005, the prosecution gave us an updated witness and exhibit list, which was eye-opening, to say the least. They were intending to use as evidence investigator notes from interviews with many detainees, some already released, and some of them US citizens in American prisons. In one way, it was not unexpected that many of the prosecution witnesses were to be FBI and NCIS investigators who were going to repeat second-hand what they had been told in interviews, as this was why the commissions were set up to allow hearsay evidence – so that the actual witnesses would not be brought to the trial. Agents would testify about the terrorist bombings in Kenya and Tanzania in 1998, and the 9/11 hijackings. Needless to say, I had no access to any of these witnesses. Nor did these incidents have the slightest connection with Hicks.

In refiling our motions to the commission, we wanted 'Australian', 'Canadian' and 'British' removed from the charge of attempted murder of coalition troops, on the grounds that those countries' forces hadn't been in Afghanistan or anywhere near where Hicks was before his arrest. The prosecution charge contended that Hicks let off explosives and fired other ordnance at coalition soldiers between September and December 2001. The prosecution would not yield, even in the face of evidence that Hicks had not fired or thrown bombs at anyone. Their reasoning was that simply by being in the area, he must have attacked *someone*.

We also challenged the review panel, on grounds I have already discussed.

As the hearing approached, the Australian media began to chase new angles with increasing vigour. Mary Robinson, the former Irish president and United Nations High Commissioner for Human Rights, called on the Australian government to increase its efforts to get Hicks out of GTMO. Terry Hicks's public profile grew, and David McLeod was not only writing letters and sending emails, but also getting them read. He had a firm control over our media message and access to Australian politicians from both sides of the aisle. Meanwhile, I took every opportunity to hammer home the difference in treatment between Australian, UK and US detainees. I had to believe Australians would not stand for the blatantly unfair treatment of one of their countrymen by his own government.

A week before the commission was due to start in November 2005, the British government informed us that it was intending to approve Hicks's application for citizenship, but in the next breath made an order depriving him of that same citizenship on the basis that he had done things seriously prejudicial to the vital interests of the UK. They asserted that he had received extensive terrorist training with known Islamic extremists. What was rather ironic was that the 'known Islamic extremists' to whom they referred were other British citizens who'd been held at Guantanamo and were brought back to Britain without ever being prosecuted at a Military Commission or in any British court. This was disappointing, but not unexpected. Nothing was ever handed to us easily; we would have to struggle for every breakthrough.

With the help of an Oxford Professor, Vaughn Lowe, we had already located a London law firm, Bindmans and Partners, that was willing to take on Hicks's citizenship case. Led by Stephen Grosz, Alison Stanley and Saadiya Chaudhary, along with barrister Mike Fordham, they would spend the next year and a half taking the case before two British courts, and winning. They quickly began litigation in the British courts to force the government to formalise Hicks's citizenship.

The defence and prosecution lawyers, the media, trial observers and Australian government representatives were scheduled to fly down to GTMO on 15 November for the restart. That was almost 100 people to be loaded onto a military C-130 transport plane. It always struck me as odd that they would go to the expense of sending 100 people to Cuba rather than one detainee to a secure facility in the United States. But if I started questioning the logic of everything about GTMO, I would have gone mad.

There was last-minute speculation about whether our federal judge was going to grant our motion to stop the commission hearing. Mark Goldman and I were working on stopping the commission hearing so the federal court would hear the case first. We had filed an injunction request, something the Department of Justice opposed. The day before we were due to leave, the decision was issued: the baby was split, giving us a stoppage of the commission and giving the Department of Justice their wish that the federal court not rule on Hicks's challenge to the commission until after the US Supreme Court ruled on the Hamdan case – a ruling that was not expected for another six months.

There were a lot of disappointed reporters. They had all been selected to go to GTMO, and now the big case was not going to happen. And throughout all this, the Howard government in Australia took every opportunity to blame the defence for delaying the Military Commission trial. We just wanted a real court to rule on the commission first. It was the US government that caused the delay, by its two-pronged offensive in delaying the federal courts and in rewriting the rules of the commission.

I had mixed feelings about the ruling. All the work that had gone into preparing thirty-eight motions and legal challenges was going to go to waste, at least for now. But one thing was clear: for Hicks, it meant more time at Guantanamo. It was important to talk to him, so I still flew down. I always found it strange to sit with him and relate the details of these complex legal arguments. They had such a direct impact on him, but at the same time he was uninvolved and probably bewildered. So much activity was happening on his behalf every day outside of GTMO, but for him, it was just another day in his cell.

When I returned to our office in DC, the sewage pipes had broken and the place was flooded. Many of my files were unusable. In response, we were moving to a new office – coincidentally the offices that were to be used by the review panel, if it ever really existed. We were also losing Master Sergeant Pierre, who was retiring. She worked unbelievably long hours for us and I could tell it was hurting her to leave the team after so long. She had developed a bond with Hicks. If we had a real end date, she would have stayed, but there was no end in sight.

Justice Collins's decision on Hicks's citizenship application came down three weeks later: the British government was ordered to register Hicks as a British citizen, and give him the full rights and entitlements that came with it. Justice Collins rejected the government's argument that they could refuse Hicks's application based on alleged conduct prior to him becoming a British citizen. The government stated that it would appeal. Given its attitude to his application, we didn't hold out much hope that the UK would rush to get Hicks out of GTMO either way.

I was scheduled to travel back to Guantanamo in the first part of December, but was snowed in. Luckily one of our paralegals, Sergeant Williams, had taken an earlier flight, and was able to give Hicks the news about his citizenship application – as well as a fresh supply of chewing tobacco.

As 2005 was coming to a close, our office was changing. Marine Colonel Dwight Sullivan had taken over from Will Gunn. I was the only lawyer left from the original six. On one quiet day in the office, Colonel Sullivan had the unenviable task of letting me know that I had not been selected for promotion to Lieutenant Colonel. I would hear the same news for the next two years.

Meanwhile, the media was taking more of an interest in Hicks's case, posing questions in their editorials to solicit a response from their audiences. It was good to see that people were beginning to see beyond the soundbites and were becoming concerned about the actual processes that were being used. They posed the question: if eventually released, should David Hicks be welcomed back to Australia? Public responses varied: some supported Hicks and others did not.

We ended 2005 on a high note with the win in the British court. The British litigation was well in hand with Grosz and Fordham, who were preparing to respond to the British government's appeal against the decision. Britain still needed to comply with the judge's order and take steps to formalise Hicks's British citizenship. What this meant was that someone from the British embassy should be heading down to GTMO to swear Hicks in. I was not confident that this would happen anytime soon. But he was now a problem for Tony Blair.

I spent the last few days of the year driving the south-east coast of the United States locating and interviewing some of the agents who had interrogated or interviewed Hicks, as a way of addressing the NCIS investigation into his alleged abuse. And so, as 2005 closed, there was some hope: we had litigation in two different countries with the chance that 2006 would bring our third.

22

Happy New Year

In a way, we were in a holding pattern. The Supreme Court's briefing schedule, which gave attorneys a timetable for their submissions, was suggesting that we would have to wait until June 2006 for a decision. The next British court hearing was several months off. We had litigation in two countries; we were still trying to figure out how to get litigation in Australia.

All we could do in the meantime was to visit Hicks as much as possible and continue to prepare for a commission, in the event that the system ever restarted. I was still shuttling his schoolwork and letters back and forth from Australia; again it felt like the only real thing I could do.

This was frustrating enough for Josh Dratel and me, but I can only imagine how it felt for Hicks. January 2006 marked the beginning of his fifth year in captivity, and one year since the release of his fellow Australian, Habib, and the remainder of the British detain-ees. More than 250 citizens from Afghanistan, Belgium, Denmark, France, the United Kingdom, Kuwait, Morocco, Pakistan, Russia, Saudi Arabia, Spain and Sweden had been released from Guantanamo Bay. Clearly if the Australian government wanted Hicks released, it would have happened. The charges against Hicks were minor, compared with some of those who had been released. One of Osama bin Laden's most loyal followers, a man who helped the al-Qaeda leader escape from Tora Bora in 2001, had been released. The Taliban's ambassador to Pakistan had been released. It had recently been reported that one of the former Taliban spokes-men was attending Yale University in 2006. So much for the 'aiding the enemy' charge! Yet Hicks remained behind, a political prisoner.

The commission office had been in place for more than three years, but no trials had been completed. But the Military Commissions office was losing the war of attrition. The prosecu-tion office was now on its fourth chief prosecutor in three years, Air Force Colonel Morris Davis having taken over in September 2005. The recently promoted Lieutenant Colonel Brubaker, the lead prosecutor on the Hicks case, left at the end of 2005 and was replaced by another Marine prosecutor. The defence team had lost Master Sergeant Pierre and also Jeffrey Lippert, who had been doing his best working from Germany while carrying out his duties as senior Defense Counsel there. It was not fair to Lippert's clients in Germany, nor to Hicks, for him to have to split his time like that. With the commissions on hold for at least six months, now was the time to make the change. Colonel Sullivan released Lippert and by June 2006, Rebecca Snyder was detailed to the Hicks case. I had worked with and trained Snyder, a University of Minnesota

Law School graduate, as a defence counsel in her first tour as a Navy JAG when we were both stationed in Yokosuka, Japan. There was no one in the Navy JAG corps who worked harder than Snyder and she was worth her weight in gold when she joined our office.

We also had four new attorneys join the CDC office – from the Army Thomas Bogar, Brian Broyles and Tom Fleener, and one new Navy JA, Bill Kuebler. When I looked at the personnel on both sides, I realised with a shock that I was pretty much the only survivor from 2003.

Since the Military Commission and federal court had stopped and the British litigation was under control, one main area I could focus my efforts on was to address the issue out in the public domain, targeting Australia. I was asked to do many US mainstream media appearances, but I began turning them down. There was no benefit in making Hicks a household name in the United States. Indeed, to get him out of GTMO, we needed the US public to care less about him, just as had been the case with the released British detainees. So when *GQ* came knocking to do a spread on me, I said no. Australia had to be the focus, so I would make four trips Down Under in 2006.

We would get some help with the media from the prosecution, with the appointment of Davis. He came out and talked in the media, much more than his predecessors Swann and Borch, and every time it was wonderful for us because he would inevitably find a way to put his foot in his mouth as he tried to defend the indefensible or he would just perpetuate the media coverage. I could not help but think what a waste of money and military personnel it was for a commission that wasn't actually operating. (It has cost the US taxpayers over $600 million dollars to operate GTMO since 2007.

The figures from 2002 to 2007 have not yet been released.)

The year of 2006 also brought a significant change at GTMO, with the professional and relatively humane Major-General Jay Hood succeeded as commandant by Navy Rear Admiral Harry B. Harris. What followed was a severe decline in Hicks's conditions. He and the other nine detainees who had been charged before the Military Commission were shifted into solitary confinement for twenty-three hours a day in Camp 5. In his new cell, Hicks had one window, if you could call a six-inch by thirty-inch frosted piece of glass a window. The window on the door into the corridor was covered over. The light in the cell was left on constantly, the quality of his food declined again, and his table and chair were taken away. He complained of constant banging and other noises. After all the hard work of the Australian consular staff to improve Hicks's living conditions over the past three years, it was all scrapped. The official reason given for this change was that the charged men had to be kept in Camp 5 because their tribunals were pending. This was BS. I suspected that the real reason was to break their spirits and push them to the point where they would give in to whatever deal was offered for a guilty plea. It made sense. In the previous year, as we had improved Hicks's conditions and he had access to better food and educational materials, he had shown more resilience when it came to his case. Now, it seemed, they wanted to try something different.

• Philip Ruddock, the Australian Attorney-General, was asked about Hicks's move into solitary confinement. Not unexpectedly, he saw nothing wrong with it. The United States had assured Australia that it was purely because some buildings had been closed down. Ruddock said he had been told that Hicks was receiving

natural sunlight. I don't know what measures Ruddock took to verify these statements.

On 6 March 2006, Prime Minister Tony Blair set out the British
government's position on Guantanamo Bay in a parliamen-
tary written statement: 'We have made it clear that we regard
the circumstances under which detainees continue to be held in
Guantanamo Bay as unacceptable. Guantanamo Bay is an anomaly
that should come to an end sooner rather than later.'

For months, the British government had been telling us that
it was trying to get access to Hicks, but had been restricted by US
personnel. I was not sure if there was a real problem, or if it was just
delay for delay's sake, as US civilian attorneys and the media had
no problem getting onto GTMO. Nor did British intelligence personnel have any problem getting access to Hicks in 2003 when they
wanted to interrogate him.

In March, I travelled to London to attend the Court of Appeal
hearing. It went as well for us as we could have hoped. The court
took a very active role in focusing on what is required for someone to have been 'disaffected' towards the Queen and when the
'disaffection' needs to have occurred, which was why the British
government wanted to prohibit Hicks from becoming a citizen.
One judge commented, 'Don't you think Mr Hicks, after four years
at GTMO, has great affection for the Queen?' We were pretty confident about the outcome, but would have to wait for the decision.

In April, the Court of Appeal handed down its decision, reject-
ing the government's arguments. As luck would have it, Dratel
and I were in Australia at the time, speaking publicly about Hicks
and liaising with his supporters, including his family. The public

meetings were not always friendly: I remember getting a hard time for suggesting that some of the guards at Guantanamo Bay had often treated Hicks with respect. Unfortunately, the Abu Ghraib scandal had tarnished the US military's reputation abroad. This trip to Australia also laid the groundwork for a future legal challenge in Australia, as Dratel, Griffin and I had an opportunity to meet with Brett Walker, a Sydney barrister, before Griffin deployed to Iraq for a few months.

Once the British decision became known, the Australian media converged on Dratel and me and we took the opportunity to renew public focus on Hicks's plight. I highlighted the difference between Britain's and Australia's attitudes to the Military Commissions:

> I think the British Government's position on Guantanamo Bay and the Military Commissions has been clear. Military Commissions do not meet international standards, Guantanamo should close, and I don't see the British government changing its position on Guantanamo Bay. There's only one UK and one Aussie national left and that's David Hicks, and after over four years it's about time he was reunited with his family and received justice.

Bob Brown, the leader of the Australian Greens party, said the Howard government had 'devalued Australian citizenship'.

'David Hicks,' he said, 'has effectively been a political prisoner of the Howard government at the leisure of the Bush administration. He should be brought home now.'

Ruddock conceded that if Hicks were released from GTMO on the initiative of the British government protecting one of its citizens from the Military Commissions, then Australia would allow him to come back home to Adelaide.

There was some unrest in Australia about Hicks 'shopping' for a convenient citizenship, and I was asked repeatedly if he was going to renounce his Australian passport. 'He's from Australia and proud he's from Australia,' I replied, 'and proud of his family heritage in the UK and he's proud to be a dual national and he just wants both of those citizenships formalised.'

We had to wait and see how the UK government would respond to its defeat in court. Would it appeal to the House of Lords or make him a citizen? As the appeal judges had dismissed the government's case unanimously, we hoped they would do the right thing and formalise his British citizenship. But we had to wait and focus on the things that we could affect.

23

Desperation

At the end of April, I returned home from Australia and took off more or less straight away for Guantanamo. When I got there, Hicks was already showing the effects of solitary confinement in Camp 5, a dark, cold warren of bare cement walls, narrow corridors and tiny cells and interrogation rooms. Camp 5 was high-tech and based on the US maximum-security prisons. Ruddock accepted the American spin on Hicks's isolation as 'single cell occupancy', the politically correct term for isolation.

They had taken everything from him. Guards were removing all of his reading material, from educational books to files on his own case. They took his letters away. His eyes, back and feet were all damaged by the lack of movement and sunlight. He wondered if he had been punished for speaking too candidly to Australian consular staff about his conditions on their previous visits, but really it was hard to tell why any of this was done. Knowing the government's pattern of incompetence, it could just have been that they spent $10 million on a new facility at Guantanamo Bay and needed someone to put in it.

When I visited him while he was kept in Camp 5, he would be transported to Camp Echo to meet me. We spent hours and hours together, talking about the case, talking about life. I felt an obligation just to stay with him as long as I could, to give him human contact, even after we'd run out of things to talk about.

Friends of Hicks, and even the Australian government, were still sending mail through me. The easiest way to ensure Hicks got mail was to have it sent to me in the US, and then for me to carry it down to GTMO, putting it all in a package with a letter and an index, so that when I returned the next trip I could verify the material had been received. I had to create a spreadsheet listing the item, the sender, the date I turned it in, and the number of pages. The mail was always getting lost – I don't know if it was because the government was trying to manipulate people, or if it was just typical incompetence. The system suffered because staff turnover was high.

As the months of 2006 passed, under the claustrophobic, icy effect of Camp 5, Hicks was becoming disengaged and disconnected from everything beyond his daily survival needs. He was demoralised and depressed. I wondered if he had given up. He hinted at contemplating suicide. I later found out he was working on a plan to obtain razor blades. He had stopped communicating with his family, and he had stopped pursuing the distance-learning classes that I had arranged for him. He was always chained when I saw him, and visibly uncomfortable. He was not truly as interested in the legal proceedings as he had been before, even when we still had appeals in the Australian and British courts. I tried to regain his interest in the litigation, but it was a struggle. He'd already won in the Supreme Court and it hadn't made any difference. He just said, hopelessly, 'If we win these other cases, where will it lead?'

Of all the years I was representing Hicks, I say unhesitatingly that 2006 was the worst. Every legal battle we had engaged in we had won, but it meant nothing. The commissions had gone nowhere, the District Court had given us the stay we wanted; even the British courts had ruled in Hicks's favour. And yet, for all these small victories, we had got him nowhere. We were just waiting for the Supreme Court now, but the Supreme Court could not free him. If we won in the Supreme Court, what would the government do? Very possibly just fix whatever the Supreme Court said was wrong and continue on. The Bush administration was against using federal criminal trials or courts-martial, so it was doubtful that a fair trial awaited Hicks. It was Bush's administration that had brought this nonsensical court system into being. And it was only Bush, when it came down to it, who could give Hicks his liberty. Bush had won re-election in 2004. It would be over two and a half years before he left the White House. The way we looked at it, Hicks might well be condemned to another two and a half years inside.

And now, 'inside' had a new meaning. Camp 5 was the realisation of General Miller's description of GTMO as an 'interrogation camp'. The solitary confinement, the lack of sunlight and the decline in Hicks's conditions took him back to what was, in some ways, worse than Camp X-Ray's dog kennels. He was a shell of a person when I first met him, and he was regressing to that state now.

The Australian government was showing some belated sense of responsibility for Hicks, awakened by media and community pressure. A group of seventy-six eminent lawyers, including four former Supreme and Federal Court judges, wrote an open letter to John Howard warning him that terrorism would destroy civilised society if Australia continued to back the detention and military trial of David Hicks. 'Whether or not David Hicks is in fact guilty or innocent is not the issue,' the letter said. 'The illegality lies in the process of indefinite detention and unfair trial by Military Commission.' They argued that the Australian government was complicit with the United States in breaking international law and 'undermining international legal order'. To counter terrorism, the world needed 'renewed and sustained commitment to the rule of law and to fundamental principles of human dignity and respect for human rights'.

'This is the shared heritage of a civilised world,' the lawyers wrote. 'Unless we are vigilant, terrorism may achieve the destruction of these values. We should not give it such a victory.' They said the Military Commission denied the right to 'an independent and impartial trial' and did not 'exclude evidence obtained by coercion, including the use of cruel, inhuman or degrading treatment'.

The letter, written through the Australian branch of the International Commission of Jurists, said Australia must follow the British in condemning the Military Commission, 'a process which expressly has no application to any American citizen . . . The imprisonment at Guantanamo Bay and the unfair trial of David Hicks by Military Commission are an affront to international legal standards, indeed all civilised standards.'

There was no doubt the Australian government was starting

to feel the pressure, which possibly made it start pushing for the unfair trial to get going. In early May, I was finally provided with the White Paper from 2003 that outlined the agreement between Australia and the US DOD on the use of Military Commissions for Australian citizens. The paper explained, as I already knew, that the Appointing Authority was the body that approved the charges and also determined what resources the defence team received, as well as having the power to rule on defence motions. This should have raised a red flag that something was not right, but I had to point it out in my meeting with Australian officials. The paper also laid out that closed sessions could occur in the Military Commission from which the accused could be removed. Australia would consent to this, despite it being in violation of any known trial procedure that would be applied to an American.

A week later, the finalised agreement was reached between the US DOD and Australia, which was signed by Hemingway and the Australian ambassador to the US, Dennis Richardson, laying out terms for any prisoner transfer. For the transfer to occur, any judgement had to be 'final': that is, beyond all appeal. If Hicks wanted to appeal his conviction, he would not be eligible to be transferred back to Australia. The agreement did, however, make him eligible, if transferred, for parole under Australian law.

At the time, I commented in the media about the agreement:

> [It] represents nothing more than another example of Australia surrendering to the US sovereignty over its citizens and application of its laws. The US negotiator was not from some neutral bureaucracy; rather, it was from the US Department of Defense, which has condemned David Hicks and set up a rigged system designed to guarantee his conviction in a Military Commission.

Thus, Australian government officials left the determination of Mr
Hicks's future, if he is returned to Australia after a conviction in
the commissions, to the legal advisor to the Appointing Authority
of the Military Commissions – the same man who says Mr Hicks
should get no credit for the four and one-half years he has served in
Guantanamo, the same person who recommends that Mr Hicks be
charged before the commission, and to whom the chief prosecutor
reports. Thus, the Australian government has compounded the
unfairness of the Military Commissions by permitting the US
to dictate the terms of Mr Hicks's imprisonment even after the
commission process has been completed.

After four and one-half years, any objective observer must
wonder if political self-interest is outweighing the rule of law, and
at what point the Australian government will represent the interest
of its citizens abroad, rather than abdicate that responsibility.

However inadequate, it was a positive to know that if he was sentenced, Hicks could go back to Australia and possibly serve out
some of his time as a parolee in the community. But this would
place him in a position of having to choose either to appeal any
conviction and rot at GTMO, or to waive any appeal and get back
to Australia. How would it really work, and how would it be used
to place pressure on him? It was hard to predict as, with everything
in the Military Commissions, we were in uncharted waters.

For Hicks, these events might as well have been happening on
the moon. The situation in GTMO was getting even worse. In
June, it was announced that two Saudi detainees and one Yemeni
had recently hanged themselves in their cells. Since GTMO had
opened, there had been forty-one suicide attempts by twenty-five

detainees. Admiral Harris showed where his sympathies lay by saying, 'They have no regard for life, neither ours nor their own. I believe this was not an act of desperation, but an act of asymmetrical warfare waged against us.' A government official told the BBC, 'Taking their own lives was not necessary, but it certainly is a good PR move. It does sound like this is part of a strategy – in that they don't value their own lives, and they certainly don't value ours, and they use suicide bombings as a tactic.' This was even too far for the Bush administration, which distanced itself from the comments. A State Department spokesman quickly stated, 'I would just point out in public that we would not say that it was a PR stunt,' and that President Bush 'had serious concerns about what had happened'.

Meanwhile at GTMO, Camp 6, Hicks's next home, was being opened up. Camp 6 was designed to permit shared cells and a large common area for detainees, like the modern military brigs where I had visited clients. The recent suicides were, however, used as justification to keep detainees in 'single cell occupancy' and not permit the use of the common areas.

Upon what information they based this leap, nobody knew. It seemed much more based on inference than fact. How they could have drawn these inferences only shows the type of minds that were running GTMO. For me, it increased my concern about how much longer Hicks could take GTMO, and the seriousness of his hints at suicide.

As each day in June went by without hearing from the Supreme Court about the Hamdan case, expectation built up among all involved in the commissions. I was preparing to testify before a classified congressional hearing on the Military Commissions, with the faint hope that I might be able to convince some in Congress to use courts-martial instead of commissions. With only six days left in June, my house was flooded by a severe summer storm, filling up my basement and up to the first floor. A friend of mine was away attending military school and left his one-bedroom apartment empty, so our family of four moved in until our place was fixed up in January 2007. I spent the next several days removing water and mud from our house, tearing our soaked drywall and scrubbing down the beams to fight the mould. I almost forgot about the Supreme Court.

Finally, the Supreme Court handed down its decision in *Hamdan v. Rumsfeld*. I stopped cleaning and put on my uniform and headed into the office, where there was a sense of celebration. Having been through this in 2004, though, I felt more of a sense of foreboding. We had won in the Supreme Court before, and then nothing changed; the Bush administration just pushed forward and no one got released.

The Supreme Court found that the Military Commission system was unlawful, as it did not comply with the Uniform Code of Military Justice (UCMJ), a law passed by Congress that incorporated the laws of war for commissions, namely the Geneva Conventions. The new system set up by the President violated the Geneva Conventions. At first glance, the decision was a victory. We celebrated in our office as if we'd won a big football game. And then reality sank in: it was only half-time.

The devil was revealed in the detail of the Hamdan decision. The Supreme Court wasn't taking issue with the Military Commissions themselves, but with the way they had been set up in 2002. Bush had two choices now: to use courts-martial, or go back to Congress to get around the UCMJ by having Congress enact a law authorising and constituting new Military Commissions.

For Hicks, the decision did have one silver lining, in a line Justice Anthony Kennedy wrote that indicated a 'duty of allegiance' was required for the crime of aiding the enemy. At least all the effort the Jenner & Block team and I had put into the amicus brief filed with the Supreme Court was not a complete waste of time.

Unfortunately, though, the real bottom line was that after four and a half years in detention, Hicks was back where he started, detained without charge or a trial date. It was Groundhog Day for him. Many thought it was a victory, but in truth it was one giant step backwards.

All the reporting on the Hamdan decision was on what a huge blow it was to the Bush administration. But then, Bush accomplished a PR masterstroke. For years, every time there had been a success or some movement towards providing access to the courts for the detainees, the Bush administration had quickly moved on. This time, President Bush went on the offensive in a televised speech, which we watched in our office. In a move that would do any stage magician proud, Bush effectively said, 'Look over here!' – a classic act of misdirection. While we were thinking about the unlawful commission system that had been running for years, Bush acknowledged that there had been secret CIA prisons for fourteen al-Qaeda kingpins, the so-called 'black' sites around the world, where Khalid Sheikh Mohammed and other 9/11 plotters had been held. Now, the President said, these men, the real terrorists, were being brought to GTMO to be tried by Military Commissions.

Bringing in Khalid Sheikh Mohammed was a beautiful media strategy, I had to admit. Importing actual terrorists to GTMO changed the dynamics. Whatever people thought about Guantanamo

Bay, it now held Khalid Sheikh Mohammed, so it had to be the right thing. This was also distraction from the secret prison issue. The use of secret prisons also spoke loudly on who was really perceived as a terrorist: the CIA had taken who they believed were the real terrorists and had given the leftovers to the DOD.

This was going to revitalise GTMO into the next presidency, and saddle the next presidency with running GTMO. Brilliant! Up to now, GTMO had been a red herring, a diversion, holding hapless small fry like Hicks. But now, it actually did hold the worst of the worst. Now the *real* terrorists were there. If you stood up against GTMO and the Military Commissions now, you were standing up for Khalid Sheikh Mohammed; you were defending this monster.

The move nullified the criticism of GTMO in one blow, and cast into the shadows the nameless hundreds of detainees who had been there for years already. Khalid Sheikh Mohammed was the rallying point for the Bush administration. The President also announced he was going to go to Congress and pass the Military Commission Act, which would in effect enshrine the majority of the original commission system as a piece of law endorsed by Congress, which would just mean more challenges through the federal court system, and, if the past was any lesson, years of delay.

The government hadn't lost with the Supreme Court decision; it had won. It gained an opportunity to bring the real terrorists into GTMO and ram a new Military Commission Act, written by Bush staffers, through Congress. They would have what they wanted: a congressional Act allowing them to try Hicks, the smallest of the small fry, at a time of their choosing. Hicks now looked like he would be in GTMO until the end of the Bush presidency, at least, unless the Australian government, or the British, stood up for justice.

John Howard's position on Military Commissions was exposed and his credibility destroyed by the US Supreme Court's findings that the commission system violated the Geneva Convention. All the legal experts were right: Howard had no legal basis for leaving Hicks in Guantanamo Bay. The German government had just secured the release of its citizen Murat Kurnaz from Guantanamo Bay. Prime Minister Howard had now left one of Australia's citizens in United States custody for four and a half years, when he had not violated an Australian law, for no other reason than personal and political obstinacy. The Supreme Court decision was an opportunity for Howard to stand up for an Australian. It was his chance to say, 'Enough.'

But he wouldn't. Howard's first statement after the Hamdan decision was to say in a media interview, 'I'm quite firm in my statement that I do not want him to come back to Australia without first facing a trial in the United States. I'm not in favour of asking the Americans to let him go without trial, because if he comes back to Australia he can't be tried, because the offences he is alleged to have committed were not crimes under Australian law at the time he committed them, and therefore he would effectively go free without charge in this country.'

So, in the view of his own country's leader, Hicks was already guilty. Of what? Howard didn't know. How should he be tried? Howard didn't know. When could he be released? Howard didn't know. All Howard knew was the position he had already dug himself into. Mistaking stubbornness for strength, he saw it as a political virtue that he would abandon his countryman to years of unlawful detention. Maybe, with an Australian election looming in 2007, he felt he could not switch positions. The Supreme Court said the system was illegal, though, giving him the perfect reason to change tack. Howard had supported Australia's ally for four and a half years, and now it was time to bring his citizen home. He could have been tough by standing up for an Australian abroad, because that was really what the test was about: whether he was tough enough to stand up for Australian citizens.

With this recent Supreme Court ruling, all the work done since I was assigned went up in smoke, and the charges against Hicks disappeared. With a Republican-controlled Congress, Bush was going to get his Act passed in a hurry, but that was at least several months away. It was not long before the Bush administration's drafts of the proposed Military Commission Act were being circulated, and it looked very much like the old system. There went any hope for a fair trial.

Following the celebrations of the Fourth of July, I headed back down to GTMO for a visit. Hicks's time back in solitary confinement was not going well. Since the recent suicides, Hicks had faced a new set of stringent conditions. He could have a pen and paper only on request, toilet paper on request, no books apart from one religious text, a half-inch-thick synthetic mattress, and one thin bedsheet. His cell light and the air-conditioning were switched on twenty-four hours a day, seven days a week. I could sense a sadness and resignation in his voice. The isolation was breaking him down; he had little hope.

The day after I left, Hicks became the first detainee at Guantanamo to receive a fax. The British government, after losing both court cases and stalling as long as they could, sent him a letter indicating that they had approved his application for British citizenship. In the same letter, they informed him: 'But I hereby give you notice of my decision to make in order for the deprivation from you of the same citizenship under section 40 of the British nationality act (as amended) on the grounds of conduciveness to the public good.' The British government based this decision on the information allegedly provided to the British security service on 26 April 2003 in Guantanamo Bay. In essence it was that Hicks attended camps with LET in Pakistan and Afghanistan and met British nationals there: the same British nationals who had been brought home never to be prosecuted, nor to have their British citizenship taken away.

A few hours later, Hicks was handed the order depriving him of his British citizenship. This set in motion the next legal battle in this process, which was going to have to take place before Britain's Special Immigration Appeals Commission. The initial issue the court would have to decide was whether or not the detention and treatment of Hicks at the hands of US forces in Afghanistan, Pakistan and Guantanamo Bay amounted to torture. In effect, a British might be the first judicial body to determine whether or not the US government had been using torture, by looking at the interrogation techniques approved by Rumsfeld. Something the Bush Administration might not be happy with.

It seemed that the British government was placing its friendship with the Australian Prime Minister above its commitment to justice. John Howard would face public embarrassment if the UK treated Hicks like it had treated its other citizens, so the British, being good allies, chose to resist. It was probably too late for Howard, though: the British had embarrassed him enough already. They had always withheld approval from the Military Commissions, and pulled their citizens out when the United States couldn't satisfy their legal requirements. Howard, on the other hand, was trapped by his own early support for the commissions.

But what was truly horrifying about the Australian government's position was that they were not pushed to it by the Americans. It was my impression now that the United States wanted to wash its hands of Hicks, and send him out of GTMO at the first opportunity. It was the Australians, on the other hand, who were insisting that Hicks stay locked away – based on the position that he had not violated any Australian law. It went to Howard's very integrity. He measured his actions by their political weight. Soon he would pay the ultimate political price.

Since the Hamdan decision, we had been waiting for the Bush administration to get Congress to pass its new Military Commission Act (MCA), which it did at the end of September, with Bush signing it into law in October. Mid-term congressional elections were coming up, and few members of the House were willing to risk being seen as 'soft on terrorists' now that KSM was at GTMO, which would be the inevitable accusation if they voted against it.

At first glance, the MCA seemed an improvement, but after a careful review it was easy to see the sleight of hand. The Geneva Conventions had to be complied with, and the Act declared that it did comply. Congress was so confident that it complied with the Geneva Conventions that the Act also prohibited any detainee facing commission from 'invok[ing] the Geneva Conventions as a source of rights'. The commission's proceedings must follow the rules of courts-martial. But it was full of exceptions and loopholes that removed any of the protections in the court-martial system.

Unlike courts-martial, it permitted hearsay evidence, and only allowed hearsay evidence to be excluded if it could be shown to be unreliable or lacking in probative value, thereby placing the burden on the defence to show why the hearsay should not be admitted. This was a 180-degree departure from the court-martial system. While courts-martial had certain rules to admit hearsay evidence, the base rule was that hearsay evidence was inadmissible. By permitting hearsay, this Military Commissions Act allowed the prosecution to use notes taken by an agent during interrogations, something that could not happen in a real military court.

The Act also dismissed the right to a speedy trial, lifted the prohibition on the use of self-incrimination in evidence, and took away the defendant's right to compel and cross-examine witnesses against him. The rubbery definition of an 'enemy combatant' took another twist, defining such a person as someone 'who has engaged in hostilities or who has purposefully and materially supported hostilities . . . who is not a lawful enemy combatant', or a person who had been ruled an enemy combatant by the Combatant Status Review Tribunal. Statements obtained by torture were excluded, but all other statements obtained were admissible if 'the totality of the circumstances' rendered the statement reliable or if it 'would best serve the interests of justice'. Statements obtained through 'interrogation methods amounting to cruel, inhuman or degrading treatment' could not be used, but *only* if they had been obtained after 30 December 2005. And the military judge did not have to adjourn a trial if a key witness was unavailable, ensuring that the government could control whether witnesses could appear or not without jeopardising the trial itself. As in the previous commission system, there was no provision guaranteeing that time spent in custody counted towards a final sentence. And finally, no other court could consider a habeas corpus writ on behalf of an enemy combatant (or even someone waiting for determination by the Combatant Status Review Tribunal). In one ironic provision, the US Congress provides immunity for violations of the US War Crimes Act committed by US citizens in violating the Geneva Convention, in the same law intended to be used to prosecute non-US citizens for violations of the Geneva Conventions.

The Act was a last-ditch face-saving effort for the Military Commissions, and it did its job. While it appeared to reconstitute the commissions in line with the Supreme Court's ruling on Hamdan, in practice it did nothing of the sort. Specifically, for Hicks, the statements he had given, under duress and possibly torture, in 2002 and up to the end of 2005 were still admissible. Hearsay evidence by other detainees or investigators was admissible, even if the detainees had been released and couldn't be found. And he could not raise any action against the fact that it had been almost five years since he had first been detained, without trial.

One of the sobering realities of this legislation was that it had been voted in by sixty-five Senators, including all fifty-two Republicans and the future presidential candidate John McCain, long a champion of Military Commissions. What this meant was there was no hope of repeal or legislative change until at least 2009, when we *might* have a Democrat president.

It was another defeat. This was an object lesson in the exercise of power. The detainees had won every legal battle, but the Military Commissions remained as rigged as ever. What hope did David Hicks have?

24

Fighting Back

The delay in creating the new Military Commissions under the new US legislation gave us time to commence litigation in an Australian court against the Howard government, and to increase the public advocacy within Australia. I was not shy to ask for help. John North, the past president of the Law Council of Australia, had returned to private practice in Sydney and was assisting McLeod, Griffin and me to identify the best legal approach against the Howard government. North had organised a meeting with Sandy Street, an Australian Reserve naval officer and barrister who would provide us with pro bono guidance on how a legal case might be run.

Our meeting with Brett Walker paid off as he offered to take the case. Everyone said, 'You won't get a better lawyer.' We assembled a team with Walker and his junior barrister, Kate Eastman. They began working on a legal strategy for challenging Hicks's detention in GTMO in the Australian Federal Court.

Walker and Eastman knew we would only have one shot at any legal challenge in Australia. It would be novel, as no such action had been run in an Australian court before, but we hoped we could get an Australian court to review the Howard government's action – or inaction – in regard to Hicks. Our first task was to find the evidence that Howard had the ability to get Hicks out of GTMO: effectively, an admission by Howard that he held the keys to the cell. Finnin and I began scouring the old media stories, looking for some statement from Howard or a minister that would provide the evidence we needed.

Initially I hadn't decided to do a media campaign on Hicks's behalf. All I had wanted in 2004, when I first spoke to the media, was to get our complaints on the public record. I might have been a bit naive, but as I came to learn that the commission was a political system and not a justice system, run by politicians not judges, it became clear that one of the main lines of attack had to be in the public arena in Australia. We put together information, gathered articles from the United States, and made sure they got to the Australian media, politicians, legal bodies and the public. I wanted to keep Australians informed of the process. People had to know, so that when we got done over by the commission, they wouldn't be fooled.

I was constantly told that Australians believe in a fair go. If this was true, shouldn't they be asked to question why the Howard government had gone so far down the commission road? Australia was deeply involved in the war in Iraq and the War on Terror, and both were highly charged emotional issues. Anti-war advocates were easy to get onside, but the challenge was getting the mainstream public to understand the unfairness of this process that had trapped an Australian, and to present it as an issue separate from whether they were pro- or anti-war. In 2004, I had travelled twice to Australia. I had been only once during 2005, with the primary purpose of investigating Hicks's background and identifying potential witnesses. In 2006, I made four trips to Australia, three of those in the last four months of the year, with the major goal of raising public awareness of the unfair treatment of an Australian citizen.

During 2006, the public became more willing to look past Hicks being 'over there' and focus on the broader issues of fair treatment for an Australian. Public opinion was swaying strongly. A petition titled 'Bring David Hicks Home' was signed by 50 000 people and sent to Alexander Downer, while a GetUp! campaign called 'Postcards to David' gathered more than 10 000 signatures from John Howard's own electorate of Bennelong. Amnesty International Australia and the Uniting Church were also very active in mobilising opinion.

More Australians were writing to their members of parliament, including Howard, Downer and Ruddock. Downer continued to repeat the same media buzz lines, such as 'There have been serious accusations made against Mr Hicks arising from acts allegedly committed by him whilst overseas,' and 'As a result of the Supreme Court's decision in Hamdan's case, the United States administration needs to decide quickly on an alternative method to try Mr Hicks in relation to these allegations,' and 'The Australian government is of the view that Mr Hicks should be brought to trial on any charges that are laid in relation to the allegations against him as soon as possible in a manner consistent with the Supreme Court's ruling. The Australian government will continue to press for Mr Hicks's case to be dealt with expeditiously and fairly.' It was as if Downer was unable to see that the Supreme Court ruling *had just found* that Hicks was not being tried fairly.

In August 2006, I made another trip to Australia to help drum up support, giving lectures, delivering an update on the Military Commission to a crowd at a public meeting in Adelaide, and appearing on the television program *Enough Rope*, where I was interviewed by Andrew Denton. This was the first time I had the chance to speak for more than a few minutes on Australian media. I did not realise at the time how large Denton's audience was: more than a million viewers. I am glad I didn't know beforehand, or I would have been even more nervous than I was! I also did a number of other television shows during the next several months, all adding to the debate. I made a return trip in November as we were still waiting for the system to get moving.

An increasing number of Australians, I discovered on my visits, wouldn't accept it any more. The Law Institute of Australia wrote an editorial in its newsletter asking for a civilian trial or a court-martial for Hicks. Beside it was a cartoon titled '2036: Counsel for the Late David Hicks Delivers his Final Tribunal Address'. Two elderly military lawyers lean on their canes before a bench of judges covered in cobwebs. In Australia, the Military Commissions had become something to poke fun at.

The shift happened in 2006. I felt it. When I went through customs, officers would say, 'Don't tell anybody I told you, but it's a shame what they are doing to Hicks.' People in the airports or on the streets were no longer coming up and saying, 'I hope Hicks rots in Guantanamo,' or 'Who cares?' They were more engaged, asking questions about the process. 'Is it really true?' 'How is this working?' 'Why is an Australian being treated so differently?' 'What crime has he committed?' The Australian Lawyers Alliance, headed at the time by President Simon Morrison and CEO Eva Scheerlinck, had assisted in organising a four-state tour of my Hicks presentation during my late 2006 visit to Australia.

The tide in Australian public opinion had turned. A Newspoll showed that 67 per cent of Liberal voters (John Howard's own party) wanted Hicks returned, 'even if he comes back a free man'. As I visited the cities, strangers came up to give me letters they had written to Hicks, to help sustain him in solitary confinement. Some had been written by children. They carried one key message: 'Australia hasn't forgotten about you.'

This sentiment went all the way up the line. In Brisbane, police officers approached me to say they supported a fairer outcome for Hicks. The Australian Catholic Bishops' Conference made a statement in Hicks's support. Members of the coalition government, including Barnaby Joyce, Petro Georgiou, Dana Vale, Judi Moylan and Bruce Baird, were raising issues within their party room on Hicks's treatment and calling for his return. Joyce's intervention was important, as he was the first member of Howard's coalition government to publicly call for Hicks's return. He did so after hearing one of my talks. It also provided a funny moment. Unwinding after my talk, I was chatting very loudly with some Brisbane police officers about rugby or something. Rebecca Snyder had to rush up and tap me on the shoulder and whisper, 'Can you keep the noise down? Barnaby Joyce is behind you giving a media conference calling for his government to bring Hicks home!'

And we had Bono in our camp as well! At U2's concert in Brisbane that month, Bono interrupted his rendition of 'Sunday Bloody Sunday' to say, 'We're calling for David Hicks to be brought back to Australia to face fair trial here!'

I'm sure there were some ministers within the Australian government who wanted me to go away quietly and let Hicks be done over in an unfair system, but that wouldn't be seeking justice for an Australian citizen. Occasionally I faced obstacles, such as when my boss, Colonel Sullivan, called to say General Hemingway had contacted him as it had been reported that I was planning to accost the Prime Minister on his morning walk around Canberra. I'm sorry to say I have never met Mr Howard, and had to tell Colonel Sullivan they had the wrong guy.

The Law Council of Australia was still hard at work. It delivered a legal opinion, signed by numerous eminent Australian jurists, to Philip Ruddock which held that Australian officials might be complicit in war crimes *against* David Hicks. The opinion stated that a Military Commission trial would contravene the Australian Criminal Code, and therefore the actions of government ministers, including John Howard, who knowingly counselled or urged 'a trial to take place before any such Military Commission . . . would constitute a war crime under the Australian Criminal Code'. I didn't hold any illusions about the likelihood of such a prosecution, but it gave a fair indication of where Australia's most senior legal minds sat.

Bob Debus, the New South Wales Attorney-General, had taken an interest in the Hicks case when it had started. With the assistance of his staffer, Damian Spruce, Debus was kept abreast of the proceedings and provided me with an opportunity to address all the state attorneys-general as well as the federal Attorney-General, Ruddock, whom I had yet to meet in person, at their annual meeting in November in Fremantle, Western Australia. Unfortunately, Ruddock would not attend my briefing on the Hicks case. I am not sure if it was because of the protestors assembled outside, calling for Hicks to be released, or the tough questions he might be unable to answer from his fellow attorneys-general.

Debus captured the feeling of the attorneys-general and, I suspect, many Australians at the time. 'Neither I, nor any of my colleagues, have any particular sympathy for David Hicks,' Mr Debus said, 'but we have a bedrock commitment to the principles by which he should be dealt with.' Those principles were enshrined in a document that was called the Fremantle Declaration, which was signed by all eight of the attorneys-general. This declaration affirmed a commitment to:

1. the right to a fair trial
2. the principle of habeas corpus
3. the prohibition on indefinite detention without trial
4. the prohibition on torture
5. access to rights under the Geneva Conventions
6. the separation of powers
7. the prohibition on the death penalty.

'These are fundamental norms of the Australian legal system,' the declaration went on, 'and we, as Attorneys-General, are responsible for ensuring that these principles are upheld in our jurisdictions.

'Australia has signed and committed to international treaties and conventions in which these rights are protected: the Geneva Conventions, the International Covenant on Civil and Political

Rights, and the United Nations Convention against Torture and other Cruel, Inhuman or Degrading Treatment or Punishment.

'We reaffirm our commitment to these international agreements and principles.'

One signature, Ruddock's, was missing.

John Howard might have been feeling the pressure mounting, because late in 2006, he said something that not only proved my suspicions correct, but was what we were waiting for. Howard admitted that he could have had David Hicks brought home, but chose not to. As well as being a brazen admission of his own cynicism, this was a legal misstep by Howard, as it gave us an opening to start legal action in Australia. Previously, we had been stopped from doing this in Australia because its government had said it had no control over Hicks while he was in American custody at GTMO. But now Howard was saying he *did* have control, and no matter how bleak the situation, we were always trying something. Two days after we filed our case, the Australian government took a page out of the Bush playbook, and counter-filed to have our case dismissed. If they couldn't win a legal point, they could delay it interminably.

As for Hicks, he ended the year feeling suicidal. He was still locked up in solitary confinement, spending twenty-three hours a day in his cell. Following repeated requests, his lights were dimmed during sleeping hours. He did not want to meet with the new consul, as he did not trust him, but I tried to patch things up by suggesting that the consul come with me on my next visit. Nor did he trust the guards, who, he believed, were reading and photographing his legal material while he was in his cell.

Hicks's back problems were worsening, and when he was told

a physical therapist would come to treat him, the therapist did not turn up.

I wrote to the Australian Department of Foreign Affairs, requesting Hicks's return (of course), but also asking for a table and chair for his cell and his removal from Camp 5 to Camp Delta, where he could at least get some fresh air and sunlight.

His condition was concerning me greatly. He was becoming increasingly institutionalised, and despaired of ever getting out. His mental state was back to when I first met him: confined to immediate issues of daily routine and survival. I could see that this was a result of his hopes having been bounced around from possibility to possibility with all the legal developments going on, on a roller coaster between expectation and depression. Under the influence of solitary confinement, his mind had shrunk into a tiny circle.

For the past two Christmases, he had been allowed a phone call with his family. In December 2006, he was too depressed to handle even that phone call. At times like these, I felt like I had achieved nothing.

As the new year began, Hicks had spent five years in US custody. On 12 January, it would be five years since Guantanamo Bay had been opened as a detention camp. The Department of Defense went on a media blitz, sending out several senior figures to put a positive spin on GTMO's fifth birthday. Among them was Cully Stimson, Deputy Assistant Secretary of Defense for Detainee Affairs, and a reserve Navy lawyer. We couldn't believe it when he put his foot firmly in his mouth, condemning the 120 American law firms who had represented detainees in court hearings. These firms, who had sent as many as 500 attorneys to Guantanamo Bay, included some of the biggest in the country, such as Shearman & Sterling and Wilmer Hale. Stimson said that their corporate clients, who included Microsoft, IBM, Harley Davidson and even Halliburton, should make them choose between representing 'terrorists' and corporations. The American Bar Association repudiated his arguments and even the White House and DOD backed away from him. It was a truly outrageous thing to say, and Stimson resigned within three weeks.

I felt like I was back in 2003, waiting for the commission system to be set up. Under the new Act, the Office of the Convening Authority (CA) for Military Commissions was created, and we were waiting on Rumsfeld's successor as Secretary of Defense, Robert Gates, to select the person to fill this role. The CA role was similar to the old Appointing Authority, approving charges, referring them to the commission, and choosing the panel members. One improvement was that the CA would not rule on defence motions. But by this time, with more delays, I seriously wondered if President Bush even wanted trials. The Military Commissions had been so dysfunctional, it began to look as though the Bush administration just wanted the process to drag out so they could hand it over to the next president, most likely a Democrat in 2009.

The Australian campaign to free Hicks gathered momentum. Terry Hicks was a recognisable, sympathetic face for most Australians, and David McLeod had provided the boost we were hoping for from an Australian solicitor who had credibility with his military background and professional manner. Mick Griffin had lined up a top legal team for our Australian challenge. Things were going well outside of the commissions. I had been invited to speak in Australia in the beginning of 2007 but I was wary of spending time away from the job of preparing the legal challenges that would need to be raised within the new commission system. The advice I had received on the legitimacy of the Military Commissions Act and offences created under it, from people far smarter than I am, gave me confidence that we would eventually win on the issue that the charges were invalid, if and when charges were ever brought. The real problem was how long that would take and whether Hicks could survive through a trial and appeal process.

The pressure upon the Howard government could not be ignored. A top Australian military lawyer, Navy Captain Paul Willee, said the commissions breached 'every single precept of natural law and justice in the criminal context'. Brigadier Lyn McDade, the Director of Military Prosecutions, said the treatment of Hicks was 'abominable', and Howard's predecessor as a conservative prime minister, Malcolm Fraser, said Hicks had been 'totally deserted by the Australian government'. Even the Australian Federal Police Commissioner, Mick Keelty, expressed his displeasure with the delay in bringing David to trial.

In order to try to defend the government's actions, Ruddock made the unusual move of writing an opinion piece in *The Age*, and even there he demonstrated his lack of knowledge of the facts when he tried to distinguish between Hicks, Mamdouh Habib and the British detainees. He wrote that Habib and the British detainees had not 'been designated as eligible for trial'; two of the British were designated with Hicks back in July 2003 and Habib was designated in July 2004. Ruddock continued to say the original charges laid against Hicks were valid offences, even though they had been nullified, and made the empty promise that he would ensure that any process was as fair as possible. He also said a detainee could not be released until he had been tried; did he not know that 300 inmates had already been released from GTMO without trial? Clearly, Ruddock's credibility in this area was shot. When asked in an interview which US law Hicks broke, Ruddock laboured:

> Well, the point that I make is that I'm not an expert in the United States law. I'm not, I think, required to, in relation to the United States, to look at the framework of law and determine for myself on the basis of the allegations made, and the truth or otherwise of the evidence that might be deduced, as to whether he be guilty or otherwise. I have asked the question of the Attorney-General of the United States, whether he has formed a view that there is sufficient evidence to warrant David Hicks being put on his trial. And he assures me that that is his considered view. I asked. That's the view I was given.

It can be depressing when a politician speaks honestly! You would hope that the Attorney-General, with a whole department at his disposal, could have worked out in five years whether Hicks had potentially violated any US law. Lex Lasry responded to Ruddock in his own opinion piece, stating, '[T]he credibility of the Australian government is drained by the fact that it apparently never considered that the original Military Commission process might have been unfair.'

The opposition Labor Party's legal affairs spokesman, Kelvin Thomson, was advocating for a trial for Hicks either in the US court system or in Australia or, if not, then his release. Labor had raised the concern that Hicks might not get credit for the time he'd already served. While the Australian government and Ruddock always claimed to have raised this with the US, they never seemed to make any headway.

To relieve some of the growing pressure on the Howard government, the chief prosecutor, Colonel Morris Davis, waded in, comparing Hicks's actions with the terrorists who bombed Bali, London and Madrid, and those who held schoolchildren in a siege at Beslan, Russia. Davis attacked me as well, claiming I was telling half-truths in the media in describing Hicks as naive and an adventurer. Davis could not help himself from talking to the media, and each time it helped us. Ironically, less than two months later, he would accuse me of violating the Uniform Code of Military Justice for speaking to the media.

Meanwhile, the commission was again grinding into gear, with the announcement that Susan Crawford was willing to serve as the Convening Authority (though she had not yet been appointed) and the issue of a new rules manual for commission proceedings. In the CDC office, we knew of Crawford as a judge on the US Court of Appeals of the Armed Forces with a reputation for supporting the government. Her career had been blessed with the patronage of Vice-President Cheney and a husband who was a Republican Party campaigner. She had been an attorney for just a few years at a local prosecutor office in Maryland before she secured a position in the General Counsel's office in the Army and quickly became the General Counsel for the Army, rising to be the Inspector General for the Department of Defense under Cheney. After becoming president, George Bush appointed her to the Court of Appeals of the Armed Forces. This was a great achievement for a person who had never served in the military and had only a few years criminal law experience right out of law school.

I used to be naive. I thought anyone who sat on a Court of Appeals had to be a highly qualified, experienced person. If you had told me that such appointments were based not on competence but on connections, I'd have called you a cynic. And yet here was a perfect example of just that: a judge in criminal courts who had minimal criminal law experience and no military court experience. My disillusionment was just about complete. This was why our country was in the state it was in. Nepotism ruled. Someone who had got through on Republican connections was now in charge of David Hicks's fate. That had always been the case, but now I saw it happening all over again, and it cemented how I was feeling.

In our office, Sullivan organised training with civilian lawyers and staff of the Federal Defender's Office, and had us go through the new manual word by word. Still we were waiting for the Military Commission regulations to be written. I sat back and thought, how did it take them five years to get to this point? Who are these bozos creating and running the commissions? This is the same DOD that is making life-and-death decisions for our service members in war?

For the first time in more than a month, I headed down to Cuba to see Hicks. His state of mind before Christmas had been the worst I'd seen, so it was important to provide him with some company. Dratel, McLeod and Griffin were coming with me, and I was keen to hear their impressions, as they had not seen Hicks as regularly as I had.

Before we left, we met with the prosecution to get a sense of whether any pre-trial agreement was possible. Davis was present, with some Department of Justice attorneys I had never met. Davis was completely unreasonable, spouting how bad Hicks was, and couldn't concede that there was any legal problem with the vague 'material for terrorism' charge, which we expected to be the main charge to be used against everyone in GTMO. Davis still believed an attempted murder charge against Hicks was valid as well. As far as a deal went, we were back at the beginning. A twenty-year sentence was the starting point, and Hicks would not receive credit for the time he had already spent in detention. It seemed to me that the main reason no one wanted to provide credit for time served was that to do so would undercut the Bush administration's view that they could hold everyone in GTMO as an enemy combatant until the War on Terror was over, at which point the clock would start running on their sentences (if they were ever sentenced). It was clear after our meeting that any pre-trial negotiations would have no chance while Davis was leading the prosecution office. He appeared to be a true believer in the corrupt system and had no connection with reality.

Bearing this unhappy news, we flew down to see Hicks. As I had feared, Dratel, McLeod and Griffin noticed an enormous deterioration in the past year. McLeod said, 'He shows all the signs of someone who has been kept in isolation for a very long time.' Hicks had been in isolation for some ten months. He was now in Camp 6, the newest structure – they were always spending more money on ways to keep the detainees locked up – which had been held out as an improvement on Camp 5, but Hicks's cement cell still only had the frosted window, and he was only allowed outside for approximately two hours a day, to go to the recreation area and occasionally shower.

The main building was an echoing cold cavern patrolled by guards who would wake any detainee caught sleeping by slamming their metal door. The food was appalling, and once cooked it was left in front of cooling ducts, making it inedible. Hicks developed chronic stomach pains and feared he was being poisoned.

Someone in the camp thought it would be a good idea to display photos of Saddam Hussein's execution between the cells and in the recreation area where every detainee had to walk.

The only thing we could do to help Hicks get through the days in isolation was bring more mail and check on the status of the mail I had brought on my last trip. We turned in a new batch of more than fifty letters, many from supporters Hicks had never met.

The isolation and removal of his reading material seemed designed to break him before his trial, applied in the same way as before his first hearing, two years earlier. It was shameful to see this happening. Our country had led the world in condemning solitary confinement in wars after it was used on American servicemen during the Vietnam War. Some of our top military leaders had spent years campaigning for the Geneva Conventions to be obeyed, so that what the North Vietnamese had done would not happen again. And here we were, doing it ourselves. It was an insult to see the Bush administration and the US military following the footsteps of the North Vietnamese.

Hicks's conditions seemed to go unchallenged by the Australian government. Ruddock had said, without the benefit of ever meeting Hicks or going to Guantanamo Bay, that Hicks was not in isolation at all, but in 'non-shared accommodation'! Ruddock also said Hicks was allowed out of his cell to mix with other detainees for reading and recreation. I don't know what his source was, but it was clearly one he was accepting without question. Downer also tried to allay concerns about Hicks's mental health, saying he had been checked by professionals. There was *never* any actual mental health evaluation by an independent mental health professional. The last thing the US government wanted was independent medical professionals evaluating the detainees. When pressed by the media on what really took place, Downer's office had to admit that Hicks's so-called mental health visitor 'is not a doctor . . . his observations are purely those of a layman and are only based on a few minutes'. But 'the quick impression' was that Hicks was 'physically healthy and mentally alert'. These walk-by reports were blindly accepted for years by Howard, Downer and Ruddock, who, having swallowed what the DOD had told them for so long, could not now start making any independent decisions. McLeod, who had actually seen Hicks, was quick to point out that such an evaluation 'reflect[ed] Mr Downer's callous indifference to David Hicks'.

It was hard to leave him, as we were his only respite from the isolation, but so much had to be done. McLeod and Griffin were returning to Australia, Dratel to New York, and I was going to DC to start preparing the numerous motions that Snyder and Finnin were working on so we could be prepared to file them when the commission started.

25

Charged Again

While we were in GTMO, the heads of several Australian law schools publicly criticised the treatment of Hicks and the Military Commissions' departure from the rule of law. The debate had moved beyond Hicks to the broader systemic issue of what the Howard government would do for an Australian citizen and how the government viewed the worth of an Australian citizen.

For the sake of his public image, Howard needed Hicks charged, and soon. On 23 January 2007, it was reported in the Australian news that he had asked the Bush administration for Hicks to be charged by mid-February. This was most likely prompted by a Newspoll that showed 56 per cent of Australians opposed the way their own government had treated Hicks. Only 27 per cent of respondents supported Howard's approach. The new opposition leader, Kevin Rudd, summed up his belief as to why opinions were shifting: 'I'm not a defender of what Mr Hicks has done or hasn't done. I am a defender of his legal rights and his human rights and they have not been honoured.' The public had gone beyond the tabloid accusations to the larger issue, which might have an impact on all Australians: would the government stand up for them or a loved one if they were being treated unfairly abroad?

Could Howard get something done if he was strong enough? Or did he know the charges were on their way, and that was why he 'demanded' them, so that he could appear to be strong? Either way, right on cue, the chief prosecutor brought two new charges against Hicks: 'providing material support for terrorism' and 'attempted murder in violation of the law of war'. They had given up flogging the dead horse of conspiracy and aiding the enemy charges.

The two charges carried a maximum sentence of life imprisonment, though Hicks had not hurt one person. Unbeknown to the defence team, prosecutors had sworn out the charges and served them on Hicks the day after we left GTMO. Was this intentional, another childish game, or just more incompetence?

In any case, these were the charges we had anticipated and were prepared to attack. The charges regurgitated the claims made in 2004 that Hicks had attended terrorist training camps and met Osama bin Laden. The prosecution still used what they knew to be false allegations, that Hicks translated manuals for al-Qaeda (he didn't know 100 words of Arabic) and conducted surveillance on the US and British embassies in Afghanistan (these embassies had been abandoned since 1989).

We were now awaiting the decision by the Convening Authority on whether to refer the prosecutor's charges to a Military Commission for trial. We thought that if we could expose the

foolishness of the attempted murder charge with sufficient pub-
licity, there was a chance it might not be referred. Such a tactic
would not be easily accomplished. While Hemingway had been the
legal advisor who had recommended the attempted murder charge
in 2004, I was unsure if, at that time, he had known that there
was no evidence that Hicks had actually shot at anyone. We had to
make sure, publicly, that this fact did not escape him. Additionally,
Hemingway was one of the people in contact with the Australian
embassy in Washington DC. While he had led the embassy astray
on issues in the past, it was possible that the staff were talking to
him about the charges and might apply some pressure.

Davis, as ever, came to our aid. Before he was chief prosecutor,
the office would only make organised, scheduled media appearances to outline specific procedures. Once Davis took over, he could
not help himself. Put a microphone in front of him and it seemed
he would say anything. We armed reporters, prompting them to
call Davis and ask him if he had any evidence that Hicks shot at
anyone. It did not take a day for Davis to step in it, admitting there
was no evidence that Hicks shot at anyone in Afghanistan. He tried
to justify the charge by saying Hicks had 'perfected his skills in killing' but did not have an opportunity to use them. Any first-year
law student could tell you that this is not a valid basis to charge
someone with attempted murder.

The Australian Prime Minister wasted no time in taking credit
for the charges: 'I'm glad that the charges are being laid and that the
deadline I set has been met . . . They are very serious charges and
that is why they should be dealt with as soon as possible.'

Yet Howard could not or would not admit the truth when con-
fronted about the complete lack of evidence that Hicks had shot

at anyone. Following Davis's comments, a reporter asked Howard: 'But the charge of attempted murder, when it's been acknowledged by the prosecution that he didn't fire a gun, isn't that extraordinary?'

'Look,' Howard said, 'you and I can't try it, we can only observe they are serious charges, and that is why it should come on and I don't intend to get into a debate about the substance of the allegations.'

There was no chance the Convening Authority would drop the charge of material support for terrorism, as that would do away with any case. Susan Crawford was not selected to stop cases or throw a wrench into Dick Cheney's creation. We had to take the offensive, promoting in the media the retrospective nature of the material support for terrorism charge, which was created in October 2006, but was being applied to conduct between 2000 and 2001 in Afghanistan. In Australia, this legal concept was referred to as retrospective legislation. The Howard government had consistently stated that creating retrospective legislation would not be an acceptable option for creating a crime to try Hicks in Australia. Yet it was apparently an acceptable option for the United States to try him in GTMO. Asked how he could apply such a double standard, Howard said, 'I don't accept the analogy,' without saying why or how.

The hypocrisy of Howard's position on retrospective legislation was profound. No less forceful was Ruddock, who repeated that he had 'been assured that there were existing laws and this is a mere codification'. Davis tried to come to Howard and Ruddock's rescue, saying material support was 'an offence that Congress recognised more than a decade ago', asserting, '[T]he difference here is the forum in which that offence can be prosecuted.'

That this was patent nonsense did not have to be stated by

me. It had been said by John Bellinger, the legal advisor to the US Department of State, in September 2006, when he said that the US's 'material support' charges did not apply outside of the US so that no such crimes 'were on our books at the time in September 11, 2001' and so could not be applied to Guantanamo detainees.

There were two statutes in the US criminal code with the title 'providing material support': 18 USC 2339A, 'providing material support to terrorists', and 8 USC 2339B, 'providing material support to a designated terrorist organisation'. The Military Commissions Act, under which Hicks was charged, modified these laws in critical ways in its attempt to apply the law retroactively. Statute 2339A prohibited support 'in preparation of or carrying out a violation of another specified US criminal statute'. What followed was a long list of US offences that the support must further. The MCA Act removed this list of US federal offences and replaced it with the non-existent, vague and retroactive offence of 'terrorism'.

Statute 2339B prohibited support to an organisation designated 'terrorist' by the US Secretary of State. The MCA Act removed this requirement. A 'terrorist' organisation could be whatever the Military Commission said it was. Further, in 2004, statute 2339B had been modified to remove the requirement that the person committing the offence be 'within the United States or subject to the jurisdiction of the United States'. The Military Commission prosecutors were now attempting to apply this 2004 amendment retroactively to events in 2001 and even before.

There was also a significant difference in the maximum punishment authorised under the Military Commissions Act compared with these US federal offences: life imprisonment versus ten to fifteen years. In one way this exposed another screw-up by the US government in not making any of our 'material support' laws that were aimed at terrorist-type activity apply outside of the US, as Congress could have. But this failure did not justify making up crimes after the fact.

With the release of the new charges, the media became manic. Australian polls were showing that the issue was going against Howard in an election year. There is no doubt that the television campaign organised by GetUp!, which began in February 2007, was contributing. Funded from public donations, the ad showed Terry Hicks and a photo of David as an eight-year-old.

> This is my son, David. He's been missing for five years – held in Guantanamo Bay. Without trial. He was born in Australia, grew up in Australia, is an Australian citizen. I love my son, but I've always said if he's done wrong he should have to face the consequences. I only ever wanted David to be given a fair trial, but I'm sure that the Guantanamo trials have been created by politicians to do one thing: guarantee convictions. Please, let's bring David home. Thank you – I'm Terry Hicks.

This was not all that GetUp! was doing. The group had mobile billboards travelling from South Australia to Canberra for the opening of parliament, as well as large stationary billboards. Brett Solomon, the director of GetUp!, said, 'This has become a political football, not a question of justice, and we want to bring his humanity back to the story.' He said the campaign for David, targeting John Howard specifically, was 'just beginning'. Anyone visiting the heart of Melbourne's CBD would have seen a giant banner hanging from St Paul's Cathedral reading 'Justice for David Hicks'. As the

Anglican Archbishop of Melbourne, Philip Freier, had put it at the time, 'When some of those liberties that we have in Western society are under threat from terrorism, we [shouldn't also] erode them from the inside.'

We got a strong sense that we had them on the ropes when the US embassy in Australia and the US State Department came to the aid of Howard and the Department of Defense's public relations machines. The State Department arranged a special briefing for the Australian media regarding the commissions, where they tried to put a positive spin on the obvious problems in the charges and claimed that Hicks was not being charged under retrospective legislation. A week later, the US ambassador to Australia, Robert McCallum, devoted an entire speech at the National Press Club to defending the US detention regime at GTMO and justifying the broken Military Commission process. The ambassador was so desperate to help, he even penned an editorial on the US policy of detainee affairs.

This did little to stem the tide in Australia or convince anyone that Hicks would receive a fair trial. In fact, it only fanned the fire, drawing more attention to the case and the flaws in the process. Each time a government official spoke, we were provided with an opportunity to respond. Our advantage was that we had truth on our side, and the audience was now seeing that. In his party room, Howard was hearing, from backbenchers such as Don Randall and Michael Johnson, that the Hicks issue was having a serious negative impact in conservative electorates.

Not to be left out, Davis jumped right in. 'One of the main criticisms,' he said, 'seems to be a false notion that the material support for the terrorism charge is something new we made up after the fact.' He tried vainly to tell anyone who would listen that it was not a new crime. This only gave others the chance to point out his shaky grasp of his own country's criminal code. Frustrated, he began taking shots at me in the media. 'Perhaps less focus on PR and more on case preparation will enable them to get Mr Hicks his day in court sooner,' Davis said. 'We look forward to getting past the hyperbole and alarmist speculation and letting the public see the facts and observe the process and then draw their own conclusions.' We were looking forward to it, too.

26

Under Personal Attack

Before the anticipated commission hearing, I had to squeeze in another trip to Australia for the Australian Federal Court hearing and to keep Hicks's case in the public's thoughts. I didn't stop while I was there: talking with lawyers and politicians, having interviews with journalists, and addressing conferences and public rallies. I travelled down to Adelaide to update Terry, Bev and Steph, and then quickly came back to Sydney for the Federal Court hearing.

My visit to attend the Australian Federal Court hearing coincided with that of Vice-President Cheney. His tour was mired in anti-war protests and the 'Bring Hicks Home' campaign. While it has been reported that Howard and Cheney worked out Hicks's plea deal on this visit, I do not believe this was true, to a point. The most Howard could have done was emphasise that he wanted the situation over and that Hicks should be back in Australia as soon as possible. If this is what happened, then all the efforts of so many were paying off. Could this have provided the motivation to get the Military Commission system to come to the negotiation table with a reasonable deal? It may have.

While in Australia, I began to receive a new wave of disturbing messages: did I know about certain inquiries being made of me? A colleague contacted me to tell me he thought someone might be trying to go after me by alleging I'd done something wrong at my speaking engagements in Australia.

Since I had first spoken out and experienced the first investigation into my media statements, I knew the rules of what I could and couldn't say, and always obeyed them, but this would not stop someone from looking into what I was doing. I made sure I always got the proper permissions to travel and speak. I filed the correct travel claims and always used the correct disclaimer. Not that the disclaimer was really needed; as if anyone might think I was an official spokesperson for the US DOD or commissions! But it did give me the opportunity to follow the Marine rule in public speaking, which was to start with a joke – I'd commence by telling my audience I was not speaking on behalf of Secretary Rumsfeld or President Bush. It usually got a good laugh. Still, I was concerned to be told that someone was looking into my affairs without my knowledge.

The Australian hearing lasted almost three days, with Walker and the Solicitor-General of Australia sparring with each other as Justice Tamberlin challenged both sides on their legal positions. The Judge invited me to sit at the counsel table even though I was not a licenced lawyer within Australia, which was quite an honour. We would not wait long for the court's decision. While I was in

Australia, the Military Commission 4.0 process was moving ahead. I didn't know it, but the day I flew across the Pacific, Hemingway recommended dropping the attempted murder charge against Hicks (even though in 2004 he had recommended going forward with basically the same charge).

Also on that day, the Defence Department announced the transfer of seven more detainees from Guantanamo Bay to Saudi Arabia. This meant 385 had been released in six years, with 390 still incarcerated. The continual release of detainees only reinforced that the Military Commission system was there for show and not to try everyone who violated the laws of war in Afghanistan. Only an unlucky few were singled out for trial, and only if their countries were not fighting for their release.

On the morning of 2 March 2007, Snyder rang me and advised that a Military Commission hearing had been convened for Hicks and only the material support charge was being sent to a commission. I had to somehow keep a handle on things while completing my commitments in Australia. I was skimming through the paragraphs of allegations rehashed from the 2004 charges, as I tried to get my uniform ready for a breakfast function organised by the Victoria Law Foundation at the State Library, where more than 200 legal practitioners, judges, politicians and the State Attorney-General, Rob Hulls, would be in attendance. With the release of the charges, I could directly address the specific issues in the Hicks case for an audience who could easily identify the problems in the process and the retrospective crimes.

It was also worth mentioning the dropping of the attempted murder charge, which only demonstrated its absurdity in the first place. One important fact was clear: all the old charges against

Hicks were gone. Australia had left him in GTMO for the past five years based on those original charges. And for five years, there had been no valid charges against him. Not one.

The dropping of the attempted murder charge, while absolutely the correct decision, did surprise me a little. Davis had certainly helped us by admitting publicly that Hicks had never shot at anyone, thus maximising the public awareness of the ridiculousness of the charge, but Hemingway had still recommended the charge in 2004. What motivated them to back down now? I didn't know if it was the lack of evidence (which had never stopped them before), public exposure or pressure from the Australian government. Whatever the reason, Davis must have been humiliated. Here was a charge he had recommended, one that the prosecution office had pushed since 2004. Since the beginning of February, he had been out pushing it in the international media. Now, on the international public stage, his credibility as a prosecutor was not even being supported by the Convening Authority. In a way I felt sorry for him.

In the interviews I was doing, the Australian media was raising the possibility of a plea deal. I never raised it myself. I didn't know if it was being mentioned behind the scenes by Davis, or if it was just something the media liked to ask about. I tried not to engage in such discussions – not that I was opposed to a plea deal, but the prosecution had been completely unreasonable and Hicks had wanted to fight when it had come up before. When I met with members of the federal government or people who might have connections, it seemed as if everyone thought Hicks was being offered a deal to come back to Australia that I was completely unaware of. I wondered if there was a disconnect between what the DOD was telling Australian officials and the truth. Imagine that. I did make one comment in the media that turned out to be fortuitous: 'You think they're going to offer him the *Godfather* deal, the deal he can't refuse?'

I had no idea how close I was to the mark.

On 3 March, I was scheduled to speak at the NSW public defenders' conference. I awoke, and reached out into the hotel corridor to grab the daily paper. I knew there were some Hicks stories coming, potentially raising the issue of a plea. Sure enough, on the cover of *The Age* was an article titled 'US Ready to Cut Deal on Hicks'. This was news to me. The basis of the story was Davis saying he would support a ten- to twenty-year deal, with Hicks serving five years in Australia. This was slightly less time than Davis had mentioned at our meeting in January. I wasn't sure what I thought of him communicating a new offer through the media.

What I didn't expect, as I flipped through another paper, was an article titled 'Mori Charges Could Be Laid after Trial'. Davis was accusing me of violating the Uniform Code of Military Justice for 'politicking' on my client's behalf. I had apparently violated article 88 of the code, which prohibits 'contemptuous' language against the President.

My initial reaction was disbelief. Did this guy really say that, or was a reporter reading too much into it? I contacted the reporter, who confirmed that it was indeed what Davis had said.

I had to read the article a few times. Whenever Davis spoke to the media it helped us, but I was shocked to think a military officer would ever sink so low as to make allegations against a fellow officer in the media. A man with honour would tell me directly, or address it with my superior officer.

My Australian mobile phone began ringing and emails flooded

my inbox. I thought Davis must have really been losing it. When prosecutors have a bad case, they often attack the defence counsel. I was very concerned because criminal allegations against a lawyer can create a conflict of interest between the lawyer and his client. This is especially so when that criminal allegation involves how that lawyer is representing the client, because then the question arises as to whether the lawyer is acting to save his own skin or to further the interests of his client. This was a serious issue that I needed to discuss with Colonel Sullivan, Dratel and Snyder. If this was a conflict of interest that couldn't be dealt with, I might have to cease representing Hicks. Until the conflict issue was resolved, I would have to watch what I said in the media.

I pondered what would motivate Davis to attack me. His allegations were reminiscent of the outlandishness of Cully Stimson's comments a few months earlier, advocating for businesses to boycott law firms that provided legal representation to detainees at GTMO. I wondered if Davis's attack would be his undoing. On a personal level, I had always got along with him, and I wondered if he'd just put his foot in his mouth again. But I would find out later that he would continue to push this issue behind my back.

In the media, he kept pressing, saying, 'Most of the defence counsel say the commissions are unfair and criticise the process as they are entitled to do, [but Major Mori] goes further than any defence counsel I've ever known.' He said it was improper for me to have alleged that the President, the Secretary of Defense and Congress 'intentionally created a rigged system that guarantees convictions in order to cover up wrongdoing' and that 'everyone involved is potentially guilty of war crimes greater than the charge against David Hicks'.

He backed down, publicly, from his statement that he wanted me charged, but privately he was forwarding his complaints to the Convening Authority's office. I suspect at this time they also found their way to the SJA and to the Commandant of the Marine Corps' office, as this would not be the last I would hear of these allegations of misconduct.

In Davis's email he wrote: 'I believe MAJ Mori's words and actions exceed what the law allows. Specifically, Article 88 of the UCMJ prohibits using contemptuous language against certain civilian officials . . .' followed by examples of my words that he thought violated the law:

'It was a political stunt. The Administration clearly didn't know anything about military law or the laws of war. I think they were clueless that there was a U.C.M.J. and a Manual for Courts-Martial! The fundamental problem is that the rules were constructed by people with a vested interest in convictions.' ·

'The system has to be written by the Secretary of Defense for the United States, which is another serious problem, that all the power sits in the Secretary of Defense's hands, and they need, the Secretary of Defense needs, a system that will guarantee convictions to justify what they've done to David [Hicks].'

'The reality is David Hicks is being left to be done over in another unfair system that is not good enough for anyone else so politicians don't have to admit they made mistakes.'

Davis went on: 'MAJ Mori's campaign is having a direct impact on the elected government of one of our closest allies in an election year and while they are supporting us in a war. An article in today's *Sydney Morning Herald* notes that Prime Minister Howard is trailing in the polls and that David Hicks is a factor.'

While there was no substance in Davis's allegations (except that Howard was trailing in the polls), once they were made 'official' by being sent to my chain of command within the commission, there was at least an appearance of a conflict of interest in my representation of Hicks, one that could not be waived without my speaking to him.

Dratel and Snyder would handle the issue by filing a prosecutorial misconduct motion against Davis, the only motion filed for the initial court session of the commission.

It was good to be back in the office as I had been travelling for twenty-four days out of the past two months, and we had a lot of work to do. Under the new rules, Hicks would be arraigned within thirty days of the referral of the charges. I could not let Davis's campaign against me throw me off.

At the same time, a report written by Australian legal experts, organised by Peter Vickery, was completed, declaring that the material support for terrorism charge was invalid. 'This is a recently invented and new war crime created with the passing of the *Military Commissions Act of 2006* on 17 October 2006,' it concluded. The next day, the Law Council of Australia sent the report to the Howard government and released it publicly. The president of the Law Council of Australia, Tim Bugg, commented, 'US authorities have, after five years of military detention, essentially conceded that Mr Hicks's alleged activities in Afghanistan in 2001 were not illegal at the time.'

The noose tightened around the Australian government's neck on 8 March, when the Federal Court of Australia ruled in our favour, dismissing the Howard government's strike-out motion of Hicks's case. We had not won the case outright, but it meant the Australian government would have to defend itself against acquiescence or, at worst, active participation in Hicks's treatment. This established that an Australian court could hear evidence and rule whether Hicks's detention was unlawful and, possibly more threatening to the United States, rule on whether the new Military Commission Act violated international law. Justice Tamberlin laid down a tight time line, setting the hearing for 24 April.

27

The *Godfather* Deal

Everything in the military is hurry-up-and-wait. The Military Commission had been no exception, with the White House rushing out the PMO in November 2001 and sitting around for almost two and a half years before anyone was charged, which set the tone for the next six years. Hicks's commission had been on the shelf for more than two years, and now the Military Commission was itself rushing. In doing so, it skipped over several requirements of its own rules. As if in haste to get the whole thing over with, Colonel Ralph Kohlmann, a Marine lawyer, one of the old presiding officers converted by the new Military Commission Act into 'military judges', detailed himself to preside over Hicks's trial and summoned us for the initial court session at GTMO on 25 March.

I wanted to try to feel out if there had been any movement on a deal. With the British and Australian court actions as well as the push within Australia for Hicks's return, this might be our best position to negotiate for some time. I did not want an opportunity to pass. This had been consistent with my approach all along. If there was a way out that minimised the risk for Hicks, we needed to find out what it was and consider it. With him deteriorating in solitary confinement, it was clear to me that he needed to get out as soon as possible.

Knowing how out of touch with reality Davis was, I felt it would be more effective to go around the prosecutor's office and approach the Convening Authority's office directly. I called the CA's office and Hemingway immediately agreed to my request for a meeting at Crystal City. I went alone; I wanted the freedom for open and frank negotiations.

After years of hearing offers of ten to twenty years, I was not prepared for what would happen at the meeting. Hemingway was one of those officers you just liked. He had been retired for a while, and had a grandfatherly demeanour. As we discussed potential options, he made the overture that Hicks could go home within ninety days.

What? I tried to keep my poker face. But in a flash, we'd gone from me expecting no chance of a deal to thinking, *This might really happen.*

We discussed the main points, such as when Hicks could leave GTMO and how much time he would have to serve once he returned to Australia. Hemingway threw around the potential of less than a year. I could hardly believe it. After all these years, they just wanted desperately to be rid of Hicks. Was it the political pressure, or the dawning reality that his case was not going to live up to the hype of the 'worst of the worst'? I did not know, and in one way, I did not care. I just wanted to get Hicks out.

As I left Hemingway's office, to await a draft of a plea deal, I hoped no one saw my Cheshire-cat grin. We had, after all, been offered the *Godfather* deal, the one we could not refuse. I was still in shock. I wanted to do something – say yes before they realised what they'd done – but could not commit to any deal without input from Dratel, McLeod, Griffin and Snyder, and then Hicks himself, not that he had a choice.

We were meant to be at Guantanamo Bay three days later. I wanted to have the key terms worked out with Hemingway. It was settled that Hicks could go back to Australia within sixty days of his court sentencing, and all confinement more than nine months would be suspended, which meant he would have about seven months behind bars when he was transferred back to Australia. I wanted to get him immediately back to Camp Echo, with an improvement in his conditions. The whole team was astonished by the terms. All the previous conversations had been about years, and now we were talking about months and days.

But we had to restrain our excitement – there would be a price to pay. He would have to plead guilty to the offence of material support to terrorism, and he would have to include a statement he had not been abused. Yet he would only be required to give an 'Alford' plea, which, under US law, is a guilty plea where the defendant does not admit that he committed the charged offence, but accepts that he will be convicted. In the Hicks case, the use of an Alford plea meant that Hicks would only be admitting that there was evidence on which he would be convicted of the made-up crime of 'material support' in the unfair Military Commission process, not that he actually committed a legitimate crime. The option of pleading guilty had to be weighed against the state he had been reduced to. I was deeply worried that Hicks would not survive solitary confinement for the length of time it might take to fight the commission, and the possible years of appeals that might follow. Add up a first appeal within the Military Commissions system, then to the DC appeals court and finally the US Supreme Court, and he could be looking at another two years at least, even if he 'won'. Personally, I was confident that somewhere along the appeals process we would successfully challenge the 'material support' charge, outside of the Military Commission system. But how long would it take?

Even with the confidence that we would win if we kept challenging the validity of this farcical charge and system, why should Hicks be asked to sacrifice himself for the cause? There was no obligation upon him to fight the Bush administration. The cause should never become bigger than the client.

Our last hope of challenging the 'material support' charge in a federal court before any Military Commission occurred ended on 23 March, when the District Court judge ruled against our motion to stop the commission. Mark Goldman had been working hard, submitting the injunction and replying to Department of Justice responses. The judge ruled that under the new Military Commissions Act, federal courts lacked the jurisdiction to consider challenges against a Military Commission. It meant that any hope of getting to a US federal court was years in the future. This closed the final door on a civilian court challenge.

I came to the conclusion that the only way out for Hicks was to plead. He wasn't going to survive two more years. He needed out. I'll admit I was hoping this might all really be coming to an end.

It might have been selfish of me to think this way, but after almost four years on one case in such an incompetent system, I had grown tired of being a pawn in a political game. The reality was that the deal they were offering Hicks was the best offer we had ever heard, and his survival depended on it.

On 24 March, prosecutors, defence lawyers, the expert witnesses, support staff and media were all bundled in together for the flight to GTMO. The media was abuzz, asking if a deal was going to happen. We had not been talking to anyone, so I was not sure if it was a leak or they were just guessing. Beyond Griffin and McLeod, nobody else in our team knew of what had been discussed. We didn't even know if the Convening Authority would accept it. So we had to work and prepare as if the trial were going ahead.

Terry and David's sister Steph flew down separately, with an Australian consular delegation and Lex Lasry, the Law Council observer. Terry and Steph hadn't seen Hicks for more than two years, so they were full of nerves and expectations.

On the trip down to GTMO, I kept pondering how I could present the plea offer and what Hicks was going to do. He would be told, 'Sign this and you go home in two months, no matter what. It doesn't matter whether you did it or not because this is an Alford plea. It doesn't matter. You're going home.'

What does someone in his shoes do? This was not some situation where he had to stand strong for fellow American prisoners of war being held by the North Vietnamese. This was upside-down. The good guys had become the bad guys. There was no principle for Hicks to fight for.

My mind was racing. When I told him what had been offered,

would he believe me? Was he capable of thinking straight? I couldn't even begin to enter his head. Would he think it was all another trick? I wouldn't believe he was leaving GTMO until I saw him strapped into a plane. When would *he* believe it? Would he be able to get a grip on this new twist?

And, of course, nothing was guaranteed. The only certainty in the Military Commission system was that nothing was certain.

The afternoon we arrived at GTMO, all the commission participants were moved into a staff housing area. I was sharing a house with Dratel, who arrived on a later flight, and McLeod and Griffin were sharing another house. Our experts McCormack and Edwards were sharing a house and were still in the dark about the potential plea deal. I handed in some letters for Hicks and went to our office, where our first pre-trial conference with military judge Colonel Kohlmann had been scheduled. Kohlmann was playing hardball in scheduling the conference when he knew Dratel would not have arrived yet. He rejected our request to delay the conference until Dratel's arrival at 6 p.m. We also asked for Hicks to be permitted to attend the conference and be moved to the commission building for court preparation, but the prosecution objected and Kohlmann took their side. We filed our objections, but Kohlmann ordered us to be there, so we had no choice.

At the conference, we asked to make a recording so Dratel could know what he missed, but Kohlmann would not allow it. He had two attorney advisors present, something I had never seen for a military judge in any court-martial. His demeanour and rulings left us in no doubt that he was intent on pushing the Hicks case through with little interference from any defence counsel.

A follow-up meeting was set for the next morning, prior to the official commencement of the commission hearing, when all the defence lawyers could be present.

After Dratel arrived, we were able to meet with Hicks to update him on the proposed pre-trial agreement and how the commission might proceed. Hicks did not look well. His skin was puffy, he had dark circles around his eyes, and his hair was long and greasy. He also seemed to be having trouble speaking coherently.

Back at our housing, we stayed up late, running through all the different potential variables in the proposed pre-trial agreement. As lawyers, we would have loved to keep fighting the Military Commission system. We had put immense work into investigating the case and preparing. We had put together a great team. We had nothing to lose, as no one expected us to win. Even to win on appeal, which was the best we could hope for, would be a wonderful feather in our cap. We were first to be tried: we would get to challenge the offences and be first in line this time to the Supreme Court. We could have been the lawyers whose client went to the Supreme Court two times and won two times. Yet we weren't going to do a day in the cell at GTMO. Hicks would be the one doing the time. What might have been best for the lawyers and our legal careers was fighting, but it would not have been what was best for Hicks.

That first day, I had been avoiding the huge media contingent in GTMO, but Davis was out and about, repeating his attacks on me for the Australian media. As well as claiming I had violated the UCMJ with 'contemptuous' language, he said, 'The defence has been very effective in peddling this notion that there is something wrong with our system. That is fiction. We're going to state facts tomorrow and I hope the world will take a look at the facts. And it is my goal to do this right, to do it fairly, and when the world looks at that, they will say they do justice.' In a few months, Davis would start singing the opposite tune when it appeared to suit his purpose.

The day began with a pre-trial conference with Kohlmann. As both the prosecution and the defence started looking through the trial schedule we were handed, I was dumbfounded. Kohlmann wanted to start the trial near the end of June, one month before even the prosecution wanted to start the trial. We had asked to complete all motions in June and October with the trial starting on 3 December, due to Dratel's other federal criminal trials that had already been set by federal judges.

We needed a break. We went upstairs to our office and fumed. It was as if Kohlmann had not even considered what we had submitted. His schedule was set in such a way as to preclude Dratel from participating in the trial. If the pre-trial agreement fell through, there was no way we could adequately prepare for a Military Commission in the two and a half months that Kohlmann was giving us. We returned to his office. Kohlmann's final words were that his way of operating was to be 'as adversarial as counsel want to be'. We left the meeting knowing what kind of judge we had if Hicks went to trial.

The hearing was to commence at two o'clock in the afternoon. We now had to decide whether to sign the pre-trial agreement or not, as it would have to travel up to DC to be signed off.

By now Hicks had been brought over to the commission building and had an opportunity to meet his father and sister. The JTF staff, while following the strict security guidelines, tried to permit as much visitation as possible. Terry had not seen his son since the hearing in 2004. While they were watched closely by the guards the whole time, I was able to get them some lunch and stretch out their time with him by just a little.

As Hicks later wrote in his book *Guantanamo: My Journey*, he had been preparing to say goodbye to his father for the last time when we showed him the pre-trial agreement document. He was that close to giving up. He described that he was angry at the document because it played havoc with his carefully laid plans to commit suicide. He wrote that it was only when he spent some quiet time with Terry and Steph, and realised how much pain his death would cause them, that he came to his senses.

We signed the document, gave it to the prosecution and emailed it to Hemingway in DC. We would get an answer sometime that day. It was as absurd, in its way, as the story of Admiral Jeremiah Denton in Vietnam, who had been filmed saying he had been well treated as a POW by the North Vietnamese, while he was blinking the Morse code for 'torture'. Hicks was signing a pre-trial agreement and stipulation of fact to the effect that he had been well treated in custody, whereas he had already documented his abuse in a US federal court affidavit and during his NCIS interview with an Australian consular staff member present. That was put even more plainly than Morse code. The more over-the-top the conditions were in the pre-trial agreement, the more it lacked any credibility.

As the hearing commenced that afternoon, Hicks's appearance shocked those in the public gallery, as he had not been seen since 2004. Observers remarked that his voice seemed broken, altered somehow by time, so that it even had a strange combination of accents. He wore the detainee scrubs provided by GTMO for what should have been a quick and relatively straightforward hearing.

Instead, Kohlmann wanted his sideshow. After asking Hicks if he understood English, Kohlmann turned his sights to Snyder, attacking her ability to represent Hicks in the commission. As he already knew, Snyder was a commissioned naval officer qualified to represent service members in courts-martial and before the military Court of Appeals, and had been detailed by the CDC office. Kohlmann would only accept that she was a civilian lawyer being paid by the US government and would not let her continue to represent Hicks even though the prosecution was not objecting to her being on the case. I sat there embarrassed for him and how he was making military lawyers look. Snyder left the counsel table and departed the courtroom.

Kohlmann then moved on to Dratel. As the rules to regulate civilian defence counsel had not been created yet, we were all flying blind, and Kohlmann was just making it up as he went along. Dratel signed a civilian attorney agreement, but with one minor change, adding the words 'presently existing' in reference to the rules and regulations that he agreed to be bound to.

Kohlmann still wanted to bully him. 'Mr Dratel's offered agreement,' he blustered, 'falls short of the required agreement to comply with all applicable regulations or instructions for counsel, including any rules of court for the conduct during the proceedings. Accordingly, Mr Dratel does not meet the requirements set forth in the United States Code for participation in this commission as a civilian defence counsel.'

In two sentences, Dratel was also off the case. Dratel asked to be heard. He stood and explained, 'I cannot sign a document that provides a blank check on my ethical obligations as a lawyer, my ethical obligations to my client, and my ethical obligations under the rules of professional responsibility for the State of New York to which I am bound.' Some more heated exchanges followed, and Kohlmann ruled that Dratel could not participate.

Dratel expressed how we were all feeling:

> What you've chosen to do essentially is to deny Mr Hicks, first with Ms Snyder, due to a tortured interpretation of the rules. And then with me, not a tortured interpretation, just a completely invalid one without any authority. It belongs to the Secretary of Defense. You've now denied Mr Hicks again another lawyer. The third lawyer, Mr Mori, has already been attacked by the chief prosecutor in a manner that's designed to intimidate him and deny Mr Hicks his zealous advocacy.

After Kohlmann kicked out Dratel, he addressed Hicks about his counsel's rights. Hicks's head must have been spinning. He said to Kohlmann, 'One's gone and now another one is going to have to go, by your choice. And now I'm left with poor Mr Mori.'

Kohlmann had done nothing but embarrass himself in the eyes of those watching. While I sat there dumbfounded, I knew something Kohlmann didn't: I knew about the deal Hemingway was offering, and that there was every chance there wouldn't be a full trial. If so, Hicks was lucky not to be tried by a judge who was looking for any excuse to rule against the defence.

The prosecution tried to ask for a recess so they could inform Kohlmann that a pre-trial agreement was being negotiated, as if to give him an opportunity to save face, but Kohlmann would not be stopped.

The next step in the hearing was for counsel to question the judge on issues that might demonstrate a bias that might preclude him from sitting on the case. I asked Kohlmann about his potential criminal liability for participating in the first Military Commission system, which the Supreme Court found violated Article 3 of the Geneva Conventions – something he wanted to shrug off as if the Geneva Conventions did not apply to him.

I made a challenge that he should recuse himself, but he was not going to. He had detailed himself to be the first judge of the first of the new Military Commissions, and he was not going to take himself off. He wanted to be part of history.

Kohlmann asked how Hicks was to plead. I asked that we be allowed to plead at a later time, which is usual practice in courts-martial.

I then turned to his setting of the trial schedule, which seemed calculated to clash with Dratel's ongoing federal court matters, but he batted that away, saying, 'Dratel is not counsel in this case.' I tried to explain how unfeasible the schedule was to be ready in less than three months.

'How long have you been working on this case?' he snapped.

'I've been working on it for three years, sir.'

'OK. How many other cases do you have assigned?'

'None, sir.'

'OK. When was the Military Commissions Act passed?'

'October 2006, sir.'

'So don't tell me you had thirteen days to work on it.'

'No, sir. We've already previously begun. But we didn't have the charge. I spent three years working on David Hicks's case for charges that don't exist any more. That work is all thrown out the window. I spent the majority of three years working under a system that no longer exists. I spent three years investigating facts to put on a defence to three specific charges that no longer exist, and yet there is an entirely new charge . . . At this point, I'm the only counsel, I would ask for more time and follow the defence's proposed schedule of having motions due in May.'

This all fell on deaf ears. Kohlmann stuck to the dates he had come up with before. We got back to our office, and the pre-trial agreement was back, signed by Crawford. It was done. There would be no lengthy trial or appeals. The prosecutorial misconduct motion would disappear; maybe this was why Davis supported the plea deal. Most importantly, Hicks would leave GTMO within sixty days. We called a new meeting with Kohlmann and the prosecution. We informed him of the agreement. A change in emotion swept over him, as if he realised he had made himself look like a fool for no reason. The deal had been done, and all his posturing had been for nought.

When Kohlmann saw the sentence portion of the deal, he seemed shocked. Clearly, he'd had something more punitive in mind for David Hicks. I got the sense that the prosecution wasn't happy either. All their work was going out the window, as the people upstairs had stepped in. The prosecution lawyers, even the judge himself, were as much victims of the political game as we were.

Meanwhile, after the close of the hearing, the Australian consular delegation, Lasry, Terry and Steph were getting ready to leave the island. They had all gone across the bay on a boat and were on the aircraft when one of the handlers came onto the plane and informed them that the hearing was going to continue that night.

The Australian delegation and Lasry, who didn't know about the plea deal, left the plane to come back and attend the hearing. Terry and Stephanie stayed on the plane and flew out of GTMO, knowing, at last, that it would not be long before they would see Hicks in Australia.

That night, the hearing recommenced and a plea of guilty was entered. The media that was attending went into a feeding frenzy. They had been feverishly filing reports about the removal of Snyder and Dratel, but now had the big story: Hicks was pleading guilty.

The entering of the guilty plea was all that would happen at that hearing. No one outside knew yet what the deal was going to mean for Hicks in terms of sentencing. And the sentencing hearing couldn't proceed until all the members detailed to the Military Commission were at GTMO. Unlike a court-martial, where a judge could sentence alone, this Military Commission required the Department of Defense to locate and gather all the members and bring them to GTMO. This would delay the sentencing hearing and the start of the sixty-day countdown until all the members could be found, taken to DC, and put on the Secretary of Defense's own jet to GTMO.

I remained slightly on edge, fearing that something was still going to go wrong. The time limit of sixty days to have Hicks transferred back to Australia would begin on the day he was sentenced. My whole goal was to get that day to happen as soon as possible, both to start the clock and so that nothing could intervene to invalidate the pre-trial agreement. I just wanted to get this hearing over with before someone woke up and said, 'Stop!'

The sentencing hearing was set to take place on 30 March; we filled the days as best we could. The Australian delegation and Lasry had packed for a two-day trip, and had to do some clothes shopping at the Base Exchange. The media spent their time hounding us to try to find out the terms of the deal. I couldn't tell them, as the commission members might read about it.

On 28 March, the world's media was focused on fifteen British sailors who had been detained in Iran for allegedly crossing into Iranian waters and were now confessing on television after five days' detention. When I saw the report, I thought about Hicks being detained for more than five years. Was it any surprise that he was ready to do anything to get out?

After three sleepless nights, the hearing finally came around. I could see that Kohlmann was not happy. His first Military Commission was fizzling out from under him. Davis was not happy either. He had been in the media condemning Hicks for months, and now the system was letting him go within sixty days. The official transcript, interestingly, redacts the names of Kohlmann, Davis and their staff, but leaves mine in. The sessions were in open court, and all names were printed in the media. Yet the judge and prosecutor's names were redacted from the transcript, as if they were ashamed of having participated.

Despite reaching this stage, I still did not believe it was happening. I would not believe it until I saw Hicks on the plane.

On the morning of 30 March, Kohlmann called the hearing to order. For the rest of the day, we would put on the charade of a trial, even though the result was a foregone conclusion. Kohlmann explained the elements of the material support charge with the stipulation of fact, and went over the terms of the pre-trial agreement. These were the facts and legalese underlying Hicks's plea.

Hicks was read these elements and facts, and he had to say, 'Yes, sir' to all of it. There was always a part of me that bridled against this and wanted to fight it. But we were past that point. And I had to remind myself that it was an Alford plea, not an acceptance that the story was true or legally valid. At the conclusion, Kohlmann found Hicks guilty.

The next part was the sentencing, which required the commission members as jury. They arrived on the Secretary of Defense's jet that afternoon, and for several hours we continued with the charade. The prosecution and I questioned each member, made challenges to some, all for no real purpose, as the sentence was predetermined.

The pre-trial agreement also required both the prosecution and defence to refrain from putting forward any evidence in the sentencing hearing. I accepted these limits, as bringing forward evidence would have meant more delay, would have left Hicks in his cell for longer, and wouldn't have had any impact, as the sentence had already been decided. At this hearing, my goal was simply to keep it moving and get it over with. I was able to make a one-minute unsworn statement on Hicks's behalf, in which I said, 'David owes apologies to many people. First and foremost, David wants to apologise to his family. He wants to apologise to Australia and he wants to apologise to the United States.'

The unsworn statement and the stipulation of fact was all the evidence the members would be provided. Kohlmann, in his rush, forgot to permit counsel to argue on sentence. I was not going to say anything, but the prosecutor reminded Kohlmann. The prosecutor started, 'Today in this courtroom we are on the front line of a global war on terrorism, face to face with the enemy. The enemy is sitting at defence counsel's table and though he is now in a suit and tie, you can be assured that when he was on the battlefield in Afghanistan with al-Qaeda going north and south trying to kill Americans, he was not wearing a suit and tie. Nor was he wearing a uniform.'

It really did not matter. The members were told the maximum they could sentence Hicks to was seven years. Having just been flown down on the Secretary of Defense's private jet for the first Military Commission in sixty years, they were unlikely to give him any less than that. I knew that under the pre-trial agreement, Hicks was going to receive an effective sentence of nine months, so for me to achieve anything in the sentencing hearing, I would have to convince these US military officers to sentence an unlawful enemy combatant to less than nine months. I always thought I was good, but I knew I wasn't that good! I had a go, pointing out that Hicks had pleaded guilty, had provided information during his interrogations, and had behaved himself for more than five years in detention.

After less than two hours' deliberation, the members came back with the maximum: seven years. The surprise was about to come for everyone. For days, the media and observers had been asking why Hicks was pleading guilty after so many years of fighting. Now they would know: Kohlmann announced that six years and three months of Hicks's seven-year sentence was being suspended, and he was to be transferred to the Australian government in fifty-nine days. Now they knew.

At the press conference that followed the sentencing, I was reserved. My job was done. Davis was trying to defend his prior public statement of how bad this detainee was, now that he'd been sentenced to only nine months. Davis complained, saying he had signed the agreement for symbolic reasons and hadn't been involved in the negotiations. I guess he had to stick to his position that Hicks was a dangerous terrorist and should be locked up indefinitely.

We were able to get Hicks back to Camp Echo, where he was allowed to have his outer door open, his books back and his chewing tobacco. He took his first steps out of the darkness he had been kept in for the past year.

That night, as the media finished filing their stories, Dratel, McLeod, Griffin, Snyder and I, along with our experts and assistant, crowded together in one of our houses for one final night together. *Team America: World Police* played as we sipped Red Stripes, ate microwaved popcorn and reminisced. Still, we reminded ourselves, it was not over until Hicks left GTMO.

The next day, the circus was flown back to DC. It was a strange feeling, as so many of the media on the plane, who had become friends and part of my life for so many years, would be gone.

28

Free

I still don't know for sure what went on behind the scenes to get the system to offer Hicks such a sweetheart deal. There were theories that it was cut during Dick Cheney's visit to Australia; that John Howard said to him something like, 'I need Hicks back. I have an election coming up and it's become a problem for me. I need Hicks out of the news. But he's got to come back convicted, otherwise I will look like I made a mistake all these years. So can you get him out, but with a conviction?'

The connection between Cheney and Susan Crawford was so close that I'm sure it wouldn't have been hard for him to convey a message to her. That is why the Bush administration and the DOD chose who they did, so they could control the process.

This is just speculation, of course. I was certainly not invited to any top-level briefings! But I find it feasible, because the one hard fact I had learnt in this entire saga was that power remained concentrated in a few hands at the very top of the Bush administration and DOD. The rest of us were just pawns.

Whether Howard finally pushed harder for Hicks's release, or Cheney pushed on his behalf, it doesn't redeem either of them. Cheney was one of those who created the system, and Howard did nothing for Hicks for five years while it was in his political interest. In the immediate aftermath of Hicks's sentencing, the Australian media went nuts. They would not drop the story until he returned to Australia, and even then I suspected he would never be truly free from media intrusion, or the fear of it. He would always be reported on, whether it was a year after he was out or ten years. The media microscope will likely follow him for the rest of his life.

Initially, they weren't as curious about the political machinations that made the deal possible as they were about the conditions in the plea bargain. The pre-trial agreement stopped him from speaking to the media for one year and from participating in legal action against the United States or US personnel. They wanted to know if the gag order on Hicks, which was part of the plea agreement, would be enforceable in Australia. Philip Ruddock said, 'I don't think it's a matter for us to enforce,' but he hinted that the Australian government did not want Hicks profiting from selling his story. The media liked to speculate that the gag order was designed to keep Hicks from speaking before the upcoming Australian federal election.

The only thing left for Hicks in GTMO was to cooperate with any military interviews, if requested. I knew by then that he had no real intelligence value, as the interrogators had put him through the wringer years before.

In early April, I flew back down to GTMO to see Hicks and ensure his conditions had improved, as promised. I'd just been up to Vermont to visit my grandmother, and while I was sitting on the plane at Jacksonville Naval Base waiting to lift off, someone ran onboard with a message. The Australian media had rehashed Hicks's statement to the British Special Immigration Appeals Commission about being maltreated in custody. None of it was new, but the media was in a frenzy and tried to make the story conflict with Hicks's gag order, creating the impression that now that he was going to be freed he was telling all. Hemingway came out accepting responsibility for the twelve-month gag order, but there were articles in Australia saying that once Hicks was back home it would not be enforceable. Another article said John Walker Lindh's family was asking for clemency, as his twenty-year sentence was far longer than Hicks's. Then there were more articles asking how Hicks might profit from telling his story.

These were all peripheral issues, but I was nervous about anything that could affect Hicks's release, which was now just four weeks away. I had to be ultra-vigilant against the possibility of anything going wrong. I spent six days visiting Hicks. We had a few conversations about how things were going to move forward from here, and what he had to expect in his seven months in an Australian prison, and then I left. The media storm quickly blew over, as they do. Everything feels on the point of maximum crisis for a day or two, and then their attention moves on. I had been through this cycle a number of times, but it still took some getting used to.

As April rolled into May, the month when Hicks would be released, the media began contacting me, trying to see if they could get his return date. Some would pretend to know when he was coming back, to see if I would slip up. Others were staking out the airport in South Australia near the Yatala prison where he was supposed to be going. They all wanted the exclusive. But I couldn't help them – my work with David Hicks was winding up.

I flew in from Jacksonville to Guantanamo Bay for the last time at 11 p.m. on 8 May. Being there felt almost as surreal as my first visit to the camp had, four years earlier. There was a sense that this was coming to an end, at least for Hicks and me, and those who had supported the fight for him. I wouldn't describe my feeling as a sense of satisfaction, but rather a sense that, at least for one detainee, the nightmare of GTMO was going to end.

Hicks and I spent the next week or so together in his cell. It was one of our nicest times. I felt sad to be breaking this tie, mixed with intense relief on his behalf and mine. I would meet Hicks in the morning and the afternoon. We sat around shooting the breeze. We even got to open the door and let some fresh air in, which was surreal. I was able to call Terry, Bev and other members of the family to tell them Hicks was doing as well as could be expected. I didn't feel I'd accomplished anything; he should have gone home a long time ago. One night I crossed the bay in a boat to meet some friends for dinner. The sea was so quiet, but the boat's speakers were playing AC/DC, which seemed apt as my connection to this Australian citizen was playing out to an end.

The day before his release, I met with Hicks. He had just woken up, and looked tired. He asked if I could be with him when he left the camp after signing his papers the next day. Unfortunately, I was not going to be allowed to be there. He wanted me to fly back to Australia with him too. I would have loved another trip to see him home, but the Convening Authority's office and, I suspect, the Australian government did not want me flying to Australia.

In a way I was glad. While the Hicks case had been my life for almost four years, it was time to move on. I would not be able to represent Hicks any more, but I would always be there to talk to him when I could. I was worried about his future, the impact the years at GTMO would have on him, and the media cause célèbre he had become. I was strongly attached to him, but had to let go.

He wanted to keep studying and was concerned about his school options. I took this as a good sign: he was thinking about the future. For so long, he had been driven into a tiny shell by his worries about the immediate present, because I do not think he could believe he had any future at all.

I went back to the office to meet McLeod and the embassy staff who were to fly back with Hicks.

The schedule for the next day came up, and Hicks needed to sign his final release documents. McLeod was there as his Australian lawyer, and from that moment Hicks would be an Australian matter, not a US military matter. I said Hicks had asked for me to be there. McLeod suggested that, as a compromise, I could be there as 'a passive observer'.

McLeod and I ate at the Cuban Club and went to the outdoor cinema, to see the movie *Zodiac*.

Hicks flew out on 19 May 2007. I met him during the day and we said our goodbyes. He told me he had more papers to sign for the Australian government. He wanted to know what I thought, and I said, 'If they give you a form, you just need to sign – it's the only way you're going to get out. It doesn't matter. Nothing matters except getting you out. If they want you to admit to the JFK assassination, you should do that too, as no one would believe it and it would get you out of here.'

Many people came to see Hicks's release. There were members of the Joint Chiefs of Staff legal office there who had flown down just for this. The JTF staff didn't want me around, and put a security cordon in place. I'm not sure what they were worried about: someone trying to *not* leave GTMO?

A kind member of staff brought me to the airstrip, where we sat in the dark waiting for the Australian plane to arrive. We could hear the noise of the plane approaching GTMO as it banked low to land, as I had done so many times. I had never seen it from this angle, on the ground and at night. The plane landed, the doors opened, and the Australian delegation came out, and members of the JTF staff spoke to them. Everyone was still waiting for the convoy to arrive, bringing Hicks from the camp. McLeod boarded the plane and disappeared inside.

Eventually the convoy arrived. Through the rows of guards forming a corridor between the vehicle and the aircraft, I could see Hicks in the bright lights. The Australian corrections staff asked the guards to remove Hicks's ankle shackles.

I can still see Hicks being let out of his chains and brought up the metal steps, slowly, one at a time. At the top, there was a pause as he took a last look back, and then he disappeared into the plane.

A few minutes later, the JTF security personnel came out of the plane and the door closed. The plane departed, and so did what had been my purpose in life for the past four years. Hicks was gone, to whatever life he could make in Australia. I went back to my lodgings, to spend my last night in Guantanamo Bay.

I'd made some friends there, and I must admit I'd had some

good times at Guantanamo: the Texas hold 'em poker nights, Mongolian barbecue, taking in a movie at the Lyceum. While Hicks would probably never miss GTMO, my experience was that of a free man and, for what it was worth, I was going to miss that quiet little base. I went back to my room. I just sat on my bed quietly pondering what happened.

You couldn't work in the Military Commission system without coming away with a feeling that you were a very insignificant part of an enormously unjust system. Hicks's release was going to be the biggest news in Australia, but no one was going to care about it in the United States. By virtue of the Military Commissions, the United States wasn't any safer, justice hadn't been done for any of the victims of 9/11, and we had degraded our own ideals. I was involved with something that was not the best part of the US military, something that was not the best part of America. In a way, as I sat there on my bed reflecting on it all, I felt ashamed.

29

Release

After a few days, the staff at Yatala prison permitted me to have a phone call with Hicks. Even though he was in jail, I got the impression that he was already feeling the massive improvement in conditions. It said a lot about where he had been.

As for myself, what was I going to do now? Getting Hicks out of GTMO had been all-consuming, and now it was over. I knew I didn't want any more to do with the political game of the Military Commissions. Each year since I'd been representing Hicks, I had screened as a military judge, just in case he was freed or I was off the case for some other reason. It was a logical next career step, a role that my experience suited me for, and one I had been approved for over the past several years. Now that I was actually available to attend the judge's course, which began after the commission hearing, I was told that the judge job was no longer an option.

I was told there was not a legal job for me and I should contact the monitor (the person who helps assigns jobs in the Marines) to see what non-legal jobs there were. I was a little pissed. The Marines had sent me to do a job and I did it to the best of my abilities. Shortly after this, Colonel Sullivan was called to the SJA for the Commandant's office to discuss how my misconduct allegation might be handled. Davis's allegations were still floating around. I had been passed over for promotion three times while I was representing Hicks. And there was still the ongoing allegation from Davis that I had used 'contemptuous' language and not worn my cover (Marine term for hat) at an event.

Luckily, a unit was deploying to Iraq and needed a lawyer so any talk of discipline went away. I was a free body so I was quickly moved out to Marine Corps Air Station Miramar, California, as the Deputy Staff Judge Advocate for the Third Marine Aircraft Wing to fill the deployment slot to Iraq. I was finally getting my opportunity to deploy. While Americans rarely showed any animosity towards me for representing Hicks, it was in Australia where people went out of their way to show public appreciation. In 2007, the Australian Bar Association presented me with an honourary membership in recognition of my work, and later that year the Australian Lawyers' Alliance gave me their civil justice award as 'recognition by the legal profession of unsung heroes who, despite personal risk or sacrifice, have fought to preserve individual rights, human dignity or safety'. Not that I felt I did anything different from what any other Marine lawyer would have done.

Late in 2007, I watched the Australian federal election campaign very closely. If it was easy to infer that John Howard had pushed for Hicks's release in a belated political move to defuse the

Hicks issue, it was also true that the Australian public saw through it. During the campaign, he looked a beaten man from the start. On election day, Howard not only lost his party their majority in the House of Representatives, but became the first sitting prime minister since the Great Depression to lose his own seat. It was tempting for me to see this as some kind of ultimate justice handed down by the people, but I'm sure there were many reasons, beyond David Hicks, for why Howard was so completely rejected.

At Christmas that year, I took the family on a holiday before I left for Iraq. I was eating breakfast on 29 December when I had my first phone call with Hicks as a free man. He'd been released that day, under a control order. In 2010 Hicks would publish a book about his life, which wasn't a bad achievement for a guy who had not finished the ninth grade. The Australian government moved to stop him from earning any money from the book, under its proceeds of crime legislation, but failed, as his guilty plea was obtained in circumstances that were unlikely to be validated in an Australian court.

Many of the creators and those intricately involved with the commission have left, while some have remained in their DOD jobs. Haynes, the careerist lawyer who was at the controls of this blight on our nation, was nominated for a position as a federal appeals court judge in 2006 and 2007. On both occasions Congress refused his nomination. He left the Pentagon in 2008, receiving a medal for his service, and went to work as an in-house counsel for a multinational corporation.

Altenburg, Hemingway and Brownback quietly departed the commissions. Others did not leave so quietly. Morris Davis, after years as chief prosecutor in which he defended the indefensible in the Military Commissions, left the commission system in 2007 under a cloud of accusations by him towards his superiors, and counter-accusations by them. As a subject of his accusations, it is hard for me to place any credence in what he claimed after leaving the commissions. The commissions would never have been created or operated without people who were willing to place self-interest above all else.

In a turnaround that makes one question what his true values ever were, Davis became a strong critic of the Pentagon's interference with the commission, and became a defence witness during the second Hamdan commission. On Hicks, Davis also turned around. Describing Hicks as a 'little guy with not a lot of education who wanted to be a big shot and went off on this adventure to Jihad', he said that there was 'no possibility' Hicks was a threat to society and his was 'the one case I did not want to start with'.

'It was a terrible case,' Davis admitted. 'We told the world these guys are the "worst of the worst". David Hicks was a knucklehead. He was just a foot soldier, not a war criminal. But when Congress passed the Military Commissions Act they authorised prosecuting material support, which is what Hicks was charged with, as a war crime. You could prosecute everyone at Guantanamo under that theory.'

The system that kept Hicks behind bars is still limping along. While the Obama administration had stated an intention to close GTMO down, it has not done so. Congress has tied his hands by passing legislation that prohibits its closure. It was reported in 2013 that more than 100 detainees remaining in GTMO were on hunger strikes, and another forty-one were being force-fed. In 2014, as I write, GTMO holds 146 detainees. Since its opening, Guantanamo Bay had been a holding pen for almost 800 detainees. Less than

3 per cent of them had been charged by the Military Commission.

In November 2009, Obama's Attorney-General Eric Holder tried to have Khalid Sheikh Mohammed and the other alleged 9/11 plotters brought to a US federal court for trial but it was blocked by many in Congress who were tied up in needing GTMO and the commission system to be a success for their own political needs. The resistance was so great that Holder had to flip-flop in April of 2011 and leave those defendants in GTMO.

In February 2013, bin Laden's son-in-law was captured and sent to a New York federal court for trial. He was convicted in March 2014 of conspiracy to kill Americans, conspiring to provide support to al-Qaeda and providing support to al-Qaeda. This timing – less than a year from capture to conviction – seems to vindicate Holder's position. The slow Military Commission process is not providing justice for either the accused or the victims.

Few GTMO detainees were guilty of any law-of-war crimes. In fact, the three original detainees convicted (of which Hicks was one) were all charged with 'material support' for terror. Finally, in July of 2014, all seven judges of the District Court of Appeals for the District of Columbia ruled 'material support' was not a valid law-of-war offence.

Hicks has long been a free man, living in Australia. He still bears the stigma of being called a 'convicted terrorist' by conservative elements of the media and fellow travellers of the politicians who left him in Guantanamo Bay. This may not last much longer, as with the help of the Center for Constitutional Rights he is fighting to have his conviction 'officially' declared invalid in accordance with the recent ruling.

While working at the CDC office and after, I was often asked, 'Why do you care, when these people were just terrorists?' You could hear this same attitude coming from the Bush administration and from members of Congress: these are terrorists, they don't deserve rights. As Senator Lindsay Graham said, 'Of all the people in the world who should enjoy the rights of an American citizen in federal court, the people at Guantanamo Bay are the last that we should confer that status on. We didn't do it for the Nazis. We shouldn't do it for these people.'

My answer was, 'Because I'm from Massachusetts.'

'What does that matter?'

I would explain that, while young Texans learn about the Alamo, we in Massachusetts learn about the American Revolution. As kids, we don't just get it through books, but we are taken to Bunker Hill, Lexington-Concord, and we walk the decks of the USS *Constitution*. We visit the site of the Boston Massacre and learn about the trial of the British soldiers accused of murdering our early patriots. We are told about John Adams, who would become our president, defending these British soldiers who had just killed innocent colonists (or 'terrorists', depending on which side you supported at the time). With pride, we learn how Adams and his family suffered harassment and his loyalty was questioned; yet he showed that we, the colonists, provided a fair trial even for our enemies.

So what kind of trial should Americans provide for even our worst enemies? It's an easy answer: a fair trial.

I was no John Adams, but the Military Commissions were not providing a fair trial. I might have been naive to hope for fairness or justice in a system that had been rigged in its design and was continually re-rigged for political purposes, but I am content to be naive. I may still be the naive schoolboy who learnt about Adams.

The Military Commission system had no credibility and will never be viewed as a fair system embodying the values of America. Part of me is still confused and upset that my country could have set up such a system. I am distressed that fellow lawyers within the US military could have set it up and supported it. Our ethical obligations are not only to provide technical and legal advice, but to ask what might be the morally correct action to take in any given situation. How could anybody who went to law school and then worked in the US military support that type of justice system? How can people in senior and influential positions place their personal ambition so cravenly, and arrogantly, above what their country stands for?

The only explanation I can peacefully come to terms with is that we had an entire generation of military personnel who had participated in part of the War on Terror. So what do you tell them? That this was nothing better than a political exercise? How do you tell military people that they have been used as political pawns? Giving court testimony in 2010, Lawrence Wilkerson, the former chief of staff to Secretary of State Colin Powell, admitted that he 'served in an administration that tortured and abused those it detained at the facilities at Guantanamo Bay and elsewhere, and indefinitely detained the innocent for political reasons'. By arresting and detaining those men, they had painted themselves into a corner from which it was 'politically impossible' to release them. The administration was trapped behind bad decisions as much as the detainees.

Just because GTMO and the Military Commissions were a fraud against the American people doesn't mean the Marine guarding the perimeter was not doing the right thing. Just because Guantanamo from a 'strategic perspective' was a poor idea doesn't mean that the sergeant who went down there for a six-month deployment didn't do a good job on the cell block.

As someone whose friends died and were injured during this war, I wanted to protect America from its enemies as much as anyone else did. When I saw David Hicks in Guantanamo Bay, I always asked myself, 'What about all those other people out there, the ones protesting and burning American flags in Pakistan? Aren't they more dangerous? What about some of the people who have been released? Why is this guy still here? It was the hypocrisy of it all. Detaining Hicks was preventing nothing. A mistake had been made in 2001, and he, we, became trapped in a political process geared to cover up and justify that mistake.

The fighting side of me wanted to go on and conquer this injustice, put those years of preparation into years of litigation. But my responsibility was to the client, not the cause. Knowing that we were on the right path provides some satisfaction, but nothing can compare to the feeling I had when I saw Hicks board that flight and leave Cuba for Australia.

After my six months in Iraq, I came back to Miramar. In February 2009, I was told I was to be promoted to Lieutenant Colonel; I had to ask the Colonel on the phone if he had the correct person. I couldn't complain as the next phone call was asking me if I still wanted to be the military judge in Hawaii.

In 2012, I finally retired from the military after spending almost twenty-nine years of my life centred on the Marine Corps. Simon Morrison from Shine Lawyers in Australia, who had been the president of the Australian Lawyers' Alliance during the Hicks case, was saying, 'Why don't you move down here?' His firm was starting a social justice section, and wanted to know if I would like to join. Of course I did!

We rented out our house in Hawaii, which gave us the freedom to give it a shot. Yet again, I was following a new, unplanned adventure. I'd loved Australia since I first visited to play rugby. For many years, fighting for an Australian to have the same rights and protections as an American, I could not understand how some of his countrymen did not see it the same way. I asked myself, would any Australian politician tolerate Indonesia or Singapore setting up a special court to try Australians? As an American, I could never imagine my government failing to stand up for equal treatment for one of its citizens.

While it was apparent to the world that the Military Commission system was illegal, only Australian ministers supported its use on one of their citizens. Detainees were returned to Albania, Afghanistan, Bahrain, Belgium, Denmark, Egypt, France, Germany, Iran, Iraq, Jordan, Kuwait, Maldives, Morocco, Pakistan, Russia, Saudi Arabia, Spain, Sweden, Sudan, Tajikistan, Turkey, Uganda, the United Kingdom and Yemen.

Only Australia was holding out, until the public began to understand the issues. In the dark year of 2006, the Australian people showed us the light at the end of the tunnel. It was they who put the pressure on John Howard to change his stance. It was they, the Australian public, who got David Hicks out. I hope that the people of Australia never forget that.

Acknowledgements

I need to thank two categories of people. First, I thank those who helped me along through my years at the Military Commissions and those who fought for justice for David Hicks well before I was assigned to his case and after I ceased representing him. Second, I thank those who have helped turn this story into sentences and paragraphs and ultimately this book.

The first group is so large that it would be impossible to list everyone. This case was long and multifaceted. It saw court challenges and political advocacy in multiple countries, grassroots mobilizing across Australia, international media interaction, and investigatory work around the globe. I regret that I cannot capture and properly acknowledge all the effort put in by so many.

I did not do this alone.

U.S. Military Commission Defense Team Members: Joshua Dratel, Elizabeth Besobrasow, LtCol Jeffery Lippert, Rebecca Snyder, MSgt Pierre (The Warrior Princess), Sgt Miguel Riostlatelpa and our Australian volunteer, Sarah Finnin. Foreign Attorney Consultants: Stephen Kenny, SA Magistrate David McLeod, Brigadier Michael Griffin.

Jenner & Block: Andrew Jacobson, Andrew Vail, David Walters, Eric Berger, Gabrielle Gold, Hillary Victor, Marc Goldman and Victoria Judes.

British Legal Team: Stephen Grosz, QC, Michael Fordham, QC, Alison Stanley, Saadiya Chaudhary and the firm of Bindmans LLP.

Australian Federal Litigation Team: Brett Walker, SC, Kate Eastman, SC, NSW District Court Judge Chris Hoy SC, Craig Lenehan, John North, David McLeod and Michael Griffin.

Center for Constitutional Rights: Barbara Olshansky, Gita Gutierrez, Irene Baghoomians, Jeffrey Fogel, Michael Ratner, Shane Kadidal, and Steven Watt. Of course, Joe Margulies while technically not CCR, took the lead in the Rasul case that litigated Hicks' claims before the U.S. Supreme Court. Joe, like Gita and Barbara, always took my calls.

Office of the Chief Defense Counsel, Office of Military Commissions: Andrea Prasow, Bryan Broyles, Charlie Swift, Douglas Harris, Dwight Sullivan, Jason Kreinhop, Kelly Redman, Mark Bridges, Michael Berrigan, Patricia Williams, Phil Leahy, Phil Sundel, Sandy Viet, Sharon Shaffer, Tom Bogar, Tom Fleener, Tom Roughneen, Wade Faulkner, Will Gunn, William Kuebler.

Office of Military Commissions: Alan Ridenour, Anthony McCloud, Clayton Trivett, Craig Lyons, Dale Cox, Dom McDonald, Donna Wilkins, Drew Brown, James Bertotti, Jeff Groharing, Jennifer Young, Karen Loftus, Keith Hodges, Kevin Chenail, Kurt Brubaker, Mark Harvey, Peter Brownback, Ron Sullivan, Susan McGarvey, Thomas Hemingway, Tim Stone, Wendy Kelly.

Experts: Antonio Cassese (In Memoriam), Cherif Bassiouni, Daryl Matthews, Detlev F. Vagts, Geoffrey Corn, George E. Edwards, George Fletcher, Jordan Paust, Michael Schmitt, Rohan Gunaratna,

Thomas Hamilton, Tim McCormack, Yoram Dinstein.

Civilian lawyers and various other professionals outside of Australia: Adam Tarosky, Ahktar Raj, Amrit Singh, Ann James, Anthony Garofano, Audre Casusol, Barbara Frey, Bob Messic, Charlie Rose, Craig King, Cy Winter, David Chick, David Cooke, David Furry, David Lerner, David Stoelting, Don Reikof, Eric Freeman, Gareth Peirce, Gary Isaac, George Nunez, Jackson Hilliard, James Vandegrift, Jennifer Minton, Jennifer Pyclik, Johnny Bardine, Jumana Musa, Karen Greenberg, LaTarsha Brown, Leah Nicholls, Leon Freeman, Liz Jones, Marisa Gonzalez, Martin Delonis, Michael Boehman, Michelle Park, Monroe Freeman, Morton Christoffersen, Neal Katyal, Neil Sonnett, Nicholas Arons, Paul Leblanc, Paul O'Neil, Peter Bergen, Rachel Meeropol, Randall Keys, Robert Fricke, Robert Nunley, Robert Watson, Samuel F. Denny, Stephen Parke, Tony Dealicante, Vaughan Lowe, William Holt.

Thanks to the many law students who provided research assistance under the guidance of Professor Madeline Morris, as part of the Guantanamo Defense Clinic, Duke University School of Law. Thanks also to the many JD and LLM law students from Indiana University Robert H. McKinney School of Law's Program in International Human Rights Law and Stetson University College of Law who under Professor George E. Edwards provided valuable legal research for the case. And, of course, thanks to Dapo Akande and the Oxford students as well.

Fair Go for David: Special thanks goes to Fair Go for David, a small group of people who fought for Hicks since he was first detained. This includes Bronwyn Mewett – coordinator; Oliver Corfe (Secretary); Zita Splawinski (Minute Secretary); Stathis Avramis (Webmaster); Keith Banfield (Treasurer); Chris Hicks;

Chris Madsen; Colin Mitchell; Graham Roberts; Irene Leighton; Jon Moore; Julie Corfe; Karen Joyce; Kevin Hremeviuc; Leslie Hopkins; Mal Fabian; Marion Mackintosh; Rosemary McKay; Stephanie Mewett; and Steve Patroni.

GetUp!: Brett Solomon, Dan Ilic (made the Hicks Cribs video), David Hernandez, Ed Coper, Jarra McGrath, Lilian Spencer (McCombs), Melanie Gilbank, Nick Moraitis, Sam Mclean, Silas Taylor and Taren Stinebrickner.

Lawyers, academics and other professionals within Australia: Thanks to the Law Council of Australia, the Australian Bar Association, and the state/territories legal bodies of Australia, and to independent legal/non-legal groups such as the International Commission of Jurists Australia, Victoria Law Foundation, Liberty Victoria and Amnesty Australia. Thanks also to all the universities that hosted my talks across the country. I thank the following within Australia, and again regret inadvertent omissions: Alex Cramb; Alistair Grigor; Amy Persson; Ben Saul; Bob Brown; Bob Debus; Brian Walters; Bruno Cara; Chris Horan; Clive Steirn; Craig Hobbs; Damian Spruce; Darren Jones; Dick Smith; Duncan Kerr; Eva Scheerlinck; Frances Bedford; Gavan Griffith; Geoff Lindell; Gillian Triggs; Glenn McGowan; Hilary Charlesworth; Jim Carlton; Joanne Kummrow; John Dowd; John Stratton; Jon Tippett; Julian Burnside; Kate McMillan; Leigh Sealy; Lex Lasry; Linda Kirk; Malcolm Fraser; Matthew Chesher; Michael O'Farrell; Natasha Stott-Despoja; Paul Mullen; Peter Holmes à Court; Peter Vickery; Peter Webb; Phil Skehan; Philip Alston; Pip Smith; Rainer Hunter; Renee Wilson; Rob Hulls; Ron Merkel; Russell Thirgood; Ruth Webber; Sara Hinchey; Stephen Estcourt; Steven Glass; Tamara Sims; and Tim Costello.

The media: The media contributed greatly. They helped raise the awareness of Hicks's plight. If I named all the members of the media I met or who reported on Hicks's case, I would still be typing. Several of the Australian journalists assigned in the US while the Military Commissions were ongoing and/or travelled to GTMO to cover the hearing who I got to know well during this period include: Karl Stefanovic, Leigh Sales, Marian Wilkinson, Michael Gawenda, Michael Rowland, and Phil Coorey, to name just a few. Thanks to Alison Caldwell, Ian Munro, Jon Faine, Mike Carlton, Penny Debelle, Ray Bonner, Tom Allard, and Verity Edwards for your efforts over those years.

The Hicks family: Terry Hicks, Bev Hicks, Chris Hicks, and David's sister Stephanie Mewett all made me feel welcome into the very personal challenge they faced. Thank you. And of course David.

The book: I probably would not have written this book without the support and encouragement from George Edwards who believed I could write it. Thanks also to Brien Hallett, Kate Eastman, Lou Coutts, Michael Griffin and Tim McCormack. Simon Morrison and Stephen Roche, for their encouragement and all the Shiners as well.

From Penguin, thanks to Ben Ball, Cate Blake, John Canty, Elena Cementon, Lou Ryan and Heidi McCourt.

Thanks to my super editor Malcolm Knox – who turned the lemons into lemonade and had the patience to sit side by side and show me the errors of my ways.

Thank you to Alice Richardson, Emily Lewis, Luke Zimbler, Natasha Robbins, and Trent Vitorrio for your help.

The Australian public: Finally, I would like to thank all the Australians I was fortunate enough to meet on the streets, in airports, in the customs lines, who came along to my talks, and those who sent messages through email and post. Your kind words of support and affirmation helped motivate me to keep up the fight then, and helped motivate me to assist Australians caught up in legal matters overseas by establishing Australians Detained Abroad (ADA) (AustraliansDetainedAbroad.org), a not-for-profit organisation that supports Australian families with loved ones detained overseas.

Photography credits:
Page 2: Top: AFP/Getty Images; Bottom: Kelly Barnes/Newspix
Page 3: Top: Brendan Smialowski/Getty Images
Page 4: [Clockwise from top left] Dick Cheney: AFP/Getty
        Images; Donald Rumsfeld: Win McNamee/Getty Images;
        George W. Bush and John Howard: Mark Wilson/Getty
        Images; Alexander Downey: Kelly Barnes/Newspix; Phillip
        Ruddock: AFP/Getty Images
Page 5: Top: Ian Waldie/Getty Images;
Page 7: Top: Sarah Reed/Newspix
Page 8: Full page: Simon Schluter/Fairfax Syndication
All other photographs author's own.